Tibetan Buddhism in Western Perspective

Tibetan Buddhism in Western Perspective

Collected Articles of

Herbert V. Guenther

Dharma Publishing

Acknowledgements

Grateful acknowledgement is made for permission to reprint the following essays:

"Excerpts from the Gaṇḍavyūha Sūtra," *Stepping Stones*, Vols. I and II, 1950-51.

"The Concept of Mind in Buddhist Tantrism," *Journal of Oriental Studies*, edited by Michael Smithies, Vol. III, pp. 261ff, Hong Kong: © Hong Kong University Press, 1956.

"Levels of Understanding in Buddhism," *Journal of the American Oriental Society*, Vol. 78, pp. 19ff, New Haven, 1958.

"The Philosophical Background of Buddhist Tantrism," *Journal of Oriental Studies*, edited by Michael Smithies, Vol. V, pp. 45ff, Hong Kong: © Hong Kong University Press, 1959-60.

"Indian Buddhist Thought in Tibetan Perspective—Infinite Transcendence versus Finiteness," *History of Religions*, edited by Mircea Eliade et al, Vol. III, No. 1, pp. 83ff, Chicago: © The University of Chicago Press, 1963.

"Some Aspects of Tibetan Religious Thought," *History of Religions*, edited by Mircea Eliade et al, Vol. VI, No. 1, pp. 70ff, Chicago: © The University of Chicago Press, 1966.

"Mentalism and Beyond in Buddhist Philosophy," *Journal of the American Oriental Society*, Vol. 86, pp. 288ff, New Haven, 1966.

"The Spiritual Teacher in Tibet," *Hermes*, pp. 226ff, Paris, 1966/67.

"Tantra and Revelation," *History of Religions*, edited by Mircea Eliade et al, Vol. VII, No. 4, pp. 279-301, Chicago: © The University of Chicago Press, 1968.

"The Spiritual Guide as Mystic Experience," R. M. Bucke Society *Newsletter-Review*, Vol. III, No. 1, pp. 22-26, Montreal, 1968.

"Towards an Experience of Being Through Psychological Purification," *A Study of Kleśa*, edited by Genjun H. Sasaki, pp. 478-493, Tokyo: © Shimizukobundo Ltd., 1975.

ISBN 0-913546-49-6; 0-913546-50-x (pbk)
Library of Congress Number: 76-47758

Typeset in Fototronic Plantin and printed by
Dharma Press, Emeryville, California

9 8 7 6 5 4 3 2 1

Contents

Introduction

Over a century ago, Alexander Csoma de Körös, who against his original intention was to become a pioneer in Tibetan studies, made the erroneous statement that "the literature of Tibet is entirely of Indian origin." He did not realize that he had come across a small, although by Western standards enormous, section of writings in Tibetan—the bKa'-'gyur and the bsTan-'gyur—and that he had been duped by the Tibetan 'propaganda' that everything the Tibetans had to offer had come to them from India. This propaganda which the Tibetans themselves eventually came to believe in, seems to have had its root in a political situation in the eighth century which the Tibetans later camouflaged with an historical hoax—the so-called Samye debate which we now, on the evidence of contemporary sources from Tun-huang, know never to have taken place. Anyhow, the statement by Alexander Csoma de Körös became the credo of the academic world and even today, despite an overwhelming evidence to the contrary, it is still fervently subscribed to both in the East and in the West. The implication is that to a large extent so-called studies in Tibetan have actually remained studies in Sanskrit or what was supposed to have been Sanskrit.

When I began my academic studies in 1936 I was naturally exposed to this climate of misinformedness and misrepresentation. It was then in 1950 when I took up my academic duties at Lucknow University and later at the Sanskrit University at Varanasi that I was given the chance to recognize the falsity of what was thoughtlessly (or should I say 'irresponsibly'?) perpetuated in academic circles all over the world. The recognition of this falsity for what it is does not imply that India did not play a significant role in the history of ideas in the rest of Asia. Her role was essentially to give a tremendous stimulus to thought, and the works that were translated from Indian sources ('Indian' must be understood as a blanket-term for everything reflecting ideas having come from India and having been absorbed and developed, maybe with an admixture of their own, by the indigenous people in the border areas of India proper and in Central Asia) bear enough evidence that the translators not only thought about the subject-matter they were going to translate, but also were aware of the problems involved. They were 'task-oriented', and it is this quality of theirs, so sadly lacking in the contemporary scene of the humanities, that made their works so precise and valuable. Furthermore, the fact that the Tibetans constantly referred to their own thinkers and to how they had understood and developed the stimulus that had come from India, rather than playing the game of correlating Tibetan words with Sanskrit terms, was decisive for my taking up the study of Tibetan thought and Tibetan Buddhism in their distinct Tibetan quality.

Much of what is discussed in Tibetan works is of a philosophical and psychological nature. Any discussion of any topic involves the use of language, whether written or spoken, and a language, in the narrow sense of the word, is made up of words. (Apart from this specific feature there are the language of gesture, the language of music, the language of the visual arts, etc., etc.) Words themselves have no meaning, but acquire meaning through their use in a specific task field. In this usage both stipulative and reportive definitions fuse imperceptibly. The important point to note is that it is always the task that determines in which sense we are going to use a word, either by selecting one of the several meanings which are already attached to the word we are going to use on the occasion, or by stipulating a meaning that is felt to be more precise and clearer than the one it already has, or by inventing a new word because we do not find one in existence for some meaning we have in mind. Never is language and its use something mechanical. But linguists keep forgetting this and also fail to take into account that language carries with it the imprint of our physical, social, and spiritual consciousness and that only as a process can it speak to us. Its end product has, quite literally, nothing to say.

Philosophy, before it is reduced to stale *isms* ('realism', 'idealism'—'Buddhism' being no exception), is a serious and demanding task because it makes us think and re-think a problem. In order to be able to do this the problem must be clearly focussed. Such a problem may be 'mind', 'matter', 'space', 'time', 'relativity', 'Being', 'Saṃsāra', 'Nirvāṇa'—there is no end to what can be thought and rethought. Again, in order to be able to focus the problem a person must be up to this task which in the realm of philosophy requires a thorough grounding in philosophical methodology and philosophical questioning, for without such prerequisites a person who is going to address himself to a problem will never be able to understand where or what the problem is. Once a problem has been recognized and focussed it will have to be elucidated. I intentionally speak of 'elucidation' and not of 'solution'. There are no solutions, only fresh problems to be elucidated and to be brought into perspective. If ever philosophy were to give a 'definite' answer not only would it have destroyed itself, it would have brought about spiritual death and the end of humanity. Elucidation means to bring to light, not to come up with pretentious-sounding answers which in fact are no answers because no questions have been asked, and which merely reinforce a widespread indifference to the advancement of knowledge and a deep-rooted unwillingness to learn because learning might involve a departure from stereotypes.

The incontestable evidence for the fact that the Tibetans were capable of thinking independently and that they, as is only natural, developed a language geared to the task of philosophical inquiry coupled with a keen insight into psychological processes—of course, not every Tibetan was or is a philosopher and, as the Tibetans themselves quite frankly admit, only very few really understand the technical writings and their implications—presents a significant phenomenon in the history of ideas and opens up a new field of research. Whenever one has to deal with a new phenomenon one soon learns that traditional ideas and concepts do not pay very well and that for the most part they have outlived their usefulness already long ago. Therefore a new approach has to be made and this necessitates a new set of concepts or new stipulative definitions. This I have attempted in the following essays of this book. They are exploratory in nature and I wish to emphasize that I never could (nor will I ever) subscribe to a mood of 'definiteness' because this mood is soporific and geared to a static conception of man and the universe and to a mechanical mode of dealing with them. Although definiteness with the deterministic interpretation displays a certain attractiveness which seems to be natural and more easy, this attractiveness is but the pervasive fallacy of assuming that everything is reducible to quantifiable platitudes.

The essays selected for this book were written at various times and in various places, always in closest contact with Tibetan scholars representing the 'Brug-pa bKa'-brgyud and rNying-ma traditions whose way of thinking offers a key to the understanding of Buddhism as a living force of 'extensive becoming' that seems to constitute the nature of human thought and human spiritual growth.

Apart from minor stylistic changes so as to ensure consistency in presentation, and a few additions for clarification of extremely concise statements, the essays have been left unaltered so as to bring out the specific implications that, where 'process' is the keynote, we have as yet no adequate language nor a corresponding conceptual framework at our disposal, and that any reduction to any static model, however comfortable such an outworn and outmoded procedure may seem, is incompatible with the actual 'facts'.

In conclusion, I want to acknowledge the benefit of stimulating discussions I had with the members of the Nyingma

Institute interested in particular aspects of Buddhist thought and practice, and with the editorial staff of Dharma Publishing, especially with Miss Judy Robertson, without whose untiring help it would hardly have been possible to decide upon a representative selection of essays.

I wish to thank my dear friend Tarthang Tulku who in many ways furthered my studies and who continues taking a lively interest in them.

Deeply felt thanks are due to my wife and to Mr. Rick Cowburn for preparing the Index.

Saskatoon/Berkeley H. V. GUENTHER

Tibetan Buddhism in Western Perspective

Excerpts from the Gaṇḍavyūha Sūtra

The *Gaṇḍavyūha Mahāyānasūtraratnarāja* is the last section of the *Avataṃsaka*, a group of texts which is mentioned directly after the *Prajñāparamitās*. Isolated sections of the *Avataṃsaka* were translated into Chinese by Lokakṣema (178–188 A.D.), Dharmarakṣa (291–297 A.D.), and Buddhabhadra (418 A.D.). The translation by Śikṣānanda (695–699 A.D.) also contains the *Daśabhūmikasūtra*. The translation by Buddhabhadra is based on the Sanskrit text which is still extant. The *Gaṇḍavyūha* is the principal authority of the Avataṃsaka school of Buddhism, which arose in China between 557 and 589 A.D., and of the Kegon sect of Japan. Parts of the text are quoted in the well-known compendium of Mahāyāna Buddhism, *Śikṣāsamuccaya*.

The text describes the idea of a Bodhisattva. The youth Sudhana travels all over India on the advice of the Bodhisattva Mañjuśrī, in order to achieve the highest knowledge of Enlightenment. He goes to all kinds of men, women and deities. Finally, by the help of the Bodhisattva Samantabhadra, the highest knowledge is revealed to him, which is essentially the vision and experience of the interpenetration of each and every thing. In the course of his travels he is sent from one teacher to another, because every one, with the exception of Bodhisattva Samantabhadra, has only a limited knowledge. In many instances these teachers tell the youth Sudhana their life-story in a form the same as that of the Jātakas. The text is in both prose and verses. The final part of the *Gaṇḍavyūha* is the *Samantabhadracaryāpraṇidhāna*, the verses in which the divine resolution of Samantabhadra is described.

The following is a translation from the instruction given by the goddess of the night Sarvajagadrakṣāpraṇidhāvīryaprabhā, 'the heroic splendor of the resolve to guard all the world', on Sudhana's question as to how long she had been in possession of her specific Bodhisattva-knowledge.

THE BODHISATTVAS' REALM OF KNOWLEDGE

O son of a noble family, in the Bodhisattvas' realm of knowledge there is no place for speculations about the aeons; therein will not be experienced or known either long duration of Saṃsāra or short duration of Saṃsāra; nor will there be experienced or known either depravity of aeons or purity of aeons, or smallness of aeons or greatness of aeons, or multitude of aeons or diversity of aeons, or manifoldness of aeons or diversifyingness of aeons, or variety of aeons. For what reason is that so? Because, O son of a noble family, the Bodhisattvas' realm of knowledge is pure in its very nature, is free from all the trammels of ideation, is beyond all the mountains of veiling obstructions. (This knowledge) rises in the (pure) intention (of the Bodhisattvas) and sheds its radiance on all the beings who will in time be led to (spiritual) maturity (by different means) according to their (different) dispositions.

In the same way, O son of a noble family, as in the disk of the sun the distinction of day and night cannot be found, nor does it reside there, but when the sun has set night is known and experienced, and when the sun has risen day is known and experienced—so also, O son of a noble family, in the Bodhisattvas' realm of knowledge (which is like unto the disk of the sun and) which knows not of ratiocination, one cannot find any thought constructions as to the aeons, nor can one find there any ideas about lives in this world, or about any paths (that one might walk). On the contrary, it is due to the fact that it takes time until all the beings have attained to (spiritual) maturity (i.e., Buddhahood) that in the ratiocinationless realm of knowledge, which has risen from the pure intentions of the Bodhisattvas, ideas and calculations as to lives in the aeons, and as to the world in general, are found.

In the same way, O son of noble family, as the disk of the sun (shining) in the clear sky is seen reflected in all the jewel-mountains, in all the jewel-trees, in all the jewel-heaps, in all the jewel-mines, in all the seas, in all the fountains and lakes, in all the vessels containing pure water, in all the (perceiving) minds of the world, yet it rises (in the sky) before the very eyes of the beings; and as the disk of the sun is seen reflected in all the particles of jewel-dust, yet this disk of the sun does not originate in the jewel-mountains, nor in the jewel-trees, nor does it at all enter into the particles of (jewel-) dust, nor does it go (bodily) into the luster of gems, nor does it proceed down into the jewel-mines, nor does it descend into the seas, nor does it enter right into the vessels filled with water, and yet it is seen everywhere within (them all)–so also, O son of a noble family, a Bodhisattva Mahāsattva, having risen from the Ocean of Existence and ascended to the sky of the Tathāgatadharmadhātu (the Buddha's Realm of Truth), abides in the sky-like field of the true nature of phenomena, resides in the sky of tranquility, (but) is seen (at the same time) in all the actual and possible existences of the world. (Though) taking upon himself the task of leading beings to (spiritual) maturity by assuming such outer forms as resemble (those of) all the beings, he is not defiled by the blemishes of the world, is not tormented by the sorrows of death and birth, harbors no futile ideas about the aeons; nor is there in his aeon the idea of long duration or short duration. For what reason is that so? Because a Bodhisattva, ever undisturbed, has transcended the troublesome distractions of ideation, minding and theorization; has understood and sees all the worlds in their true state, that is, that they are like a dream; has profoundly grasped the fact that all the worlds are like a display of jugglery (*māyā*); has grasped the profound knowledge that the realms (of existence) are unsubstantial; looks at things as they really are; is beheld by all creatures by reason of his great devotion characterized by an all-comprehensive compassion, since he has taken upon himself the task of leading all creatures to (spiritual) maturity.

In the same way, O son of a noble family, as on big rivers a ferryboat is constantly engaged in and never gets tired of carrying people across to the other shore, so long as the boatman lives, nor does the ferryboat halt at the other shore, nor at this shore, nor does it come to a stop in the middle of the water—so also, O son of a noble family, a Bodhisattva is (ever) busy with ferrying all the beings over the rivers and currents of the world in the boat of the Great Perfections. He does not shrink with fear from the other shore, neither does he stay complacent at this shore; on the contrary, he is constantly busy with ferrying the beings over. He accepts the diversity of the aeons and leads the life of a Bodhisattva which has been prepared for during immeasurable aeons, but he does not lead the life of a Bodhisattva by harboring such an idea as that it will take a long time to transcend the aeons.

In the same way, O son of noble family, as in all the spheres of the world, be they evolving or revolving or expanded, the sky of infinite space, the richness of the Dharmadhātu, cannot be apprehended by means of thought constructions, is pure by nature, undefiled, unobstructed, a whole, not long (or short), not fathomable, not restricted to time, sustaining all the fields of action—so also, O son of a noble family, the sky of knowledge born from the pure intentions of the Bodhisattvas and encircled by the winds of (their) great resolutions, does not get tired of preventing beings from falling down over the precipice of woeful existences, does not know of any anxious deliberations when leading them on the right path, never takes rest while engaged in firmly establishing the beings on the ways to Omniscience, is not perplexed by the host of ego-centered passions (*kleśa*), and is not defiled by the evils of this world.

In the same way, O son of a noble family, as ten things are not to be found in an (illusory) man created by jugglery (or magic), though he may possess all the major and minor limbs–Which ten?–Coming and going of his own accord, coldness, warmth, hunger, thirst, joy, anger, (the succession of) birth, old age, illness and death, as well as pain–so also, O son of a noble family, ten properties are not to be found in a Bodhisattva whose body has been produced by the magic of knowledge, who is not different from the Dharmadhātukāya, who is born in all forms of existence in this world, who lives throughout the aeons in order to lead all beings to (spiritual) maturity–Which ten?–Yearning for the world, indifference to all the actual and possible existences of this world, sensual inclinations towards worldly objects, attitude of retaliation, desire for enjoyment, experience of sorrow, torment by all the ego-centered passions, fear of objects and of all the actual and possible existences (of the world), desire for continued (mundane) existence or the tendency to become absorbed in it.

IN PRAISE OF BODHICITTA

[In his desire to learn the way of a true Bodhisattva, the indefatigable youth Sudhana comes to the Bodhisattva Maitreya, who after having extolled Sudhana's earnest longing for enlightenment and for the accomplishment of a Bodhisattva's career, delivers the following panegyric on the all-comprehensive properties of the Bodhicitta. The translation is made from the last chapter but one of the *Gaṇḍavyūha*].

O son of a noble family, the attitude characterized as being bent on Enlightenment (*bodhicitta*) is the seed of all the virtues of the Buddhas. It is like a field, because in it grow all the bright virtues of the world; it is like the earth, because all the world takes refuge in it; it is like water, because it washes away all the impurities due to self-centered passions; it is like the wind, because it is present everywhere in the world; it is like the fire, because it burns all the remaining undergrowth of wrong views; it is like the sun, because it fills the whole world with splendor; it is like the moon, because it makes the disk of resplendant virtues grow; it is like a lamp, because it radiates the light of the Dharma; it is like the eye, because it sees what is plain and what is not plain; it is like a path, because it leads into the fortress of omniscience; it is like an (excellent) ford, because it abolishes all bad fords; it is like a carriage, because all the Bodhisattvas ride in it; it is like a door, because it is the main entrance to the behavior of all the Bodhisattvas; it is like a palace, because it is the place for meditation and spiritual culture; it is like a garden, because it is suitable for the enjoyment of the Dharma; it is like a cave, because it protects all the worlds; it is like a place of shelter, because it brings what is good for all the world; it is like a foundation, because all the Bodhisattvas walk on it; it is like a father, because it protects all the Bodhisattvas; it is like a mother for all beings; it is like a nurse, because it protects against all dangers; it is like a king, because it subdues the attitudes of all who have still to strive, of all who have no longer to be instructed, and of all who are Pratyekabuddhas; it is like an overlord, because it is most excellent as regards all vows; it is like the great ocean, because all virtues and jewels are gathered together in it; it is like the great Meru, because it has the same attitude toward all beings; it is like the world-enriching mountain, because all the world takes refuge in its round; it is like the Himalaya, because it makes the herb of wisdom grow; it is like the mount Gandhamādana, because it is the support for the odor of all virtues; it is like a lotus flower, because it is not defiled by worldly things; it is like a well-trained steed, because it is free of all viciousness; it is like a driver, because it precedes the entering into the teaching of the Mahāyāna; it is like a physician, because it heals the illness consisting in self-centered passion; it is like a furnace, because it purifies all unwholesome things; it is like a diamond, because it pierces everything; it is like a smelling-box, because it wafts abroad the fragrance of the virtues; it is like a huge flower, because it is pleasant to be seen by all the world; it is like a cool sandal (paste), because it assuages the heat of craving; it is like an ornament, because all the Dharmadhātu moves in it; it is like the king of the physicians, Sudarśana, because it extirpates all diseases originating in self-centered passion; it is like the surgeon Vigama, because it extracts the thorn of all evil propensities; it is like Indra, because it rules over all the mental faculties; it is like the god Vaiśravaṇa, because it banishes all poverty; it is like the goddess Śrī, because it is an ornament of all virtues; it is like an ornament, because it adorns all Bodhisattvas; it is like the all-destroying fire at the end of a Kalpa, because it consumes all evil deeds; it is like the king of the physicians, Anivṛttamūla, because it makes all the qualities of a Buddha grow; it is like the jewel in the hood of a serpent, because it removes all self-centered passion; it is like the surface of a well, because it removes all blemishes; it is like the Wish-fulfilling Gem, because it actualizes all virtues; it is like an auspicious jar, because it fulfils all desires; it is like the Wish-fulfilling Tree, because it rains down oranments of virtues; it is like a garment on which swans are printed, because it is not connected with the evils of saṃsāra; it is like a thread of cotton, because it is radiant by nature; it is like a ploughshare, because it clears the field of the evil propensities of all beings; it is like an iron arrow, because it destroys the Satkāyadṛṣṭi; it is like an arrow, because it hits the mark of miserableness; it is like a sword, because it overpowers all self-centered passions; it is like armor, because it destroys wrong attentiveness; it is like a dagger, because it cuts off the heads of self-centered passions; it is like the blade of a sword, because it destroys arrogance, infatuation, vanity and hypocrisy; it is like a razor, because it slays the propensities; it is like the flag of heroes, because it casts down the flag of arrogance; it is like an axe, because it fells the tree of ignorance; it is like a hatchet, because it cuts asunder the tree of miserableness; it is like a weapon, because it protects against all miseries; it is like a hand, because it safeguards the body of the Perfections; it is like a foot, because it is the foothold of all virtues and wisdom; it is like a chisel, because it scrapes away the wrappings of ignorance; it is like a hoe, because it roots up the view of Satkāyadṛṣti; it is like tweezers, because it pulls out the thorn of the propensities; it is like a friend, because it delivers from the fetters of this world of woe; it is like substantial matter, because it obstructs all that is useless; it is like an instructor, because it knows all the paths that lead to the conduct of all Bodhisattvas; it is like a treasure, because it is inexhaustible in merits; it is like an excellency, because it is inexhaustible in wisdom; it is like a mirror, because it reflects the images of all phenomena; it is like a lotus flower, because it is not defiled; it is like a great river, because it carries the vessels necessary for the attainment of the Perfections; it is like the king of the serpents, because it makes the Cloud of Dharma rain; it is like life, because it sustains the great compassion of all the Bodhisattvas; it is like the elixir of life, because it leads to the realm of the immortal ones; it is like a net, because it envelopes and drags along all people that are to be lead (out of this world); it is like health, because it spreads health everywhere; it is like an antidote, because it counteracts the poison of karma and carnal lust; it is like a spell, because it takes away the poison of all that is improper; it is like a storm, because it uproots all obstacles and hindrances; it is like the jewel island, because it is a mine for those qualities that belong to Enlightenment; it is like a clan, because all bright qualities are in it; it is like a market place, because it is frequented by all the merchant-like Bodhisattvas; it is like the elixir of life, because it purges from all the obstructions due to karma and self-centered passions; it is like honey, because it fulfils all the requirements for omniscience; it is like a path, because it leads all the Bodhisattvas toward the fortress of omniscience; it is like a vessel, because it contains all bright virtues; it is like a downpour of rain, because it lays the dust of self-centered passions; it is like a platform, because it points out the position of all the Bodhisattvas; it is like a lodestone, because it attracts also the liberation of the Śrāvakas; it is like beryl, because it is immaculate by nature; it is like sapphire, because it overpowers all the worldly knowledge of all the Śrāvakas and Pratyekabuddhas; it is like a watchman in the night, because it arouses those who sleep, lulled by self-centered passions; it is like clear water, because it is not disturbed; it is like a bracelet of pure gold, because it illuminates the realm of what has been created and the accumulation of what is profitable; it is like the king of the mountains, because it towers above this triple world; it is like a shelter, because it does not betray those who have taken refuge in it; it is like profit, because it counteracts all that is not profitable; it is like a vision, because it gladdens the heart; it is like the implements for a sacrifice, because it satisfies all the world; it is like reason, because it is the most excellent attitude in the world; it is like a treasure, because it comprises all the qualities of a Buddha it is like a solemn promise, because it comprises all the vows as regards the activity of the Bodhisattvas; it is like a guardian, because it protects all the world; it is like a protector, because it averts all that is evil; it is like a net, because it catches all enemies, the self-centered passions; it is like Indra and Agni, because it burns all the impressions, propensities, and self-centered passions; it is like the noose of Varuṇa, because it pulls out those who are to be led out of (this world); it is like a sanctuary for the world together with its gods, men, and demons.

FRIENDS IN THE GOOD LIFE

[Sudhana is directed to the Boy Śrīsaṃbhava and the girl Śrīmati who, after having told him about their spiritual realizations, give the following account of the importance of the company of and the aid rendered by spiritual friends].

O son of a noble family, you must be unwearied in your search for friends in the good life, you must never feel contented with (merely) seeing friends in the good life; you must never feel satisfied with (merely) conversing with friends in the good life; you must never abandon your intention of being in the company of friends in the good life; your effort of paying respect to the greatness of friends in the good life must never grow feeble; you must never adopt an antagonistic attitude as regards the counsels and instructions given by friends in the good life; you must feel no doubt about the acquisition of merits by friends in the good life; you must never harbor any dubiety as to (the ability of) the friends in the good life to show the way out (of the snares of the world); you must never have any ill-will when the friends in the good life act contrarily to the commonly accepted wordly usage as regards the means they adopt; you must never, either in body or in mind, withdraw from increasing the satisfaction of friends in the good life. Why must you never do so? (Because,) O son of a noble family, the foundation of the Bodhisattvic life of all the Bodhisattvas rests (primarily) on friends in the good life; the coming to ripeness of the merits of all the Bodhisattvas starts with friends in the good life; the rivers of the original vows of all the Bodhisattvas have their source in friends in the good life; the seed of the good to be reaped later by all the Bodhisattvas has been planted by friends in the good life; the necessary (bodily and spiritual) requisites of all the Bodhisattvas have been prepared by friends in the good life; the excellent light of the Dharma (shed by) all the Bodhisattvas proceeds from friends in the good life; the purity of the gateway to liberation (as exemplified by) all the Bodhisattvas originates in friends in the good life; the acquisition of learning by all the Bodhisattvas is linked up with friends in the good life; the meritorious qualities of all the Bodhisattvas rest firmly in friends in the good life; the purity of intention of all the Bodhisattvas has its root in friends in the good life; the firm resolution of all the Bodhisattvas to awaken (in the sentient beings) an attitude directed toward the realization of Enlightenment has originated with friends in the good life; the light of the countenance of all the Bodhisattvas on which understanding, reaching as far as the earth and the ocean, shines, is gazed at by friends in the good life; the excellent treasure of purity of all the Bodhisattvas has been collected by friends in the good life; the light of knowledge of all the Bodhisattvas has been kindled by friends in the good life; the excellency of the original vows of all the Bodhisattvas lies in the hands of friends in the good life; the uniqueness of happiness rests on friends in the good life; the distinct conviction about the rise of all the Bodhisattvas is the clan of friends in the good life; the secrets of all the Bodhisattvas are the treasure house of friends in the good life; the Dharma mines of all the Bodhisattvas are the mines of friends in the good life; the sprouts of quick apprehension by all the Bodhisattvas are tended by friends in the good life; the oceans of knowledge of all the Bodhisattvas are made to swell by friends in the good life; the treasures in the treasure-houses of all the Bodhisattvas are protected by friends in the good life; the accumulation of merits by all the Bodhisattvas is guarded by friends in the good life; the purity of births of all the Bodhisattvas is created by friends in the good life; the Dharmamegha (the Dharma clouds sprinkling the nectar of the good life) of all the Bodhisattvas has risen through friends in the good life; the entering of all the Bodhisattvas upon the paths leading to liberation is the granary of friends in the good life; the Buddha-Enlightenment of all the Bodhisattvas is gained by pleasing friends in the good life; the behavior of all the Bodhisattvas is directed by friends in the good life; the development of spiritual values by all the Bodhisattvas is illumined by friends in the good life; the going through the world by all the Bodhisattvas is pointed out (to them) by friends in the good life; the greatness of mind and intention of all the Bodhisattvas is described by friends in the good life; the huge power of love (*maitrī*) of all the Bodhisattvas has risen from friends in the good life; the huge power of compassion (*karuṇā*) of all the Bodhisattvas has been generated by friends in the good life; the superiority of all the Bodhisattvas has been collected by friends in the good life; the (seven) characteristics of Enlightenment of all the Bodhisattvas (discrimination of the true and the false; zealous striving; joy; riddance of all grossness and weight of body and mind; power of remembering; concentration; and freedom from any selfishness and looking out to the world of selfishness from this selfless standpoint) has been created by friends in the good life; the sacrifices for the welfare (of all sentient beings made) by all the Bodhisattvas originate with friends in the good life.

O son of a noble family, kept back by friends in the good life the Bodhisattvas do not fall into the pits of woeful existences; surrounded by friends in the good life the Bodhisattvas do not turn away from the Great Career (Mahāyāna); exhorted by friends in the good life the Bodhisattvas do not forsake the teachings of the Bodhisattvas; guarded by friends in the good life the Bodhisattvas do not come under the power of bad friends; protected by friends in the good life the Bodhisattvas do not lose the essential qualities of Bodhisattvas; directed by friends in the good life the Bodhisattvas go beyond the world of ordinary men; taught by friends in the good life the Bodhisattvas do not lower themselves to the level of Śrāvakas and Pratyekabuddhas; shielded by friends in the good life the Bodhisattvas have risen above the world; tended by friends in the good life the Bodhisattvas are not defiled by worldly things; guarded by friends in the good life the Bodhisattvas are irreproachable as to their behavior in all walks of life; uplifted by friends in the good life the Bodhisattvas do not leave (unfinished) whatever (task) they have begun; taught and guarded by friends in the good life the Bodhisattvas cannot be attacked by the defilements of selfish actions; having gained their strength from friends in the good life the Bodhisattvas are invincible (to attack) by all the armies of Māra; relying on friends in the good life the Bodhisattvas increase in the (seven) characteristics of Enlightenment.

Why is that so? (Because,) O son of a noble family, the friends in the good life clear away and purify the veiling obstructions (on the way to Enlightenment); the friends in the good life turn (you) away from the pits of woeful existences; the friends in the good life make (you) realize what must not be done; they restrain (you) from all things conducive to laziness; they dispel the darkness of ignorance; they snap the fetters of preconceived ideas; they make (you) go beyond the world of relativity; they uproot the conventions of the world; they liberate (you) from the fetters of Māra; they extract the thorns of suffering; they liberate (you) from the brushwood of ignorance; they make (you) pass safely through the deserts of preconceived theories; they ferry (you) over the floods of being; they drag (you) out of the swamp of lust; they make (you) turn away from bad roads; they show (you) the way toward Enlightenment; they make (you) take upon yourself the tasks of the Bodhisattvas; they have (you) firmly established in the (spiritual) realizations; they lead (you) on the way toward Omniscience; they cleanse the Divine Eye; they make the attitude directed toward Enlightenment grow; they engender Great Compassion; they describe the (Bodhisattvas') behavior; they counsel (you) as to the perfections; they make (you) reach the various levels of spiritual growth (*bhūmi*); they distribute the (various kinds of) patience; they cultivate all the seeds of good to be reaped later; they prepare all the necessary (bodily and spiritual) requisites; they confer all the qualities of the Bodhisattvas; they make (you) reach the feet of all the Buddhas; they show (you) all (good) qualities; they make (you) take upon yourself all tasks for the sake of (all sentient beings); they fill (you) with enthusiasm as regards the realizations; they show the gateway to liberation; they keep (you) away from the roads that lead to destruction; they illuminate the doors of the Dharma light; they make the clouds of hearing the Dharma rain; they destroy all self-centered passions; they make (you) turn away from all preconceived theories; they make (you) enter into all the Buddha-qualities.

Furthermore, O son of a noble family, friends in the good life are a mother, because they give birth (to Bodhisattvas) in the Buddha families; friends in the good life are a father, because they bring immense good; friends in the good life are a wet-nurse, because they protect (the Bodhisattvas) from all evil; friends in the good life are a teacher, because they educate (the Bodhisattvas) in the disciplines of the Bodhisattvas; friends in the good life are guides, because they make (the Bodhisattvas) walk on the way of the perfections; friends in the good life are a physician, because they free (the Bodhisattvas) from the disease of self-centered passion; friends in the good life are the Himalaya mountains because they make the herb of knowledge grow; friends in the good life are heroes, because they protect (the Bodhisattvas) against all dangers; friends in the good life are servants, because they make (the Bodhisattvas) cross the floods of existence by the (bodily and spiritual) supplies (they give); friends in the good life are pilots, because they make (the Bodhisattvas) reach the jewel island of Buddha-wisdom.

Therefore, O son of a noble family, thinking about (the value of having friends in the good life) in this way you should eagerly call on friends in the good life: with a mind that is like the earth, because it does not change by carrying all burdens; with a mind like the diamond (*vajra*), because its firm resolve cannot be broken; with a mind like the world-encircling mountain, because it does not let through any suffering; with equanimity, because it generates knowledge as desired; with a mind like a pupil, because it is not averse to all the universal spiritual powers (*abhijñā*); with a mind like a common servant, because it is not fastidious in taking up all sorts of work; with a mind like a wet-nurse, because it does not get frightened by self-centered passion; with a mind like a skilled laborer, because it skillfully takes up whatever has to be done; with a mind like a duster, because it sweeps away all pride and conceit; with a mind like the full moon, because it does not change phases; with a mind like a thoroughbred horse, because it leaves behind all roughness, with a mind like a chariot, because it carries the heavy burden (put upon it by the Guru); with a mind like a Nāga, because its attitude is tamed and noble; with a mind like a rock, because it does not shake nor tremble; with a mind like a dog, because it is not angry; with a mind like a Caṇḍāla boy, because it is without pride and selfishness; with a mind like an inmate, because it has no sense of superiority; with a mind like a boat, because it does not tire of coming and going; with a mind like a bridge, because it crosses (over to the other shore) by the precepts given by friends in the good life; with a mind like a good son, because it looks up to the face of friends in the good life; with a mind like a prince, because it fulfills the order of the King of the Dharma.

O son of a noble family, you must consider yourself as a patient, friends in the good life as the physicians, their instructions as the remedy, and spiritual realizations as the cure of illness. O son of a noble family, you must consider yourself as a wanderer, friends in the good life as signposts, their instructions as the way, and spiritual realizations as the actual walking over fields. O son of a noble family, you must consider yourself as a man wanting to go to the other shore, friends in the good life as the shipowner, their advice as the point of embarcation, and spiritual progress as the boat. O son of noble family, you must consider yourself as a cultivator, friends in the good life as the Lord of Rain (Indra), their instructions as rainfall, and spiritual realizations as the growing of crops. O son of a noble family, you must consider yourself as a pauper, friends in the good life as the God of Riches, their instructions as wealth, and spiritual realizations as the abolition of poverty. O son of a noble family, you must consider yourself as a pupil, friends in the good life as the teacher, their instructions as the arts to be learned, (and spiritual realizations) as the mastery of the arts. O son of a noble family, you must consider yourself as an audacious one, friends in the good life as heroes, their instructions as the dealing of blows, and spiritual realizations as the destruction of enemies. O son of a noble family, you must consider yourself as a merchant, friends in the good life as the helmsman, their instructions as jewels, and spiritual realizations as the acquisition of jewels. O son of a noble family, you must consider yourself as a dutiful son, friends in the good life as father and mother, their instructions as the family tradition, and spiritual realizations as the non-decline of the tradition. O son of a noble family, you must consider yourself as prince, friends in the good life as ministers of the King of Dharma, their instruction of political science, and spiritual realizations as the crown of the King of Knowledge, the turban of the Dharma, and the maintenance of the towns of the King of the Dharma. O son of a noble family, with a mind that has been trained in this way you must call on friends in the good life.

Why is that so? (Because,) O son of a noble family, the Bodhisattvas who, pure in their intentions regarding friends in the good life, follow the precepts of friends in the good life, grow as regards their seed of good like the grass, shrubs, herbs, and trees on the Himalaya mountain. They become a vessel for all the Buddha-qualities like the ocean for water. They become a mine of all virtues like the great sea of jewels. They awaken the attitude directed toward the realization of Enlightenment like gold (purified) in the heat of a fire. They rise above the world like Mount Meru out of the ocean. They are not defiled by the things of the world as the lotus flower is not defiled by water. They do not live together with a detestable life just as the ocean does not keep company with putrid corpses. They increase in bright qualities like the moon in the bright half of the month. They illumine the Dharmadhātu as the sun illumines Jambūdvīpa. They make the bodies of the original vows of the Bodhisattvas grow just as young boys are reared by their father and mother.

ALWAYS READY TO HELP

[Wandering all over the world in order to learn and to live the life of a Bodhisattva, the youth Sudhana is directed by Sthāvarā, the goddess of the earth, to Vāsantī, the goddess of the night, in Kapilavastu. Soon after the sun has set, Sudhana sees "Vāsantī, the goddess of the night, sitting on the jewelled lion throne of lotus shape, wondrously fragrant, in a palace of many colored, incomparable gems high up in the sky over the city of Kapilavastu; lovely, charming, and glorious with her golden-hued body, her dark, soft, rich hair, her dark eyes, dressed in precious ornaments, wearing a beautiful red garment, with a crown in her single braid, adorned by the disk of the moon, and on whose body is visible the splendor of all the stars, planets, constellations, and heavenly bodies." Then, after having saluted her with due respect and asked her about the way towards omniscience and where to stand in order to be excellent in all one's deeds for the benefit of the world, the goddess of the night answers]:

O son of a noble family, I am in the possession of the Bodhisattva emancipation called The Door Toward Discipline of the World Illumined by Dispelling the (Spiritual) Darkness of all Sentient Beings. I have love (*maitrī*) even toward those beings who are crooked in mind; I feel sympathetic joy (*muditā*) even toward those beings who have not yet trodden the way of meritorious deeds; I have equanimity (*upekṣā*) toward beings who are straight in mind and crooked in mind. I intend to purify those who are defiled; I intend to set on the right path those who have gone the wrong way; I intend to inspire sublime ideals in those who have mean ideals; I intend to increase the feeling of strength in those who feel themselves weak. I intend to turn away from the remorseless wheel of the world and its paths those who delight in a world of relativity (and pain). I intend to put firmly on the way toward omniscience those beings who are inclined toward the (limited) Śrāvaka and Pratyekabuddha careers. Thus intending and thus keeping (my intention) always in mind, O son of a noble family, I am endowed with the Bodhisattva emancipation called The Door Toward Discipline of the World Illumined by Dispelling the (Spiritual) Darkness of All Sentient Beings.

In a dark and murky night when hosts of ghosts walk about and crowds of robbers set out, when vicious people roam about in all quarters of the world and a net of black clouds covers the sky, when the air is filled with the filth of dust and smoke and adverse winds and rain storms shake the earth, when the sun, moon, and multitude of stars have disappeared and one cannot pierce the darkness with one's eyes—in such a night, those beings among the wayfaring people—who have set out by sea or by land, through mountains or forest deserts, through jungles or foreign countries, to other villages or to other quarters of the world, to the intermediate regions or on other ways, or on the great ocean —may meet with an untimely end of their voyage. On their way by land they are killed; on their way through the mountains they fall into deep ravines; on their way through forest deserts they are deprived of food and drink; deceived by the multitude of trees and shrubs and reeds they lose the direction; on their way into foreign countries they are killed by highwaymen; on their way to other villages they are destroyed by viciousness; on their way to other quarters of the world they miss the direction; on their way to the intermediate regions they lose the way; and on their way by other roads they meet perdition. O son of a noble family, to these people I am a refuge in various ways and by various means: To those who go by sea I show the way to the jewel island by dispelling adverse winds and clouds, by making them pass over a rough sea, by dispersing treacherous storms, by calming the force of the huge waves, by liberating them from the fear and danger of whirlpools, by illuminating the regions, by setting them on the right sea path, and by showing them the shore, I am a refuge to them in the form of a convoy, a caravan leader, a king, an elephant king, a tortoise king, an Asura king, a Garuḍa king, a Kinnara king, a great serpent king, a goddess of the sea, and a fisherman. All this stock of merit I transfer (to all the other sentient beings). I wish I might be a refuge to all sentient beings in order to turn them away from all suffering. To those beings who go by land, who have lost the direction in a dark and murky night of delusion on an earth which is covered with reeds, thorns, stones, and gravel, frequented by terrible poisonous snakes, uneven with mountains and valleys and full of dust and dirt, shaken by adverse winds and rain storms, painful to touch owing to its cold and heat, dangerous because of its beasts of prey and lions, and roamed by crowds of murderers and highwaymen—I am a shelter in the form of the sun, the rising moon, a meteor, a lightning flash, the circle of the planets, the splendor of palaces, the constellations and heavenly bodies, a god, and a Bodhisattva.

And I adopt this mental attitude that by this stock of merit I may be a shelter to all sentient beings in order to dispel the darkness of all selfish passions. To those beings who go through the mountains, are in fear of death, have fallen into the power of desire for fame, are desirous of the banner of glory, are in need of food, are prey to greed, are in need of help, are solely bent on achieving worldly things, are fettered by the selfish love for child and wife, perish in the thicket of theorization, are oppressed by all sorts of pains, fears, and dangers—I am a refuge in various ways and by various means: by procuring them hidden shelters in mountains, by bringing them fruit, roots, and food, by creating rivulets and lakes, by bringing them remedies against heat and cold, by showing them the right way, by making them hear the cry of sparrows, making them hear the shouts of peacocks, through the luster of the medical herbs and the splendor of a mountain deity. To those who have gone into caves and caverns and grottos of the mountains, and encounter many difficulties and dangers, (I am a shelter) by creating a smooth surface and by dispelling darkness and murkiness.

And I adopt this mental attitude that, in the same way as I protect beings who have gone into the mountains, I may be a refuge to those who have fallen into the ravines of the world and are attacked by the demons of old age and death. I show the right path for walking to those also, who in a dark and murky night are deceived by the net of trees and shrubs, who are surrounded everywhere by the tree-like sensuous objects, whose way is blocked by the hardships of grass, water, thorns, and trees, who have penetrated into the thicket of trees, creepers, and forests, whose hearts are frightened by the roaring of tigers, whose minds are troubled by not having fulfilled their duties, are attacked by all sorts of fears and dangers, and who do not know the way out of the thicket of the jungle.

And I adopt this mental attitude that by this stock of merit I may liberate from all suffering, those beings who have gone into the thicket of theorization, are entangled in the net of desire and experience all sorts of suffering, fear, and danger in the world. To those beings who have gone into forest deserts in a dark and murky night I am a shelter, by creating happiness for them, showing them the way and putting them in a state of fearlessness and peace.

I adopt this mental attitude that by this stock of merit, after having liberated them from all suffering I may put on the way toward omniscience in the realm of peacefulness those beings who have gone into forest deserts and have gone the way of evil.

O son of a noble family, those who have gone into foreign countries and provinces, who suffer the hardships connected with going to foreign countries and provinces, I encourage in various ways and by various means I make them free from the attachment-like entering into foreign countries and provinces.

I adopt this mental attitude that by this stock of merit I may draw away all sentient beings from the attachment to the substratum of the psycho-physical constituents (*skandhas*) and put them firmly in the realm of omniscience which does not know of any (limited and limiting) substratum.

O son of a noble family, those who have gone into villages, who are tied down by the fetters of houses and dwellings, who, in a dark and murky night, are afflicted by the hardships of a householder, I encourage by various encouragements—when their minds are disturbed I treat them with the gift of the Dharma, and when I have made them rejoice in the right spirit I put them firmly in the Dharma which is no home (in the conventional sense).

I adopt this mental attitude that by this stock of merit I may draw away all sentient beings, who are attached to the village of the six senses' activity spheres (*āyatana*), from roaming about in the sensuous objects of the world and its walks and put them firmly in the realm of omniscience.

O son of a noble family, to those who in a dark and murky night have lost the direction in the regions beginning with the East or in the intermediate regions or in all regions, who think that the plains of the earth are rough ravines are that the elevations are depths and the depths are elevations, and who are confused as to the regions, ways, and countries—I bring light (to such beings) in various ways and by various means. To those who want to go out of this world, I show the door; to those who want to walk I show the way; to those who want to cross (the ocean of existence) I show the ford; to those who want to enter (the realm of peace) I show the house; to those who want to see I show the quarters of the world, the depths and heights of the earth, I show the plain and the rough parts of the earth, I show all the various forms and shapes. To those who set out on the way I show towns, townships, frontier towns, residences and capitals; to those who suffer from heat and thirst I show lovely places of rest with fountains, lakes, ponds, lotus lakes, rivers, parks, and gardens; to those who are afflicted by the separation from those whom they love I show such manifold and lovely forms as the mother, father, wife, friend, counsellor, relative, and the consanguineous.

And I adopt this mental attitude that, in the same way as I bring light and luster in a dark and murky night to those beings whose eyes are stricken with blindness and who are disorientated, so that they may not recognize things, so also I may with the light of great wisdom dispel the darkness of ignorance, make (beings) embrace supreme Enlightenment, show by the all-auspicious Mahāyāna the way toward the realm of knowledge (*jñānabhūmi*) of Buddha, make visible the Tathāgatabhūmi, the range of power of a Tathāgata, the ocean of omniscience, the realm of Buddha Knowledge, the sphere of power of a Buddha, the acquisition of the ten powers [giving complete knowledge of (i) what is right or wrong in every condition, (ii) what is the karma of every being, past, present, and future, (iii) all stages of dhyāna and samādhi, (iv) the powers and faculties of all beings, (v) the desires and trends of every being, (vi) the actual condition of every being, (vii) the direction and consequence of all laws, (viii) all causes of morality and of good and evil as they really are, (ix) the end of all beings and Nirvāṇa, (x) the final destruction of all illusion], the power of a Buddha's control [over all that is good so that it may not be lost (*dhāraṇī*)], the unique body of all the Buddhas.

Having shown all this, (I) firmly put in the Samatā Knowledge of all the Buddhas those who have fallen into the long night of Saṃsāra, who are lost in every direction, who have fallen into the darkness of ignorance, whose eyes are veiled by the veil of ignorance, who are confused in their ideas, minds, and conceptions, who believe that to be durable which is transitory, who believe that to be pleasure which is suffering, who believe that to be the Ātman which is not the Ātman, who believe that to be purity which is not purity, who cling to a belief in a (permanent, individual) soul, who are attached to the psychophysical components (*skandha*), the chemico-cosmic elements (*dhātu*), and their field of interaction (*āyatana*), who are confused about cause and effect, who have trodden the way of evil actions, who kill what is living, who take what is not given to them, who lead a life of sensual indulgence, who tell lies, who bring others into bad repute, who use harsh words, who talk for the mere sake of talking, who are covetous and malevolent, who cling to wrong views, who do not respect mother, father, Śramaṇas, Brāhmaṇas, gods, and men, who indulge in illicit love, who are overpowered by (the greed for) evil gain, who have become stuck in wrong conceptions, who do not acknowledge the Tathāgatas, who endeavor to put an end to the promulgation of the Dharma, who carry the banner of Māra, who kill Bodhisattvas, who hate the Mahāyāna, who destroy the attitude directed toward Enlightenment (*bodhicitta*), who defame Bodhisattvas, who are matricides, who hate those who do no wrong, who blame the noble ones, who associate with those who do not lead the life of an honorable man, who hate what belongs to the Stūpas and the Saṅgha, who are against father and mother, who commit heinous crimes, and who are on the verge of the abyss.

O son of a noble family, as a refuge I stand also for those beings who are ill and exhausted by long illness, whose body has become weak, who are aged, old, and overpowered by the vicissitudes of old age, who are without protection, who are destitute and poor, who have met with misfortune, who are in a foreign country, who are in strange quarters of the world, who are in prisons, tortured, and are about to be executed. O son of a noble family, in various ways and by various means I help eliminate the illness of those beings who are ill. Those who are aged and overcome by the vicissitudes of old age I help by not (creating) an interruption in respect, attention, and readiness to serve them. To those who are without protection I offer protection. Those who are destitute and poor I help with money and gold. Those who have met with ruin I support by a common goal. Those who have gone into a foreign country I lead back to their home-country. Those who have gone into the wrong direction I lead into the right direction. Those who are in prison I liberate from their fetters. Those who are tortured I release from the pains of torturing. To those who are to be executed I give the hope of life.

I adopt this mental attitude that, in the same way as I am a refuge to the beings by protecting them against all sorts of fears and dangers, so also I may encompass them in the sublime Dharma and liberate them from all selfish passions, making them transcend birth, old age, illness, death, lamentation, suffering, affliction, and tribulation, putting them in the company of true friends (and thus liberating them) from the fear of all evil existences and states of punishment, supporting them by the jewel gift of the Dharma, instigating them to irreproachable deeds, making them accept the purity of the body of the Tathāgata, and establishing them firmly in the understanding of that realm which is absolutely without old age and death. In various ways and by various means I am refuge also to those beings who have gone the wrong way, who have entered the thicket of all sorts of theorization, who have given themselves up to futile resolutions, who are addicted to sensuous objects in body, speech, and mind, who are unrestrained in their conduct, who give themselves up to the performance of all sorts of vows and penance, who believe him to be the supremely Enlightened One who is not the supremely Enlightened One and who believe the supremely Enlightened One not to be the supremely Enlightened One, who are engaged in terrible mortification of their bodies, who venerate the springs, lakes, ponds, rivers, mountains, rivulets, directions of the sky and the intermediate directions (as holy objects), and who have fallen into the power of evil friends. All these who follow bad views I draw away from the path leading into the abyss of bad existences. Putting them into the right view about worldly matters I engage them in the achievement of divine and human happiness. I create this mental attitude that, in the same way as I liberate these beings from the misery of such evil things, I may establish all sentient beings on the noble, supra-mundane way of the Pāramitās and make them never recede from omniscience and by the all-auspicious great resolution lead them to omniscience and not bring them from the sphere of the Bodhisattvas back to the realm of ordinary beings.

THE DIAMOND OF OMNISCIENCE

[The Bodhisattva Maitreya, who has described to the youth Sudhana the glories of Enlightenment-mind, gives now a vivid illustration of the power of the diamond (*vajra*) of omniscience. From the similes used by Bodhisattva Maitreya it becomes obvious that omniscience, which is the unfoldment of Enlightenment-mind is, as the outcome of a most strenuous spiritual effort, a most positive and active state of mind, wherein not only an inexhaustible reservoir of possibilities lies hidden, but in which all these possibilities are utilized. What the diamond of omniscience destroys is death and decay; whereon the diamond of omniscience rests is life and health].

O son of a noble family, just as a diamond is not found in any other jewel mine than in a diamond mine or in a gold mine, so also the awakening of omniscience, which is like a diamond, is not found in any other jewel mine of good qualities in the disposition of beings than in the diamond mine of Great Compassion for the protection of beings, or in the great gold mine of the foundation of the knowledge of the Omniscient One. O son of a noble family, just as the roots of a special kind of tree called Rootless are not seen, although all its branches, leaves, foliage, and blossoms are seen on the trees, so also the root of the awakening of omniscience is not perceived, although all its flowers of wholesome knowledge and universal power are seen as a net in all the existences of the world. O son of a noble family, just as a diamond does not shed its luster in any other setting, nor can it be held in a setting full of holes, but only in a setting not full of holes, so also the diamond of the awakening of omniscience does not shine in a setting of beings who have mean intentions, are of bad character, have a vicious mind, are lazy, whose faculty of recollection fails them, and who are poor in insight; nor can it be held in those sieve-like beings who have fallen from their resolution and who have an unstable mind, but it can be held only in the jewel-mounting of a Bodhisattva's resolution. O son of a noble family, just as a diamond pierces all other jewels, so also the diamond of the awakening of omniscience pierces all the jewels of the dharmas. O son of a noble family, just as a diamond cuts all stones, so also the diamond of the awakening of omniscience cuts all the stones of theorization. O son of a noble family, just as a diamond, even if it be broken, excels all other jewels and all other gold ornaments, so also the diamond of the awakening of omniscience, even if it be broken by not having achieved the fulfilment of its resolution, excels all the gold ornaments of the merits of the Śrāvakas and Pratyekabuddhas. O son of a noble family, just as a diamond, even if it be broken, dispels all poverty, so also the diamond of the awakening of omniscience, even if it be broken into pieces, dispels all the world's poverty.

O son of a noble family, just as the diamond sphere (*vajradhātu*), however small it may be, is characterized as splitting all jewels and stones, so also the diamond sphere of the awakening of omniscience, however small the object from which its starts may be, is characterized as splitting all ignorance. O son of a noble family, just as the diamond is not found in the hands of an ordinary man, so also the diamond of the awakening of omniscience is not found in the hands of those gods and men who have ordinary intentions and who have only a low stock of merits. O son of a noble family, just as a man who does not know the examination of jewels, who is ignorant of the qualities of diamond jewels, does not experience the specific qualities of a diamond, so also an individual of low intellect and standing, who is ignorant of the qualities of the diamond of Great Wisdom which is Enlightenment mind, does not experience the specific qualities of omniscience. O son of a noble family, just as a diamond cannot decay, so also the diamond of the awakening of enlightenment mind which is the cause of omniscience, cannot decay. O son of a noble family, just as the impact of the diamond (weapon) cannot be sustained even by a great warrior, unless he has the power and strength of the Mahānārāyaṇa (weapon), so also the impact of the great diamond of the awakening of omniscience cannot be sustained by Śrāvakas and Pratyekabuddhas, even if they be great warriors, but only by Bodhisattvas who are surpassing by the strength of the Mahānārāyaṇa (weapon) which is the limitless stock of merits as the cause of omniscience, and who are most resplendent. O son of a noble family, where no other weapons are successful the diamond (weapon) is victorious and is not destroyed, so also, where the weapon of resolution of Śrāvakas and Pratyekabuddhas are not successful either in bringing the beings to (spiritual) maturity or in living the hard life (of a Bodhisattva) in the three times (of past, present, and future), there the Bodhisattva, who has taken the weapon of the great diamond of the awakening of omniscience, is unrelaxingly victorious and never defeated.

O son of a noble family, just as a diamond cannot be sustained by any other part of the earth than by a diamond basis, so also the diamond of the supply for the firm resolution of the Bodhisattva to lead beings out (of the world of relativity) cannot be sustained by Śrāvakas and Pratyekabuddhas, nor can their intention be supported by anything else but the firm basis of the diamond of the awakening of omniscience. O son of a noble family, just as the water spreads in the great ocean, because it is a vessel not full of holes and having a firm basis, so also the stock of merits of a Bodhisattva, which is based on the transference (of merit) having a holeless and firm basis of the diamond nature of a Bodhisattva, does not get exhausted in all existences of the world. O son of a noble family, just as the great earth rests on a diamond basis and is not torn nor does it collapse, so also the solemn vows of the Bodhisattvas, resting on the firm basis of the diamond of the awakening of omniscience, are not destroyed nor do they collapse in all the three worlds. O son of a noble family, just as a diamond is not soiled by water, so also the diamond of the awakening of Enlightenment mind is not soiled or spoiled by the water of selfish actions and selfish passions, or by associating itself with all activity. O son of a noble family, just as a diamond is not burned by any firebrand nor is it heated, so also the diamond of the awakening of omniscience is not burned by the firebrand of all the world's suffering, nor is it heated by the fire of selfish passions.

O son of a noble family, just as the seat of the Tathāgatas, the Arhants, the Supremely Enlightened Ones, who are sitting under the Bodhi tree, who are fighting Mārā, and who have awakened toward supreme Enlightenment, cannot be borne by any other place of the earth but by that earth which is the diamond center of Trisāhasramahāsāhasra, so also the rapture of the foundation of the power of the great stock of merit of the Bodhisattvas–who have devoted themselves to the realization of supreme Enlightenment, who lead the life of (a Bodhisattva), who fulfill the Pāramitās, who gain peace of mind, who ascend the various stages (of integration, *bhūmi*), who transfer their merits (to the beings of all worlds), who live up to the revelation (made about them by the Buddhas of all ages), who arrange the necessary requisites (both spiritually and physically) for the treading of the way of all the Bodhisattvas, who hold the Dharma clouds of all the Tāthagatas–cannot be encompassed by any other mind than by the awakening of omniscience which is the solid center of the diamond of all firm resolutions and knowledge.

O son of a noble family, the awakening of omniscience is endowed with these and other immeasurable and ineffable merits. And so also beings who direct their minds toward the realization of supreme Enlightenment are, have been, and will be endowed with such merits. Therefore, O son of a noble family, you have made a great gain in having directed your mind toward the realization of supreme Enlightenment and in seeking the way of the life of a Bodhisattva for the acquisition of (these) merits.

THE BODHISATTVA

[The youth Sudhana is directed by the Goddess of the Lumbinī grove to go to Gopā, a maiden of the Śākya clan, who is supposed to give him further instructions as to the life and work of a true Bodhisattva. Sudhana respectfully greets Gopā and asks for instructions in the following way: "Lady, I have set my mind upon Supreme Enlightenment, but I do not know how the Bodhisattvas live in the world without being defiled by the vices of the world. (I know that) they have awakened to the fact that all the dharmas are basically the same and (that) they do not take their stand on the levels of the Śrāvakas and Pratyekabuddhas. They have attained the splendor of the Buddha-nature and do not cut off the way of how the Bodhisattvas act. They have taken their stand on the Bodhisattva-bhūmi and see the realm of the Buddhas. They have transcended all the walks of life in the world, and yet they are walking in all the walks of life in the world. They have the perfection of the Dharmakāya, infinite splendor, and (miraculously) produce the visible body (*rūpa-kāya*). They are fully aware of the fact that all the dharmas have no characteristic of their own, and yet they show the aspects and shapes of all the world by their own body. They know that all the dharmas are ineffable, and yet by speech, etymology, and examples they teach the Dharma to sentient beings. They know that all the dharmas have no individuality of their own, and yet they do not slacken their efforts to educate the world of sentient beings. They know that all the dharmas have neither origin nor end, and yet they do not slacken in their efforts to pay homage to all the Tāthāgatas. They know that all the dharmas are without action and its fruit, and yet they never slacken in their effort to perform salutary actions." But before he is able to address Gopā with these words he is told about his future greatness by the Goddess Aśokaśrī].

Then the youth Sudhana took leave of the Goddess of the Lumbinī grove, Sutejomaṇḍalaratiśrī (Beauty of Pleasure in the Brightness Circle), and went to the great town of Kapilavastu; and while he was cultivating, embodying into his life, amplifying, following, exercising, mastering, thinking over, and discriminating the Bodhisattva emancipation called 'The view of the miraculous manifestation of the birth of the Bodhisattvas as regards all the factors in innumerable aeons' he came to the deity of the Bodhisattva assembly called 'Splendor of the Reflection of the Dharmadhātu'; and while he came there the deity of the Bodhisattva assembly called Aśokaśrī went with ten thousand deities of the house toward the youth Sudhana and addressed him in the following way:

"Welcome are you, great man, surpassing (all) in great knowledge, whose mind is resolved to cultivate the unimaginable Bodhisattva emancipation, who walks the palace of (immaculate) wide dharmas, whose gaze is turned toward the city of the Dharma, who has found peace in embodying into his life the mode of skilfulness of the infinite number of Bodhisattvas, who is shone upon by the splendor of the ocean of merits of the Tathāgatas, whose gaze is turned toward the knowledge of how the whole world is educated, who follows the mantra of the knowledge of all sentient beings' mode of action, whose mind is turned toward proper conduct, who is moved by the pains and pleasures of the world, who is resolved to increase (the good), who is on the way of understanding the nature of all Tathāgatas. As I see you walking the pure path of right and profound conduct with unblinking eyes (I know) that in a short while you will have obtained the unsurpassable ornamental purity of the Tathāgatas' body, speech, and mind, and that you will walk in the world with a body adorned by the major and minor auspicious signs and a mind adorned with the light of knowledge of Him who has the ten powers (i.e., the Buddha). And as I see your firm and strong energy (I know) that in a short while you will see the Buddhas of the three times, that you will acknowledge the Dharma-clouds of all Tathāgatas, that you will enjoy the pleasure of the palace of tranquil dharmas of the attainment of all Bodhisattvas' meditation, emancipation, and concentration, and that you will see the profound Buddha-emancipation. You will accept the going to, seeing, attending to, and instruction by friends in the good life, you will not slacken in applying yourself to acquire these merits, you will not recede from this, you will not repent (your step), nor will there be any stopping, any veiling, any hindering by Māra or by Māra's armies or by (other) deities. Therefore, after a short while you will bring joy to all sentient beings."

Having been thus addressed, the youth Sudhana answered the Goddess of the Bodhisattva assembly, Aśokaśrī, with the following words: May it be so, O Goddess, as you say. Goddess, I find supreme joy in the appeasement of the burning fire of the emotions of all sentient beings. I find supreme joy by the stoppage of the karma bearing fruit in the realm of all sentient beings, by all sentient beings' finding happiness, by all sentient beings' coming to irreproachable actions. Goddess, when the beings affected by various objects, actions, and emotions, distracted in mind, fall into bad existences or when, in good existences, they suffer various bodily and mental pleasures and pains, then the Bodhisattvas are grieved, deeply grieved. In the same way, O Goddess, as a man who is ridden by desire has a single dear and lovely son, and his son's major and minor limbs are cut asunder, this man, because of his being ridden by desires, would be extremely sad and discontented, so also, Goddess, Bodhisattvas leading the life of a Bodhisattva are grieved, deeply grieved, when they see that beings have fallen into the three bad existences through their own actions and affects. On the other hand, when the beings, because of their having taken to good conduct in body, speech, and mind, after death are reborn in good existences, in the heaven, or in the world of the gods, and among men and gods experience bodily and mental happiness, then a Bodhisattva is highly happy, content, and satisfied, exalted by joy, enthusiastic and blessed in mind. But, Goddess, the Bodhisattvas do not aspire for omniscience for selfish ends, nor do they seek various worldly pleasures and delights, nor do they aspire to various sensuous pleasures in the world of sensuality, nor are they fettered by tendencies or desires; nor is their mind bent on associating with various beings, nor are they greedy for the sweet taste of the pleasure of meditation, nor are they shrouded in various veils (of cognition and emotionality), nor do they indulge in the pleasures of the world.

Furthermore, O Goddess, the Bodhisattvas have the firm resolve to comprise the whole world by producing Great Compassion as regards the beings who have ventured out into the ocean of existence, who are tormented by immeasurable hardships. They are seen to live the life of a Bodhisattva in the world in bringing the beings to maturity by the power of producing the firm resolve (to work for the good of the world) by Great Compassion. They produce the firm resolve to pay homage to all the Tathāgatas, seeking omniscience (and the end of) all veiling obstacles (in the way) of sentient beings. They never get tired in their resolve to pay homage to the Tathāgatas. While in the Bodhisattva career they lead the life of a Bodhisattva—when they see the defiled realms they produce the firm resolve to purify all the Buddha-realms. While purifying the oceans of the defiled realms and while seeing the differences of the realms of all the sentient beings they produce the firm resolve (to attain) the nondifferent sublime purity of the Dharmakāya. While seeing the beings with defiled body, speech, and mind they produce the firm resolve (to attain) the ornamental purity of all beings' body, speech, and mind. While seeing the beings deficient and of impure minds they lead the life of a Bodhisattva purifying the mental actions of all sentient beings, and they never get tired.

Thus, O Goddess, the Bodhisattvas are leading the life of a Bodhisattva which has neither an end nor a middle, and they do not get tired. Thus leading the life (of a Bodhisattva) they are an ornament for the world with its gods, because they generate happiness for man and gods; they are (like) parents, because they bring to life Bodhisattvas; they are a nurse because they (make the beings) walk the way of the Bodhisattvas; they are the protecting deities because they guard (men) from the danger of falling into bad existences; they are great sailors, because they ferry across the ocean of existence; they are a refuge, because they stop the fear of all the Māras and passions; they are a shelter, because they bring calmness and coolness; they are a ford, because they lead to the ocean of all Buddhas; they are navigators, because they bring (people) to the jewel island of the Dharma; they are flowers, because their mind is flowering in the virtues of all the Buddhas; they are ornaments, because they emit the luster of wide and wholesome knowledge; they cause joy, because they are all-benevolent; they are those who may be approached, because they do not let others down; they are all-auspicious, because they are lovely to be looked at; they bring light, because they emit rays of knowledge; they create light, because they carry the lamp of the Dharma; they are illuminating, because they purify the disposition of those who will become enlightened; they are commanding generals, because they crush the actions of Māra; they are the sun, because they emit a net of knowledge-rays; they are the moon, because they rise (in the world) like the moon in the sky; they are the clouds, because they shower the rain of the Dharma upon the whole world. Thus, O Goddess, the Bodhisattvas are dear to all sentient beings.

Then the deity of the Bodhisattva assembly, Aśokaśrī, together with ten thousand deities of the houses, showered lovely celestial flower-garlands and scented powder and jewel ornaments upon the youth Sudhana and, surrounding him who entered the abode of the Bodhisattvas, she addressed him with the following verses:

> "Rarely there arise in the world the Victorious Ones, the suns of knowledge, setting their mind upon Supreme Enlightenment out of Compassion for all sentient beings.
>
> In many thousands of aeons it is difficult to see them who are the sun of knowledge in the large sky for a world wrapped in the darkness of ignorance.
>
> Having seen the world dejected and engulfed in the darkness of ignorance, out of your own (world) you have come full of compassion.
>
> With pure intention you endeavor to enlighten those who will be enlightened; you seek the company of friends in the good life and you do not care for your body or your life.
>
> You have no place, no house in this world; you have no home, you are not pressed, without attachment like the sky.
>
> You lead the supreme life of a Bodhisattva, the radiant light of which is wholesome; you emit rays of knowledge in a world that rises and sets.
>
> You do not flee away from the world and you are not defiled by the world; without attachment, you live in the world like the wind in the sky.
>
> Like the all-consuming fire at the end of time, like an ever-glowing lamp, strongly like the fire you lead the life of a Bodhisattva.
>
> Like a lion, a great hero, powerful, full of strength, surpassing all in knowledge you live unconquered.

Whatever currents there are of methods in the ocean of the Dharmadhātu, you go into them, O Hero, served by faithful friends."

When the Goddess of the Bodhisattva assembly, Aśokaśrī, had thus praised the youth Sudhana she followed him closely out of love for the Dharma.

The Concept of Mind in Buddhist Tantrism

Insufficient information about the meaning and purpose of the Tantras and the misconceptions that were the inevitable result have been responsible for dismissing the study of Tantric thought in a rather high-handed way. Yet it is precisely this dismissal of Tantrism, fortified by a refusal even to consider its claim, that has jeopardized a better understanding of Buddhist philosophy, because it has failed to realize that a philosophy which begins with and insists on immediate experience is naturally different from a philosophy which starts with a hypothesis and remains essentially speculative. This failure, first to ascertain the starting-point and then to evaluate the subsequent presentation from the initial standpoint of immediate experience, has succeeded in watering down Buddhist philosophy till it looks like some other more or less 'rational' system that could be swallowed with but little discomfort. Nevertheless, the fact remains that immediate experience is the key-note of Buddhism. Experience, however, is a term belonging to the group of process-product ambiguities: the same word stands for the process and the product of that process. But while ambiguous words which are closely related in their meanings are most apt to be misleading, 'experience' should prove an exception precisely because of this 'ambiguity' of process-product. Taken as process-product, experience is symbolific activity, and the symbol itself is always the product or the end-phase of the process, never its beginning. Bearing this point in mind we should be able to avoid the fallacies of both phenomenalism and idealism which make the end the beginning.[1] Since experience has the quality of knowledge and knowledge seems to have to do with that which we are accustomed to call mind, mind is of paramount importance.

Although it is assumed that we know pretty well what is meant by 'mind' and 'mental', we should have considerable difficulties in giving a clear definition of the meaning of these terms. Actually, no satisfactory definition has ever been given. It will, however, be admitted by most people that such occurrences as thinking, feeling happy or sad, believing, wishing, doubting and such experiences as seeing, hearing, smelling, tasting and perceiving, generally are mental. In this way 'mental' would be a term designating a common quality of events which would be said to be states of a certain mind. But from here the ways part, and several conceptions about what a mind is are possible, none of them being able to claim absolute validity, though each of them has a certain amount of plausibility.

If it is already difficult to know what we mean by these terms 'mind' and 'mental' in our own language, it will be readily admitted that it is still more difficult to ascertain the meaning of what is translated by 'mind' or 'mental' from Eastern texts. The question, whether the authors of the original texts actually meant the same as we do by those words about whose meaning we ourselves are not quite clear, should always be present, not only

---

[1]It is unfortunate that 'idealism' should have become the name of what actually is some form or other of 'mentalism'. As C. D. Broad, *The Mind and Its Place in Nature*, p. 654, has shown, mentalism is no guarantee of idealism. Traditional mentalism as represented by Berkeley, Leibniz, Hegel, and M'Taggart—Ward and Bradley may also be mentioned—is untenable. In addition to Broad's analysis see also F. S. C. Northrop, *The Meeting of East and West*, p. 114 *seq*. Nor can phenomenalism be said to be an improvement of mentalism or to have solved the difficulties which mentalism encountered. The introduction of sense data seems more a regression to realism.

when translating texts but still more when dealing with a systematic presentation of Eastern philosophies.[2] Otherwise the already existing ambiguity will only serve as an admirable means to misrepresent Eastern ideas.[3] Although we cannot dispense with language, language is a treacherous instrument which very often creates problems where there are no problems at all.[4]

It has been customary to translate the terms *sems* (Skt. *citta*) and *sems-las byung-ba* (Skt. *caitta*) by 'mind' and 'mental event' respectively. But this translation, however philologically correct, does not tell us much until we know what is meant by these terms in their relation to each other. At first sight, the relation is comparable with that which common sense assumes to exist between the 'thing' and the 'states of the thing'. In this particular case, mind (*sems, citta*) would be the 'thing' and mental event (*sems-las byung-ba, caitta*) would be the 'state of the thing'.

---

[2]Edwin A. Burtt, "Basic Problems of Method in Harmonizing Eastern and Western Philosophies," *Essays in East-West Philosophy*, ed. by Charles A. Moore, University of Hawaii Press, Honolulu: 1951, p. 115 has said: ". . . a number of specific studies of rather limited problems need to be carried out before we will be in a position to formulate hypotheses of significant comparative relationships that will have any chance of proving more than premature and superficial." It is very deplorable that his advice should have remained unheeded. In the field of Sanskrit, Pali, and Tibetan studies not a single study of the meaning of the technical terms has been performed. The only exception is Wilhelm and Magdalene Geiger's *Pali Dhamma* in 1923! But translations of Eastern texts are produced by the ton.

[3]Even so distinguished a scholar as W. T. Stace, *Time and Eternity, An Essay in the Philosophy of Religion*, Princeton: 1952, is apparently not aware of the fact that "The nihilism of the Buddhist is a curiously distorted and eccentric version of the genuine religious intuition" (p. 20) is a statement on the basis of insufficient information.

[4]This statement is fully endorsed by Buddhist philosophers. Padma-dkar-po says in his *Phyag-rgya-chen-po'i man-ngag-gi bshad-sbyar rgyal-ba'i gan-mdzod*, fol. 22*b*:

> If at the time of instructing those who are to be taught and to be brought to spiritual maturity, words and letters or symbols and signs are not made use of, no mutual understanding (between teacher and disciple) is possible. Hence Saraha has said:
>
> If the Guru does not express his instruction in words,
> The disciple will not understand anything.
> How else could the flavor of Sahaja
> Be communicated to another individual?

Mind (*sems, citta*) is considered to have an inherent tendency to assume a certain state of such and such determinateness when conditioned in such and such a way, so that properly speaking we know the state of a certain mind rather than this mind itself, although we tend to continue speaking of a mind since the states are states *of* this mind: "This mind under consideration, when it has been changed by conditions such as traces and dispositions, should be known as only a state of mind."[5]

But mind also has the inherent tendency to assume its 'natural' state when left alone: "Mind, in the absence of conditions, is without memory and association and is *śūnya*."[6] This tendency is compared with what happens when we allow disturbed water to become calm and transparent again: "Like muddy water which becomes pure by itself when it is not interfered with."[7] This characteristic of mind, to assume a certain state when subjected to certain conditions and to pass back into its

---

On fol. 23*b* of the same work he states:

> In the *De-kho-na-nyid-la 'jug-pa* is said "According to the diverse interests and mental capacities of those who are to be taught, the teaching is diversified only as to the words used so that those who are to be taught may attend to the instruction." This means that according to the words they have heard individuals follow Reality. Therefore by such and such words the mind of such and such individuals is brought to such and such doctrine. But although in Reality there cannot obtain any differentiation, the Buddhas impart their instruction as if there were some differentiation.

Language serves the function of 'drawing attention', as may be seen from Saraha's words (*De-kho-na-nyid-kyi man-ngag-rtse-mo do-ha'i glu* = *Tattva-upadeśa-śikhara-dohā-gītā, bsTan-'gyur, rgyud*, vol. zhi, fol. 127*a* [Derge ed.]):

> In what I, Saraha, say
> There is not so much as an atom of Being.

Wittgenstein would have liked Saraha if he had known him.

[5] *Doha-mdzod-kyi snying-po-don-gyi glu-'i 'grel-ba* = *Dohākoṣa-hṛdaya-artha-gīti-ṭīkā*, by gNyis-med-avadhūti, *bsTan-'gyur, rgyud*, vol. zhi, fol. 74*b*, (Derge ed.). In the following this work will be referred to only by folio number.

[6] Fol. 76*a* śūnya (*stong-pa*) is mostly translated by 'void', 'empty', and the noun Śūnyatā (*stong-pa-nyid*) by 'insubstantiality'. Such translations are utterly wrong. Śūnya and Śūnyatā mean 'nothing' in the sense of 'not standing for any conception at all'. Śūnyatā has nothing to do with the philosophically antiquated concepts of substance and its negation.

[7] *bSre-'pho'i lam-skor-gyi thog-mar lam-dbye-bsdu*, fol. 81*b*.

original state when the conditions have been removed, may be called the causal characteristic of mind.[8] The causal characteristic does not belong to any of the states of mind, though they are caused by it, but only to mind itself.

In this connection it is even possible to distinguish various orders of causal characteristics. We may say that it is a first-order causal characteristic of mind to pass into a certain state when conditioned in a certain way and to pass back into its natural state when the conditions do not obtain any longer. Conditioning may happen in such a way that mind loses the first-order causal characteristic of changeability and acquires the second first-order causal characteristic of staying in the particular state into which it has been brought by certain conditions. This feature of losing the first first-order causal characteristic and gaining the second first-order causal characteristic may be termed a second-order causal characteristic. Since this process is assumed to be reversible, mind may be said to possess also the second second-order causal characteristic of losing the second first-order causal characteristic and regaining the first first-order causal characteristic. This is evidently implied in the statement that mind has to be tanned like a hide in order to make it flexible again.[9]

We further notice the following characteristics. This mind is sometimes 'pure', sometimes 'muddy and having the determinable characteristic *d*' and sometimes 'muddy and having the determinable characteristic d_1' and so on. As is stated: "When mind is not pure it is given the name of 'sentient being' and when it is pure in itself it is given the name of 'Buddha'."[10] Or, it is said:

> When there is no mind, no minding, no intellect, no sensation, no perception, no memory and association, what then is the mind of a sentient being?–Sentient being can be spoken of only as long as these function-events operate.[11]

---

[8] I owe this term to C. D. Broad, *The Mind and Its Place in Nature*, p. 432.

[9] *Phyag-rgya-chen-po'i man-ngag-gi bshad-byar rgyal-ba'i gan-mdzod*, fol. 52*b*.

[10] Fol. 104*b*.

[11] Fol. 94*a*. Cf. also fol. 81*a* and 82*a*.

The designation 'sentient being' is just a particular determinable characteristic as are the other forms of being, viz., denizens of hell, spirits, animals, gods, demons. All these classes are so many determinable characteristics of mind in its 'impure' state. They are not causal and may be said to belong to the mind in the sense that they belong to all the successive states of a mind.

Finally there is the completely determinate form which these determinable characteristics assume in the various statuses of mind and which is defined more precisely as 'memory and association' (*dran-pa*), 'discursiveness' (*bsam-pa*) or covering the whole field of sentient life, 'Saṃsāra' (*'khor-ba*):

> What ordinary people understand by concentrative meditative attention is discursiveness, discursiveness is memory and association, memory and association are creative activity, creative activity is Saṃsāra.[12]

Inasmuch as memory and association are of primary importance in all our mental operations, the term for them, *dran-pa*, has been used to include all other operations as well.[13] Memory and association are characterized as 'fleeting' (*yal-ba*): "Memory and association are fleeting like mist,"[14] or they are termed 'accidental' (*glo-bur*): "Memory and association appear accidentally,"[15] and since they dim the clear light and radiance of mind they are spoken of as "the stain of accidental memory and association."[16] As completely determinate occurrences they belong to the states of a mind rather than to the mind itself. Hence these completely determinate events are linguistically distinguished from mind (*sems*, *citta*) by the term *sems-las byung-ba* (*caitta*) 'that which has originated from mind'.

To sum up: Like a material thing and its changing states, mind (*sems*) under certain conditions assumes a certain state and returns to its 'natural' state as soon as the conditions that brought

---

[12]Fol. 95*a*.

[13]Almost synonymous are *yid*, *sems*, *rig-pa*, *blo*, *rnam-par-shes-pa*. See note 10 where the passages in which this enumeration occurs, have been mentioned.

[14]Fol. 75*a*.

[15]Fol. 93*b*. The Tibetan term *glo-bur* is also synonymous with our terms 'incidental', 'adventitious', and 'fortuitous'.

[16]Fol. 74*b*.

about the change or deviation from the natural state, are no more. By dividing up the history of a mind into successive adjoined slices, it is found to have certain determinable characteristics which belong to all the slices and which are termed 'sentient being' (*sems-can*) and it is further found to have even the more determinate or primary characteristics of 'having a state which is memory and association' (*dran-pa*). That is to say, mind having assumed a certain determinable status of, say, a human being, and retaining this status throughout its history of a human mind, has completely determinate occurrences of these determinable characteristics, viz., memory and association. This analogy of mind with a material thing has important consequences. Just as there are many things in our world (so at least common sense asserts), so there are also many minds, each individual being a certain 'mind'. But not only does such a conception of mind account for the differences that exist between individuals or individual minds, it also allows for the variety of mental operations, because every event of memory and association may be a different determinable event of the determinable characteristic 'human being', without ever failing to be a state of this mind under consideration. Moreover, it allows for the variety of all life. Just as memory and association in a human being have a man-ish or woman-ish determinateness, so also an animal's mental operations have a distinctly animal-ish determinateness. So far the analogy of mind with a material thing has worked out very well. It can be advanced one step further.

When a thing changes from one state into another its primary characteristics, a definite color or a definite shape, may be different, but since these states are states *of* the thing, we say that the thing has changed. At the same time we tacitly assume the thing to persist through its changes, and so we seek for causes producing changes. There are three causes which produce changes of what is termed mind. They are appearance (*snang-ba*), traces and dispositions (*bag-chags*), and symbolism in the widest sense of the word (*brda*):

> While the Sphere of Mind, being pure, is not stained by the dirt of perception against the apperceptive mass of memory and association as background which is only accidental, under the conditions of appearance, traces and dispositions, and symbolic expression, it emerges as anything.[17]

'Appearance' (*snang-ba*) is a term which, when left unspecified, is apt to mislead us into the assumption that it refers to a three-term relation of appearance which stood at the beginning of modern science and subsequent philosophy. Although this theory presented many difficulties to the modern mind, it remained hardly unchallenged until recent times.[18] Since the Buddhist conception of appearance does not presuppose a doctrine of absolute space as the common matrix of all objective constituents of perceptual situations, a three-term relation theory is not implied by 'appearance'. Nor is 'appearance' equivalent with illusion which may be said to be a stronger term for the denial of the reality of the world.[19]

The Buddhist conception of appearance begins with an analysis of perceptual situations which contain a sense-field with an outstanding sensum (*yul*). This is apprehended (*'dzin*) by entering into a certain specific relation with feeling and expectation (*zhen*). The apprehension together with feeling-emotions and expectations gives the situation the specific external reference: all of which is the perception of an external object and termed 'appearance' (*snang-ba*). It is a complex phenomenon of mental activity and in the widest sense of the word it expresses the ordinary dual mode of cognition involving a perceiving subject which owns the specific perceptual situation (*yul-can*) and the perceptual situation with its sense-field and sensum therein (*yul*). Being constructive activity, symbolific in creating the symbols of subject and object as its end-phase or product, appearance is a deviation from mind in its 'natural' state or, to

---

[17]Fol. 77*b*, Three causes are also mentioned, fol. 96*b*.

[18]C. D. Broad, *The Mind and Its Place in Nature*, p. 161 *seq.*
F. S. C. Northrop, *The Meeting of East and West*, p. 78 *seq.*

[19]W. T. Stace, *Time and Eternity*, pp. 122, 77.

put it more precisely, since the 'natural' state is also an occurrence, appearance is a relinquishing of pure sensation (*rang-rig*).

> Although as far as instantaneous experience is concerned there does not obtain any duality, by not recognizing it as such, there is no emergence of pure sensation. Due to this failure a first instant is born as a sense-field (*yul*), and a subsequent one as apprehension and feeling-expectation (*'dzin-zhen*). The perception of an external object is the rising of constructive mental activity (*rtog-pa*) or 'appearance' (*snang-ba*). But by cognizing whatever arises as what it is, there is Śūnyatā, perception being pure and leaving no trace because of the non-origination of apprehension and feeling-expectation. While these two topics, appearance and Śūnyatā, on the side of appearance seem to be different from each other, on the side of immediate experience (*so-so-rang-rig*) they are not different, hence the primary characteristic (of mind) is the non-duality of appearance and Śūnyatā.[20]

This passage contains a number of terms which will be explained later on. Here it is important to note that while we have no difficulty in recognizing 'appearance' as an occurrence, a change of a thing, it is more difficult to recognize persistence in a state as an occurrence. But this is what the Buddhist texts make clear. By terming mind 'instantaneous' (*skad-cig-ma*) it is pointed out that there is no logical justification for distinguishing between the two cases of mind *having* a certain state such as designated 'sentient being' or *being in* a certain state such as is termed 'Buddha'. Both states have primary characteristics: 'sentient being', 'ignorance' on the one side and 'Buddha', 'knowledge' on the other. Apart from the fact that there is no logical justification for assuming the two cases to be absolutely different, any differentiation (differentiating evaluation) would destroy the unity of 'mind'. Hence Saraha declares:

> Although the manner of pointing out a Buddha or a sentient being
> may be different,
> They (i.e., sentient being and Buddha) are born together,
> as are knowledge and ignorance.[21]

---

[20] *bSre-'pho'i lam-skor-gyi thog-mar lam-dbye-bsdu*, fol. 119*b*.

[21] *sKu'i mdzod 'chi-med rdo-rje'i glu* = *Kāyakoṣāmṛtavajragīti*, *bsTan-'gyur*, *rgyud*, vol. zhi, fol. 109*b*.

The next point to note is that 'appearance' is tied up with feeling-expectations. They are causally dependent on 'traces' left by past experiences (*bag-chags*) which are mentioned as the second condition favoring a change of mind. However, if the apprehension of the sensum (*yul*) fails to excite these traces which cause specific modifications in the general mass of feeling and thereby evoke the specific external reference, then we have a case of pure sensation (*rang-rig*), as is clearly stated: "Unchanging, without an external reference, free from a specific feeling-tone, of the nature of (unchanging) bliss."[22] These traces are not experiences themselves, either conscious or unconscious, nor are they themselves mental events or processes, but are just certain qualities of the mental events of a total state of mind. Since Buddhist philosophers scorn the idea of a Pure Ego, there is no stuff to be the matrix of traces in the literal sense of the word.[23] The relation between our ordinary conscious experiences and the qualities of them may simply be called 'mental relation and qualities'. Every experience modifies the relation and qualities by being imposed on the content and structure of each successive state. Thus there are 'traces' as regards relations (*'dzin-pa'i bag-chags*)[24]and 'traces' as regards qualities (*nyon-mongs-pa'i bag-chags*).[25]

The third condition is 'symbolic expressiveness' (*brda*). It is of three types: expression by body or overt activity (*lus-kyi brda*), expression by speech or language (*ngag-gi brda*), and the formulative activity of the covert level, the inner forum of thoughts and images, mind (*yid-kyi brda*).[26] This term *brda* has

---

[22]*Phyag-rgya-chen-po'i man-ngag-gi bshad-sbyar rgyal-ba'i gan-mdzod*, fol. 31*a*.

[23]To a certain degree the Vijñānavādins are an exception. They consider the *ālayavijñāna* as the container of all possibilities. However, they insist that their *ālayavijñāna* must not be confused with the Ātman or Pure Ego of the non-Buddhist schools, because this *ālayavijñāna* is a Central Event. For the analysis of Pure Ego theories and Central Event theories in Western philosophy and psychology see C. D. Broad, *The Mind and Its Place in Nature*, p. 558 *seq*.

[24]*rTen-'brel kho-bo lugs-kyi khrid chos thams-cad-kyi snying-po len-pa*, fol. 4*a*.

[25]*bSre-'pho'i lam-skor-gyi thog-mar lam-dbye-bsdu*, fol. 8*a*.

[26]Fol. 93*ab*.

not so much the meaning of 'sign' indicating anything in our actual surrounding, but that of 'symbol' representing things and ideas; it takes the place of things that we have perceived in the past or that we can merely imagine by memories and creative phantasies or that might be in future experience. At whatever level of expressive life it may be found, *brda* is frought with connotations, denotations, or other meanings. We act, we speak, we think–and all this is symbolific activity of that which we are wont to call 'mind', and all this appeals as much to the intellect as to feeling and emotions. But mind itself is a symbol, and a symbol invites us to a quest for meaning and quest for meaning is philosophy. While for all practical purposes we may divide and classify symbolific activity into bodily gesture, vocal expression, and thought, the quest for meaning leads us to the symbols of 'appearance' (*snang-ba'i brda*), of 'Śūnyatā' (*stong-pa'i brda*), and of 'unoriginatedness' (*skye-ba-med-pa'i brda*).[27] As a matter of fact, "The whole of reality is subsumed under Appearance, Śūnyatā, and Unoriginatedness."[28]

Every move we make, every word we speak, and every thought we harbor, is expressive formulatedness and falls under the symbol of 'appearance'.[29] Appearance, however, as has been shown above, is activity of mind or more precisely, a state of mind, but as a state of mind appearance cannot be separated from mind. This is expressed in the formula that 'appearance and mind are indivisible' (*snang-sems-dbyer-med*).[30]

This leads us back to the initial premise of the causal characteristic of mind: "The root of all and everything is mind."[31] Taken at its face value this assertion seems to point to some sort of mentalism which may be termed 'subjective mentalism' or

---

[27]Fol. 93*ab*.

[28]Fol. 81*a*. Cf. fol. 98*b*.

[29]Fol. 83*a*: "Appearance and the symbolic expression of body, by speech, and by mind are all the symbol of appearance."

[30]*Phyag-rgya-chen-po'i man-ngag-gi bshad-sbyar rgyal-ba'i gan-mdzod*, fol. 34*a*.

Phyag-chen-gyi zin-bris, fol. 6*a*.

[31]Fol. 76*a*, 92*b*.

even 'solipsistic mentalism' on account of such statements as the following ones: "The whole of reality is one's own mind"[32] or "Apart from one's own mind there does not exist any other entity."[33] But certainly, even if it should be conceded that it is mind which gives us knowledge of reality, it is still a tremendous leap to the conclusion that mind is the true and only reality. And as the statement stands, it is easy to see that the problem of the whole of reality being mind is a pseudo-problem. Hence it has to be rejected, as it was rejected by the Tantrics and Mādhyamikas. Mentalism is as little an answer to man's perennial problem as is realism. The rejection of mentalism is contained in the words that "Mind is no mind at all,"[34] or as Saraha expressed it:

> He who understands that from the very beginning there has been no mind,
> Realizes the Mind of all Buddhas in all three times.[35]

Hence it is impossible to point out the 'root' of all and everything: "Since mind is not found as an entity, there is also no root to be shown,"[36] and more comprehensively: "Since the foundation of sentient beings is without roots, the foundation of Buddha-knowledge is equally without roots. This rootlessness is the root of enlightenment."[37] Or, it is said that "Mind, in the absence of conditions, is without memory and association and is *śūnya*."[38]

To understand what is meant by *śūnya* or mind and Śūnyatā,

---

[32]*Do-ha-mdzod ces-bya-ba phyag-rgya-chen-po'i man-ngag* = *Dohākoṣa-nāma mahāmudrā-upadeśa*, *bsTan-'gyur*, *rgyud*, vol. zhi, fol. 122*b*.

[33]Fol. 98*b*.

[34]*Lam-zab-kyi rnam-par-bshad-pa zab-lam-gyi snye-ma*, fol. 8*a*.

[35]*Do-ha-mdzod ces-bya-ba phyag-rgya-chen-po'i man-ngag*, fol. 122*b*. 'Mind' with a capital letter is used to distinguish it from mind as a term holding a variety of mental events together. The Tibetan language uses for 'Mind' two terms: *dgongs* and *sems-nyid*. The former is almost always combined with *sangs-rgyas* = Buddha. Both terms are synonymous with Śūnyatā in the sense of 'unconceptualizable'.

[36]Fol. 76*a*.

[37]Fol. 76*b*.

[38]Fol. 76*a*.

it is necessary to refer to the great division within Reality between that which exists and that which does not exist. Much attention has been given to 'existence' within the history of philosophy and it has been described to the effect that whatever exists appears to be actually and literally in time and that it can occur in a proposition only as the logical subject. In this sense, any state of mind, or since a state of mind is an occurrence, any mental event, is certainly the kind of entity which can be the logical subject of a proposition and since it appears to have a temporal position, it may legitimately be said to be existent. This description of existence tallies with the first part of the following statement:

> The mental event (memory and association) or existence, and this mind or non-existence—because in the absence of conditions there is no memory and association—both dissolve in that which is unoriginated.[39]

This statement introduces a new concept 'that which is unoriginated' (*skye-ba-med-pa*) in addition to 'mental event' which is said to be something existent (*dngos-po*) and 'mind' which is declared to be non-existent (*dngos-po-med*). Because of the importance of this passage it will be useful to divide it into three parts:

(*a*) mental event or existence
(*b*) mind or non-existence
(*c*) that which is unoriginated.

For the present we shall be concerned with the existence and non-existence of mental events and mind respectively. It is commonly held that every state of mind is part of the history of some mind which endures for some time, and has other earlier and later states which are held together by some relation characteristic of the sort of phenomenon which we are accustomed to call 'mental'. The peculiar fact about the series of successive mental events is that it appears as a unity of center and not as a mere unity of system. It is the nature of this center that is the crucial problem. Even in Buddhism it has found different ex-

---

[39]Fol. 85*ab*.

planations. There is complete agreement between the various schools of Buddhist thought only in so far as the supposition of this center being a Pure Ego is ruled out. The Vijñānavādins, continuing the line of thought of the realistic Sarvāstivādins (with the difference that for the Vijñānavādins only mind has real being), were inclined to conceive of this center as something existent in the manner of a central event, while the Tantrics and Mādhyamikas maintained that the variety of mental states and events is directly interrelated in certain characteristic ways and that there is no particular center whether this be a Pure Ego or a Central Event. In this view 'mind' is an abstract, a fact about certain mental events and their interrelation. Mind, not being a particular which alone can be said to be existent (though it may be questioned whether this can be maintained), is therefore non-existent, as the second part of the above quotation declares. However, the fact that we can think about that which does not exist has tempted many philosophers into holding that there are different 'modes of being', so that in the present case, states of mind exist or have being in one sense, and mind has being in another sense, for which the word 'subsist' is sometimes used. Actually this is nothing but a reintroduction of ontological considerations and only serves to confuse the issue, because in this case 'non-existence' becomes an individual object of precisely the same type as state of mind. The only difference is that in one case a positive ontological postulate, 'existence', is used and in the other case a negative one, 'non-existence', is used and in the other case a negative one, 'non-existence', is used. more validity or sense than the other. Hence it is possible for sKye-med-bde-chen to assert that "Appearance and Śūnyatā are artifacts, because they are accidental,"[40] and more explicitly:

> When the meaning of 'beyond intellect' has been fully understood and comprehended, it will be realized that 'appearance' is accidental, because it is due to certain conditions; and also

---

[40] *Do-ha mdzod ces-bya-ba spyod-pa'i glu'i 'grel-ba don-gyi sgron-ma = Dohākoṣa-nāma-caryāgīti-arthapradīpa-nāma-ṭīkā*, by sKye-med-bde-chen, *bsTan-'gyur, rgyud*, vol. zhi, fol. 36*b*.

> 'Śūnyatā' is accidental, because a 'constructed Śūnyatā' is bound to collapse.[41]

This rejection of both existence ('Appearance') and non-existence ('Śūnyatā'), which by some exiguous reasoning was turned into subsistence, is a rejection of all ontological considerations and argumentations. It also states quite clearly that the statement 'mind does not exist' is equivalent to 'mind is unreal', and it is not possible to say that 'being unreal' is a property which can belong to something in the same sort of way as, for instance, the property 'being blue'. Moreover, terms such as 'being unreal' as well as 'non-existent' do not stand for any conception at all. They are used to deny existence, not to affirm

---

[41] *Ibid.* sKye-med-bde-chen touches here the logical interdependence of Being and Nothing, whose observation is usually attributed—wrongly—to Hegel. What is more, sKye-med-bde-chen's expression reminds us of the analysis given by Martin Heidegger, "What is Metaphysics?" tr. by R. F. C. Hull and Alan Crick in *Existence and Being*, ed. by Werner Brock, Henry Regnery, Chicago: 1949, p. 363:

> But, even apart from the questionableness of this relationship between negation and Nothing, how are we, as finite beings, to render the whole of what-is in its totality accessible *in itself*—let alone to ourselves? We can, at a pinch, think of the whole of what-is as an 'idea' and then negate what we have thus imagined in our thoughts and 'think' it negated. In this way we arrive at the formal concept of an imaginary Nothing, but never Nothing itself. But Nothing is nothing, and between the imaginary and the 'authentic' (*eigentlich*) Nothing no difference can obtain if Nothing represents complete lack of differentiation.

But the 'authentic' Nothing—is this not once again that latent and nonsensical idea of a Nothing that 'is'? Heidegger's 'imaginary Nothing' is equivalent to sKye-med-bde-chen's 'constructed Nothing (Śūnyatā)' (*byas-pa'i stong-pa-nyid*) and see his statement on fol. 34*b* that also 'the absence of memory and association is a relational term (to the presence of memory and association)' (*dran-med kyang ltos-pa'i chos yin te*). But although Heidegger insists that the 'authentic Nothing' has no positive existence, it seems that in spite of himself he deals with Nothing as if it were in reality something, p. 370:

> Nothing is neither an object nor anything that 'is' at all. Nothing occurs neither by itself nor 'apart from' what-is, as a sort of adjunct. Nothing is that which makes the revelation of what-is as such possible for our human existence.

With the first part of this statement the Buddhists would agree, but not with the latter. While it shall not be denied that certain similarities exist between Buddhist Tantrism and Western existentialism, there is a marked difference. In existentialism Nothing is revealed in dread, boredom, anguish (Sartre's favorite term), in Tantrism Śūnyatā is experienced in bliss and happiness.

special modes of existence. But if mind is unreal or non-existent, in the view of the assertion that "states of mind are not different from mind itself,"[42] the attempt to attribute existence to states of mind is futile and meaningless, if we understand anything else but a description by it. We may say that 'states of mind exist' in the sense that 'there are states of mind', i.e., '*x* is a state of mind for a suitable *x*', but we cannot say of this suitable *x* that it exists. That states of mind have no existence in the sense of 'this exists', while they may be said to exist in the sense that their existence is nothing else but the possibility of their being placed in a certain system, in this case, in the cognitive-emotive system of our world of experiences, is often expressed by similes, among which 'sky-flower' is the most usual one. Thus, while 'sky' as a term for vastness and intangibleness is used to symbolize 'mind' as not being a thing, 'sky-flower' is a symbol for something equally unreal, not being a thing: "In this way mind is like the sky and the mental event memory and association is like a sky-flower."[43]

The upshot of the discussion is that the Tantrics as well as the Mādhyamikas insist on the fact that ontological speculations, whether they move in positive or negative terms, are senseless and that any introduction of ontological considerations is a deviation from the Middle Path as living experience and is a stagnation in dead concepts. This rejection of ontological considerations is most clearly expressed in the third part of the above quotation, viz., that "existence (positive term) and non-existence (negative term) dissolve in that which is unoriginated." Padma dkar-po points out that this term 'that which is unoriginated' does not stand for any conception at all: "It is not used to demonstrate something that is unoriginated, because in this case it would fall under the category of non-existence."[44] (As will be remembered, non-existence is often

---

[42]*Phyag-rgya-chen-po'i man-ngag-gi bshad-sbyar rgyal-ba'i gan-mdzod*, fol. 55*a*.

[43]Fol. 82*b*.

[44]*bSre-'pho'i lam-skor-gyi thog-mar lam-dbye-bsdu*, fol. 78*a*.

spoken of as if it were a special mode of existence, while actually it denies existence. Hence to avoid confusion a new term or operational concept had to be coined). Still more succinctly the same author declares with respect to the problem of Reality:

> As to ultimate Reality a distinction must be made between the so-called incidental ultimate reality, which means that as an object for our analysis, which takes into account every angle of the problem, it is unoriginated, Śūnyatā, limitlessness; and the final ultimate reality, which even the Buddhas cannot demonstrate by saying 'This is it', because, due to the fact that it defies every analysis when subjected to the four alternatives possible for any subject, viz., being, non-being, being and non-being together, and neither being nor non-being, every attempt to 'grasp' (i.e., to conceive) that which does not stand for any conception at all (*gshis*) as something 'graspable' (i.e. conceivable, conceptualizable) is not beyond bewildering ignorance![45]

In other words, the nature of reality and of ourselves is such that it is in itself incapable of being conceptualized. It cannot be apprehended by any kind of conceptualizing intellect (*yid*),[46] and it cannot be understood by any process of analysis and re-synthesis of concepts, although it operates also in this process.

This analysis should make it abundantly clear that advanced Buddhist thought cannot be equated with any '-*isms*', for to do so is the error of introducing premises which Buddhism is at pains to eliminate from its reasoning because they prove to be utterly meaningless.

Apart from the facts that by the determination of 'mind' as 'unoriginated' (*skye-ba-med-pa*) in the sense that 'mind' is nothing but an operational concept without any denotatively given content, the important point to note is that all ontological speculations are out of place and that the idea of a mind-stuff is

---

[45] *Phyag-rgya-chen-po'i man-ngag-gi bshad-sbyar rgyal-ba'i gan-mdzod*, fol. 46*a*.

[46] *yid*, Skt. *manas* is that function-event which is particularly concerned with conceptualization. Hence *yid-la mi-byed-pa* (Skt *amanasikāra*) 'not to conceptualize' is of decisive importance.

totally gratuitous, and that, therefore, this determination also effects a change from causal laws to laws of functional dependence. For while causal laws relate to the modes of changes of things, or substantive particulars, laws of functional dependence relate to the correlation of sets of properties. Such correlation is the essence of what is commonly termed 'meditation' or 'Yoga'. In order to be able to correlate various sets of properties, it is necessary to have an operational formula, and since in this correlation we ourselves are involved, the analysis of 'mind' as the basis and fount of our life is but the beginning of Buddhist philosophy. It is important to note this point, because under these circumstances philosophy is not a purely academic pursuit, as it tended to be during the European mediaeval world and in many respects still continues to be, but is looked to for a way of life, for reasoned guidance in conduct. Hence philosophical analysis is meant primarily to 'lay the foundation' (*gzhi gtan-la-'bebs-pa*) for subsequent operation and at the same time to give the operational formula as an effective tool into the hands of him who starts correlating the different sets of properties that make up his spiritual life. Laying the foundation, from which later on 'meditation' starts as part of conduct, is described as follows:[47]

> While the source of the progressive (instabilizing) development as indicated by the twelve topics in the Inductive Principle of Functional Relation[48] is ignorance (*ma-rig-pa*) and the source

---

[47] *rTen-'brel kho-bo lugs-kyi khrid chos thams-cad-kyi snying-po len-pa*, fol. 1 *seq*.

[48] *rten-'brel*, Skt. Pratītyasamutpāda. This term is mostly translated by 'Causal Nexus'. This translation dated back to a time when it was assumed that causality is the essence of science, and that the Pratītyasamutpāda in Buddhism must be a statement (a proposition) about the world. Apart from the fact that science is not concerned with terms but with relations, the *Pratītyasamutpāda* is not at all a proposition about the world. It is a leading principle, a way of eking out of nature as many uniformities as possible. Hence all reference to causality should be avoided. Buddhist philosophy is complicated enough in itself, and it will certainly not help to have recourse to such ambiguous terms as 'cause' which B. Russell, 'On the Notion of Cause' in *Mysticism and Logic*, Pelican Book, p. 171 describes as "so inextricably bound up with misleading

of the regressive (steadying) development is knowledge (*rig-pa*) where all ignorance has ceased, by investigating the momentary experience (*shes-pa'i-skad-cig-ma*) oscillating between the two types of ignorance and knowledge, from a higher point of view, it is permissible to state that Freedom (*rang-rgyud-pa*), by deviating from its steady state, becomes (A) Ignorance mistaken about Reality, because this deviation blurs the view of Ultimate Reality.[49] By perpetually deviating from what has appeared, it first becomes (B) Ignorance mistaken about the relation between cause and effect of our action, because this deviation obscures mind as the owner of cognitive situations. The first aspect (A), the instabilizing bewildering experience having come about by traces and dispositions[50] since beginningless time, is because of its incessancy termed 'divisive activity' (*rtog-pa*) or 'the most subtle'. From the latter aspect (B) proceeds an experience which is divided into sense-field and sense-perception or into subject and object and which by clinging to this duality is characterized by a thoroughgoing dualism. It is termed 'division' (*rnam-par rtog-pa*) or 'the subtle'. From this state of duality there arises the variety (of our world) not limited as to number and shape. The infinite possibility of 'bewilderment' (*'khrul-pa*) appearing as the multiplicity of all that is visible or heard about in this triple world. It is termed 'the imagined' (*kun-tu-rtog-pa*) or 'the coarse'. The result of these causes and conditions is Saṃsāra. But by experiencing this momentary instabilizing experience as such, the stream of divisive activity (*rtog-pa'i rgyun*) is stopped, bewilderment becomes disentangled precisely there where it was entangled, and this is Nirvāṇa. As Saraha says:

> When mind is fettered there is bondage,
> When it is free there is no doubt.[51]

---

associations as to make its complete extrusion from the philosophical vocabulary desirable." Moreover, the topics (twelve members) of the Pratītyasamutpāda do not follow logically from the premises; the Pratītyasamutpāda is inductive, not deductive.

[49]'View of Reality' does not mean that A sees B; there is as yet no division into subject and object. Such division is restricted or veiled liberty.

[50]Traces and dispositions are one of the triad of conditions bringing about a veiling of liberty and knowledge. The nature of them has been explained above.

[51]Saraha's *Dohākoṣa* 44.

And from the *'Jam-dpal-gyi lta-ba mdor bstan*:

> When mind is fathomed by comprehensive understanding
> There are no more any traces and dispositions.

The fact that the sphere (*dbyings*) in which neither bewilderment nor non-bewilderment have any place whatsoever, is nevertheless the Inductive Principle of Functional Relation which is only a fiction[52] due to it rising as incessant cognition as far as mere appearance (as symbolific activity) is concerned, is stated to be the non-duality of Saṃsāra and Nirvāṇa or the Genuine Buddha Mind, so that 'incessant as to appearance' it is the basis of the Inductive Principle of Functional Relation; 'non-existent' it is the basis of Śūnyatā; 'not staying in any differentiation' it is the basis of unity,[53] and 'impartial' it is the basis of pervasiveness. As is stated by Yan-lag-med-pa'i rdo-rje (Anaṅgavajra):

> Because of unoriginatedness non-existent,
> Because of incessancy functionally related;
> Out of the disappearance of existence and non-existence
> There is origination of unity.

In this way, Mind (*sems-nyid*) as unconceptualizable Reality (*gnyug-ma*) pervades mind as a contingent phenomenon. All intellectual attempts to concentrate on mind are covetousness, and all intellectual attempts to avoid mind are animosity. While such contingent factors as covetousness and animosity throw us into Saṃsāra, it is by plunging into their contingency without ever affirming or negating mind that they become the cause of the rising of illumining comprehensive knowledge instead of turning into covetousness or animosity. To give an example: Water as such pervades ice as an accidental occurrence and therefore out of ice, water comes forth. The division of water into the two topics of 'nature of water' and 'changeability of water' is a gratuitous affair. Whether you make a division between water and ice or not, there is always water, and this holds good for the ultimate. In brief, when it appears in its genuineness it is termed 'appearance in itself' (*rang-snang*), and when it appears in its contingency it

[52]*sgyu-ma-tsam-du*. There is nothing fictitious about the 'leading Principle', all that is meant is that it is no object at all.

[53]*zung-'jug*, Skt. *yuganaddha*.

is termed 'bewilderment appearance' (*'khrul-snang*).[54] As is expressed by kLu'i byang-chub (Nāgabodhi):

> When Śūnyatā is infected by traces and dispositions,
> Śūnyatā turns into existence:
> Just as water swept by a cold wind
> Becomes frozen and is ice.

As will have been observed, the further the analysis of 'mind' proceeds, the farther the substantive particular 'mind' disappears and instead of it there are sets of properties. Properties are not individual objects, they are particulars which we can think of and with which we can operate even if there are no objects which possess these properties. Such properties are referred to by such terms as 'being incessant' (*ma-'gags-pa, 'gag-med*) and 'being invariable' (*'gyur-med*) for which also the operational concepts *gdangs* and *gshis* are used respectively. The former term, *gdangs*, is specified in the following way:

> Since *gdangs* is 'being incessant', it is capable of becoming everything and anything, and this fact is termed the basis and fount of manifoldness. But since becoming a manifoldness occurs only under suitable conditions, 'being incessant' is intellectually spoken of as 'owner of all causal characteristics'.[55]

The suitable conditions which are here referred to are those of appearance, traces and dispositions, and symbolism, as was pointed out above. At another place it is said:

> That *gshis* which is being invariable is the cause of purity in itself, and the *gdangs* is termed the basis and fount of the pure and impure (as which we interpret our experiences on the reflective level), because it is capable of turning into everything and anything.[56]

---

[54] On fol. 4*a* of the work from which this passage is given in translation it is stated that " 'appearance in itself' (*rang-snang*) is termed so because all that rises as incessant creativity from the *gshis* or the unoriginated Dharmatā, is not different from the delightful play of sole illumination in pure sensation" and "bewilderment appearance (*'khrul-snang*) also termed 'appearance other than in itself' (*gzhan-snang*) is appearance affected by the traces of the subject-object division, because it appears without being existent."

[55] *bSre-'pho'i lam-skor-gyi thog-mar lam-dbye-bsdu*, fol. 64*b*.

[56] *Ibid.*, fol. 66*a*.

Although *gshis* and *gdangs* are substantive words, in no way are they used as implying entities in themselves. They are mere operational concepts. Reality is not such that anything can be abstracted from it and declared to be existent in itself and graded into something less real or unreal and something more real. To do so is to move in concepts about arbitrarily selected slices from reality and to have lost sight of reality. This is explicitly stated with respect to Mahāmudrā (*phyag-rgya chen-po*), another term for Reality and the *leitmotif* in Tantrism; its division into *gshis* and *dgangs* being utterly gratuitous.

> Mahāmudrā which itself is impartial is split up by the intellect which forever falls into opposites, and appears as *gshis* and *gdangs*. This splitting up of Reality is exactly like what happens in the case of any person whatsoever who is looked at by an observer either as a friend or as an enemy. In its aspect of *gshis* Reality is asserted to be unchanging bliss and in its aspect of *gdangs* it is asserted to be Śūnyatā possessing all causal characteristics. The former aspect is the ultimately real and the latter aspect is the relatively real.[57]

This distinction between the 'ultimately real' and 'the relatively real', which is characteristic of mysticism and all philosophical systems that are rooted in mystic illumination, is not only at variance with the conviction many people probably have, that Reality is one and indivisible, it also introduces gradation into Reality so that there is something more real than another,[58] from which assumption it is not difficult to arrive at the conclusion that Saṃsāra is unreal and worthless and Nirvāṇa alone is real and valuable, or to formulate other propositions to the same effect. Such statements, however, are not factual statements that can be empirically verified; they are expressive of an experience which may be tentatively described as an awareness of becoming-existing against a background of Being. To avoid misunderstanding I had better say at once that 'Being'

---

[57]*Phyag-rgya-chen-po'i man-ngag-gi bshad-sbyar rgyal-ba'i gan-mdzod*, fol. 32*b*.

[58]For this doctrine of acosmism see W. T. Stace, *Time and Eternity*, p. 122 *seq*.

with a capital letter does not necessarily imply something ontologically given. Only on the reflective level, which is already a subsequent phase in experiencing, may an experience give rise to metaphysical assertions and ontological considerations, which are all of no avail in helping us to *live*. It gives high credit to the Buddhist Tantrics that they never lost sight of Life and successfully avoided the trap of the literalist error by knowing full well that the function of language consists also in being a means to 'draw attention to', and by making use of critical analysis, after that to which attention had been drawn had been expressed in language. The ontology of the slices we have cut from Reality are not the problem; it is, rather, the relation that holds between that which we have cut off and termed 'the ultimately real' (*gshis*) and 'the relatively real' (*gdangs*)–'being invariable, without origination (i.e., not standing for any conception at all)' and 'being incessant, capable of becoming everything and anything'. For it is only the basis of knowing what it 'means' to say that A stands in a certain relation to B that we can work out our life so that thereby it may become nobler, freer, and happier than it could otherwise be.

The relation that holds between the 'ultimately real and unconceptualizable' and the 'relatively real which is capable of becoming conceptualized' is a symmetrical transitive relation having the formal nature of identity, as is made explicit by the use of the term 'co-nascent' (*lhan-cig-skyes-pa'i de-kho-na-nyid*). Hence the indivisibility of Reality or the relation between the two truths can be expressed only as follows: "*gshis* is ultimately beyond truth and *gdangs* is commonly beyond falsehood by virtue of co-nascence."[59] In other words, that which is unconceptualizable cannot be asserted to be truth, but we and our world are not an illusion, are not falsehood, but truth. This distinguishes Tantrism from all other forms of mysticism. Such a view which is the foundation from which our

---

[59] *Phyag-rgya-chen-po'i man-ngag-gi bshad-sbyar rgyal-ba'i gan-mdzod*, fol. 35*b*.

See also *bSre-'pho'i lam-skor-gyi thog-mar lam-dbye-bsdu*, fol. 78*b*.

life will have to be built up, has one important consequence: The reality of man and of his world proceeds from 'livingness', not from anything that mind as a formulatedness of livingness can codify; for objectified knowledge is always removed from truth. Long before Kierkegaard and the modern existentialists the Buddhist Tantrics knew that 'truth is subjectivity'.

The Levels of Understanding in Buddhism

Buddhism calls itself a career (*yāna*), a progress through life, and what it teaches is designed to fulfil this purpose: to lead man out of his unregenerate state of naive common-sense to enlightenment or reality knowledge. In more familiar terms this means that a complete change of attitude is aimed at, which it is certainly not too incorrect to define more precisely as a shift from a discursive thought situation to an intuitive cognitive situation. The means by which this change is brought about are meditational concentrative processes. Already in the earliest strata of Buddhism intuitive knowledge and meditational practices leading to it have been emphasized. However, in course of time, the methods have become more and more elaborate and refined and it is therefore from the Mahāyānic phase of Buddhism that a much clearer picture of both the methods and their attendant phenomena may be obtained. Here I shall not deal with the methods, in the first place, but with the salient features that mark the transition from one situation to the other and I shall try to give as precise statements as are possible, which is all the more necessary because the presentation of Eastern philosophical problems for the most part thrives on the ambiguity of terms due to the complete absence of semantic studies in this particular field.

Buddhist texts, as a rule, make a distinction between the 'assumed' meaning (*drang-don*, Skt. *neyārtha*) and the 'real' meaning (*nges-don*, Skt. *nītārtha*) of the teachings,[1] a distinction which roughly corresponds to the various degrees of the student's intellectual acumen. This distinction as such has nothing to do with the spiritual development aimed at, but it is evident from the general trend of Buddhism that the 'real' meaning can be understood only when the student's intuition has been developed to a certain extent and depth. It is this fact that has been emphasized in those texts which are concerned with the actual living of the Buddhist tenets–the Buddhist Yoga texts.[2]

Starting with a quotation from the Tibetan scholar and saint Mi-la-ras-pa, which in concise terms outlines the salient features of the various levels of understanding, Padma-dkar-po declares:[3]

> Venerable Mi-la said that
>
> In whatever way the outer world may appear
> It is error[4] when one does not intuitively understand it;

---

[1]See *Abhidharmakośavyākhyā*, pp. 174; 704. *Madhyamakavṛtti*, p. 43.

[2]In the following analysis I have made use of the following texts. In the course of the article they will be referred to by their abbreviations given in parentheses:

(a) *Phyag-rgya-chen-po'i mang-nag-gi bshad sbyar rgyal-ba'i gan-mdzod* (*Phyag-chen gan-mdzod*)
(b) *Phyag-chen-gyi zin-bris*
(c) *rNal-'byor bzhi'i nges-pa rab-tu dbye-ba phyag-rgya chen-po'i bshad-pa thams-cad-kyi bla-ma* (*Phyag-chen bla-ma*)
(d) *Phyag-rgya chen-po rnal-'byor bzhi'i bshad-pa nges-don lta-ba'i mig* (*Phyag-chen rnal-'byor mig*)
(e) *rNal-'byor bzhi'i bshad-pa don-dam mdzub-tshugs su bstan-pa* (*rNal-'byor mdzub-tshugs*)
(f) *Phyag-rgya chen-po lnga-ldan-gyi khrid-dmigs yid-kyi snye-ma* (*Phyag-chen snye-ma*)
(g) *bSre-'pho'i lam-skor-gyi thog-mar lam dbye-bsdu* (*bSre-'pho'i lam skor*)

[3]*Phyag-chen gan-mdzod*, fol. 21*b seq*.

[4]*'khrul-pa*, Skt. *bhrama*, *bhrānti*, offers great difficulties for a proper translation. It essentially means a deviation from Reality, hence 'error' includes everything in the perceptual field which we should call a veridical and a delusive situation. Even our veridical situation is likened to the perception of a white shell as yellow by a man affected by jaundice, and the curing of the disease is the awakening to Reality. See for instance *Phyag-chen gan-mdzod*, fol. 62*a*.

For those who intuitively understand it
it appears as the Dharmakāya.
The consummatory stage on which one does not
experience any appearance
Is said to be pure like the cloudless sky.[5]

There are three situations: the situation of non-intuition (*ma-rtogs-pa'i skabs*), the situation where intuition begins to function (*rtogs-pa shar-ba'i skabs*), and the consummatory situation (*mthar-thug-pa'i skabs*). These situations are also to be known as the status of a man of ordinary common-sense, the status of a Bodhisattva, and the status of a Buddha.

In the first situation there may be an assertion as to freedom from duality (*gnyis-med*, Skt. *advaya*)[6] or coincidence (*zung-'jug*, Skt. *yuganaddha*),[7] but intellectually there remains the world of appearance in a dual way or the differentiation into opposites, because the world of appearance in a dual way has not been given up. Since, following the dictates of the intellect, the persons in this situation hold to reciprocally exclusive assertions[8] such as that error remains error, non-error, non-error, relative truth relative truth, and ultimate truth ultimate truth, they busy themselves with the 'assumed' meaning of things. People of low intelligence (i.e., people who do not venture into the realm of critical philosophy) feel compelled to call this (assumed meaning) the Truth.

As to the second situation it has been stated that "when the

---

[5]Comparisons with the immaculate sky abound in Yoga texts.

[6]There is a marked distinction between the *advaya* of the Buddhists and the *advaita* of the Vedantins. *advaya* refers to knowledge which is free from the duality of the extremes, while *advaita* is knowledge *of* a differenceless Brahman. The term *advaya* often implies the futulity of engaging in a knowledge governed by the duality of extremes. On this distinction between *advaya* and *advaita* see T. R. V. Murti, *The Central Philosophy of Buddhism*, p. 217.

[7]The literal meaning of this term is 'bound together, forming a pair'. However, Padma-dkar-po, *Phyag-chen gan-mdzod*, fol. 102*b*, referring to the definition of this term given in *Pañcakrama* V, makes it clear that the 'pairness' is a unity and not comparable with the unity two horns form on the head of a bull. An example from chemistry will serve to clear the Buddhist conception of this term. Silver-chloride is not understood by the investigation of either silver or chloride, so *yuganaddha* is not understood by investigating the one or the other of its components.

[8]In a wider sense this definition refers to what we call the Laws of Thought.

conception of the world of appearance in its dual way has subsided there is intuition of non-duality." Due to this (intuition) all interpretative concepts (*rnam-rtog*, Skt. *vikalpa*) rise as the Dharmakāya, all emotions (and the destructive conflict into which they ordinarily lead man, *nyon-mongs*, Skt. *kleśa*) as ambrosia, and all error as intuitive knowledge (*ye-shes*, Skt. *jñana*,)[9] and since it is no longer possible to make divisions or differentiations into opposites it is due to this basic feature that then the two truths (i.e., relative truth and ultimate truth) have become indivisible (*dbyer-med*), or (what is the same,) that the beneficial expedients (*thabs*, Skt. *upāya*) and the analytical appreciative understanding of things (*shes-rab*, Skt. *prajñā*) have become indivisible—and many other statements to the same effect—so that there is only one truth, viz., the ultimately real truth. Furthermore, rGyal-dbang-rje expresses this idea in the following verse:

> As soon as the nature of the interpretative concepts is known,
> Whatever rises has the ring of the Dharmakāya.

And the Great Saraha says:

> When intuition has come to function everything is this;
> Nobody will get anything but this.[10]

This is the 'real' meaning.

In this third case it may suffice to quote what rGyal-ba'i dbang-po has said about the statements made by the intellect of the human beings as regards the Buddha-viewpoint:

> To measure the sky with a yardstick,
> To cut up the all-pervading into little bits:
> Though there is no sense in doing so, many people do so.

---

[9] These combinations are often mentioned. For instance, *Phyag-chen-gyi zin-bris*, fol. 7*a*; *Phyag-chen gan-mdzod*, fols. 21*b*; 81*a*; 95*b*; *rNal-'byor mdzub-tshugs*, fol. 11*a*; *bSre-'pho'i lam-skor*, fols. 64*a*; 69*b*; 74*b*; etc. etc. There is a marked distinction between *jñāna* (Tib. *ye-shes*) and *prajñā* (Tib. *shes-rab*) which is often overlooked. The former is an intuitive mystic knowledge, while the latter is analytical. T. R. V. Murti in his *Central Philosophy of Buddhism* constantly translates *prajñā* by Intuition. This is against all evidence. *prajñā* is 'discrimination, analytical knowledge' (*dharmāṇāṃ pravicaya*), but its mode is different whether it operates in an intuitive attidue or an ordinary common sense attitude when *prajñā* is called *mati*. See *Abhidharmakośa* II 24 and *Vyākhyā*.

[10] *Dohākoṣa* 18.

While here three levels of understanding have been pointed out[11] nothing has been said about their inner relation. Further, while from purely logical considerations it would be sufficient to have only the distinction between the 'assumed' and the 'real' meanings of the teaching, the introduction of a third level, the 'consummatory situation' (*mthar-thug*, Skt. *niṣṭāgata*), is obviously necessitated by practical considerations. In all developmental processes man is but too easily inclined to lose sight of the actual goal and, if not actually falling away from it, at least to remain stuck halfways. Therefore the ideal or goal has to be reintroduced as an additional level to the already existing two levels.

The actual process of spiritual development and maturation, however, begins when the individual feels necessitated to change his outlook. It is at this moment that again three different cognitive situations can be distinguished. These three situations are: first to think about the goal, then to apprehend it and thereby to be in a more intimate contact with it, and finally to have a clear view and knowledge of it in a purely non-conceptual manner. With the attainment of the last mentioned situation the foundation (*gzhi*) has been laid from whence it is possible to walk the path (*lam*) to the goal (*'bras-bu*), for knowledge is according to the Buddhist conception given to man that he may act. It has further to be noted that the three situations mentioned are distinct levels and not phases within one situation. In other words, the levels of understanding represent distinct attitudes which have an equally distinct bearing on action. The emphasis is thus on the *how* and not on the *what*, and it is precisely this feature that distinguishes Buddhism from the other Indian systems which, to judge from the available best material, were mainly concerned with ontological questions.

About the distinctive features of the various levels Padma-dkar-po declares:[12]

---

[11]These three levels are levels in their own right and not stages within one level. They must not be confused with the three stages assumed by the Mīmāṃsakas.

[12]*Phyag-chen gan-mdzod*, fol. 42*a seq*.

> At the beginner's stage there is only discursiveness (*go-ba-tsam*); at the stage of interested practice [*mos-pa-spyod-pa*, Skt. *adhimukticaryā(bhūmi)*] there is the apprehension (*myong-ba*) of reality in a general way; (at the final stage there is) pure intuition (*rtogs-pa*). Since through it there is no chance that doubts will not be destroyed, it is the attainment (*grub*) of what is called the dispelling of doubts from within[13] independent of syntactically formulated sentences.[14]

Of these three stages a fuller account has been given by Dvags-po-lha-rje[15] and since his words have an immediate bearing on the topic under discussion they may be given here:

> The beginner's level is the period for the Path of the Acquisition (of the necessary prerequisites for spiritual development) (*tshogs-lam*, Skt. *sambhāramārga*), because one is about to bring to maturity the as yet immmature stream representing one's existence. The level of interested practice is the period for the Path of Practical Application (*sbyor-lam*, Skt. *prayogamārga*), because one is only interested in the meaning of śūnyatā. At this time miserliness and other vices which are opposed to the practice of the perfections, emotional conflicts which can be got rid of by seeing them, as well as all the postulates which veil the knowable as to its real nature have been bent head-down so that they cannot rise again. The Bodhisattvas' levels extend from the first level called 'The Joyous One' to the tenth level called 'The Dharma Cloud'. So also it is said in the *Daśabhūmikasūtra*:

---

[13]A fuller definition has been given in *rNal-'byor mdzub-tshugs*, fol. 7*b*: "The dispelling of doubts from within is said so, because on account of having directly intuited the natural and real disposition (*gnas-lugs*) of all entities the discursive understanding of reality in a general way and all doubts have subsided in their own place."

[14]This latter part of the quotation refers to the nature of *kalpanā* or a cognition the content of which is capable of being associated with verbal expressions (*abhilāpasaṃsargayogyapratibhāsapratiītiḥ kalpanā*). Valid, however, is only perception free from *kalpanā* (*kalpanāpoḍhaṃ pratyakṣaṃ*). See *Nyāyabindu*, chapter I.

[15]*Dam-chos yid-bzhin-gyi nor-bu thar-pa rin-po-che'i rgyan zhes-bya-ba theg-pa chen-po'i lam-rim-gyi bshad-pa*, fol. 108*a*. See on this work my article *Dvags po lha rje's "Ornament of Liberation," JAOS*, vol. 75, pp. 90 *seq*. and its fully annotated translation *Sgam.po.pa, The Jewel Ornament of Liberation*.

> O sons of the Victorious One, these are the ten levels of a Bodhisattva: the Bodhisattva's level called 'The Joyous One,' and . . . .[16]

Here, the first level 'The Joyous One' is the occasion for the Path of Seeing Reality (*mthong-lam*, Skt. *darśanamārga*) to come into existence, it is the intuition of śūnyatā as a reality.

As is evident from these passages, the beginner's level is distinctly a thought situation and discursive in character. It chiefly consists of judgments about reality or, what is the same due to what at first sight appears as mentalism in Buddhism,[17] about the status of mind. I use the term 'chiefly' here, because I do not want to deny that there may be something intuitive in the thought situation. Obviously this is meant also by the statement that *rtogs* which essentially is pure intuition, is synonymous with all kinds of understanding such as discursiveness and apprehension,[18] although the thought situation is defined more precisely as "To understand the status of mind by hearing and thinking about it."[19] What happens in a discursive situation is that reality is split up and various meanings and evaluations are assigned to the parts. Thus Padma-dkar-po declares:[20]

> The Mahāmudrā (or Reality) which itself is devoid of contraries is split up by the intellect which (for ever) falls into

[16] *Daśabhūmikasūtra*, p. 5.

[17] I follow here the distinction C. D. Broad, *The Mind and its Place in Nature*, p. 654, makes between Idealism and Mentalism. The Buddhists were Idealists in holding that the highest and most sublime, Buddhahood, becomes manifested in greater and greater intensity in course of the individual's spiritual development. However, in holding that there is only mind (*cittamātra*) or even mindness (*cittatā*, Tib. *sems-nyid*) they were mentalists. Further, while materiality was for them at best delusive, mentality was emergent. This characterizes the aspect of Buddhist thought to which the Yoga texts mentioned in note 2 belong. There have been other schools of Buddhism which one would have to characterize in a different way. But this is outside the scope of the present analysis.

[18] *Phyag-chen-gyi zin-bris*, fol. 7*a*.

[19] *Ibid.*

[20] *Phyag-chen gan-mdzod*, fol. 32*b seq.*

contraries, and through this splitting up reality makes its appearance as pure being (*gshis*) and pure creativity (*gdangs*).[21] (This splitting up) is exactly like what happens in the case of any person whosoever who (just is, but) is looked at by the observer either as a friend or as an enemy. With respect to its pure being (*gshis*) it is posited as unchanging great bliss (*'gyur-ba-med pa'i bde ba chen po*) and with respect to its pure creativity (*gdangs*) it is posited as the śūnyatā endowed with all excellent occurrents (*rnam-pa'i mchog thams cad dang ldan pa'i stong pa nyid*). The former is ultimately real (*don dam*, Skt. *paramārtha*) and the latter is relatively real (*kun-rdzob*, Skt. *saṃvṛta*).

I shall give an analysis of the technical terms later when I have mentioned the other factors involved in perception. Here it may be pointed out only that 'ultimately real' is a provisional ultimately real, the 'real' ultimately real itself being inaccessible to any attempt of verbalization or conceptualization. This Padma-dkar-po points out in the following words:[22]

> Ultimately real is a conventional or provisional ultimately real, inasmuch as the object of discrimination which views every angle of it is (still) predicable as being 'unoriginated', 'void' (*śūnyatā*), 'devoid of contraries' and so on. But the consummatory ultimately real means that even the Buddhas cannot point out that this is it, because not allowing itself to be investigated by the four alternative views on a subject, void, non-void, both together affirmed, and both together denied, to take the Ultimate (*gshis*) as some thing (*gang-du gzung-yang*) would not be beyond the error under which the oridnary perceiving subject operates.

This statement is in full accord with the assertion that the Ultimate or pure being (*gshis*) is in the truly ultimate sense beyond even truth, while the pure creativity (*gdangs*) which is inseparable from pure being and forming with it a unity and not

---

[21]The term *gdangs* is sometimes written *mdangs* and *dvangs*. Its connotation is that of light, *gshis* is pure being and always true, *gdangs* is relatively true in so far as it refers to pure perception, always false is the belief about the item perceived. See also *Phyag-chen gan-mdzod*, fol. 62*a*.

[22]*Phyag-chen gan-mdzod*, fol. 46*a*.

a mere aggregate as such like anything that admits of being expressed in concepts or words, is relative, but in this relative nature it is thoroughly true,[23] the error not lying in our perception of reality but in our beliefs about reality. For just as the ultimately real may be distinguished into a provisional ultimately real and a real ultimately real, so also the relatively real is really relatively real and erroneously relatively real; and it is from the really real that, as has been pointed out above, the two truths are said to be indivisible. This then explains that metaphysical position of Buddhism, which contends that all judgments involve us in the thought of one all-embracing system of reality of which each true judgment declares a part of it. Certainly a conch, to use a frequently employed item, is not an attribute of reality, but its existence is bound up with the existence of the whole universe. It is real in its being (*gshis*) and in its being a conch (*gdangs*), but it is not real in the sense that the sensum by which the particular object manifests itself is directly determined by the physical object or guarantees the existence of a physical object.[24]

Without going further into the description of a discursive thought situation it is obvious that a totally different situation is given if instead of hearing or thinking or reasoning about a thing we actually apprehend and experience it. Here the various factors of the particular situation are not merely co-existent and may be selected for inspection, but are related in a perfectly unique manner to form the perfectly unique kind of a whole which we call the 'experience of so-and-so.' In order to experience a thing it is necessary to concentrate upon and to pay closest attention to it.[25] Now what happens when we are looking at something with interest and attention is that our awareness

[23] *Phyag-chen gan-mdzod*, fol. 35*b*; *bSre-pho'i lam-skor*, fol. 78*b*.

[24] Cf. *Phyag-chen gan-mdzod*, fol. 62*a*.

[25] Nine stages are distinguished in concentration. See *Mahāyānasūtrālaṅkāra* XIV 14 and commentary. A fuller explanation is found in *Phyag-chen gan-mdzod*, fols. 89*a*–90*b seq*.

of the sensum in this particular situation loses its external reference by insensible degrees and approaches pure sensation. The favorite simile to describe what happens is the sky. Because of its nature of being a vast expanse of blue and of possessing the least disturbing qualities which are likely to divert the attention of the observer, in giving closest attention to it, every chance is given that the perception of it melts into pure sensation, an event which Saraha aptly describes in his verse:

> By repeatedly looking at the state of the sky which is pure
> from the very beginning
> Seeing (the sky as an external object) melts away,[26]

and which his commentator, gNyis-med-avadhūti, explains in the following manner:

> The real nature of mind, when no conditions for its becoming obscured arise, is known by looking at it first as the perceptive activity against the background of the apperceptive mass of the flux of mnemic persistents; by looking at it again it is known as being unoriginated; and by once again looking at it it is known as inaccessible to reasoning.[27]

On the other hand, in this vast expanse of blue clouds come and go in an unceasing and ever changing manner, out of it they appear and back into it they fade, but the sky persists, and in this way the sky also serves as a simile for the wondrous unity of pure unchanging being and continuous creativity. As Padma-dkar-po points out:[28]

> Since there is nothing more vast (*stong-pa*, Skt. *śūnya*) than the sky it is used as a simile: just as one can easily know that the sky is spotless when the conditions for its becoming overcast disap-

---

[26] *Dohākoṣa* 36. The usefulness of the sky in achieving pure sensation has been taught by Mi-la-ras-pa, as may be gleaned from the quotations in *Phyag-chen gan-mdzod*, fols. 72*a*, 91*a*.

[27] *Do-ha mdzod-kyi snying-po don-gyi glu'i 'grel-ba* (*Dohākoṣa-hṛdaya arthagīti-ṭīkā*), fol. 75*b* (*bsTan-'gyur*, section *rgyud*, vol. zhi, Derge edition).

[28] *bSre-'pho'i lam-skor*, fol. 81*b*.

pear, similarly one can know the nature of the incessant creativity going on (*gdangs*). Further, the multitude (in which the creativity manifests itself) is made by the intellect. On the side of the created items there is difference among each other; in reality, however, all the differences are something single: just like gold remaining in itself one single substance and the same though it may have been turned into a variety of ornaments. But when the gold is left by itself and not continuously worked into ornaments, though it may be turned into a variety of them, it is at peace with itself, just like muddy water which by itself becomes clear when it is not disturbed.

> "Like water, gold, and the sky,
> It is spoken of as pure because of its purity."[29]

The first simile explains how the incessant (creativity) appears in a manifold of forms; the second simile explains how even at the time when a manifold of forms has appeared pure being remains unchanged; and the third simile points out how pure being left in its originality becomes the result.

What is given in an experience may on subsequent reflection be looked at from various angles, either as the situation in which the particular experience could happen or as the experience itself. The former is known as 'tranquillity' (*zhi-gnas*, Skt. *śamatha*), obviously called so because through and after the concentrative and attentive processes a certain harmony and peacefulness is obtained. The experience itself is designated by the technical term *rtse-gcig* (Skt. *ekāgratā*) which I propose to translate by 'a unique kind of whole'. 'Tranquillity' and 'unique kind of whole' are therefore synonymous[30] and have the same qualifying attributes. Thus,

> tranquillity has the essence of feeling, transparency, and absence of interpretative concepts (*bde gsal mi-rtog-pa*).[31]

and

---

[29]According to the *bZhi-chos zhal-gdams*, fol. 3*a* this has Nāropa as its author.

[30]*rNal-'byor mdzub-tshugs*, fols. 6*b*–7*a*.

[31]*Ibid.*, fol. 2*a*–*b*.

> at the time of there being a unique kind of whole the view that only mind exists is firmly established. There is absence of interpretative concepts as subject and object, there is knowledge as awareness and transparency, and there is its essence feeling. Thus feeling, transparency, and the absence of interpretative concepts (*bde-gsal-mi-rtog-pa*) abide in the unique kind of whole (*rtse-gcig*).[32]

The term 'absence of interpretative concepts' (*mi-rtog-pa*) is intimately connected with what was referred to as the view that only mind exists. This view is the rejection of the common-sense belief in physical objects as ontological items corresponding to the epistemological object of a particular perceptual situation. It further declares that the notion of a physical object is a category and defined by postulates (*rnam-par rtog-pa*, Skt. *vikalpa*) which are as innate principles of interpretation superimposed on and applied to what is given in pure sensation. The view that there is only mind takes into account the subjective part in cognition—and the unique contribution of Buddhism to Indian philosophy is the discovery of the subjective, hence its role is comparable to the one Kant played in Western philosophies with this distinction that the Buddhists did not consider the so called *a priori* categories to be absolutely necessary. Therefore, however important the subjective is it is not ultimate and so the view of there being only mind is but provisional and an intermediate stage in the whole of the developmental process.[33]

But not only is 'physical object' an interpretative concept, so also is the idea of a 'self,' and both are said to be absent in the experience called 'a unique kind of whole'. This total absence of all interpretative concepts is borne out by direct experience. The following considerations may assist in understanding what is meant by the Buddhist statement. In a perceptual situation which is indicated by the phrase "I see the sky" there is an objective constituent which is an outstanding sensum in a wider sense field and which has a certain external reference beyond

---

[32]*Phyag-chen rnal-'byor mig*, fol. 11*b*.

[33]*Lankāvatārasūtra* X 256 *seq*. Quoted in *Phyag-chen gan-mdzod*, fol. 36*b*.

itself by virtue of which I speak of the sky, all this being related to me in an asymmetrical two-term relation. Now, as can easily be verified by anyone who takes the time to concentrate and to contemplate, it is a fact that to the same degree as the sensum loses its external reference which, speaking more precisely, is the non-inferential belief about the perceived content as being a three-dimensional object in space and time, also the notion of the perceiving self fades away. In other words, the approach to pure sensation is a progressive absorption and, indeed, the attainment of the unique kind of whole (*rtse-gcig*) is called 'absorption in which feeling and the Void have become the predominant feature.'[34] This absorption in which the notion of a physical object and of a self equally fade away is therefore not an identification of the subject with the object or of the object with the subject. For identification and the judgment of identity is a purely intellectual process moving in postulates and can at best give only knowledge 'about' but not direct knowledge. Since in the 'unique kind of whole' all judgments and beliefs are absent, all that one can say about it is that it is a mode of knowing (*shes-pa*) which is non-postulational, immediate, 'intuitive'.

So far only the objective side of a perceptual situation has been taken care of. There is also a subjective constituent. This is a mass of feeling which, as the quotations have shown, does not vary at all in quality 'unchanging great bliss', *'gyur-ba med-pa'i bde-ba chen-po*). It is with this mass of feeling that the apprehension of the sensum enters into a specific relation which cannot be analyzed any further and which is technically known as 'coincidence', 'unity' (*zung-'jug*, Skt. *yuganaddha*).

That this mass of feeling is called 'unchanging' has its ground in the fact that in pure sensation the apprehension of the sensum fails to excite traces which can cause specific modifications in the mass of feeling, which is the case when in ordinary perception a sensum of a specific kind is apprehended. For in this case certain traces left by previous experiences are excited and, in turn, arouse certain emotions that effect a modification in the mass of feeling as the pleasantness, unpleasantness or indif-

[34] *Phyag-chen rnal-'byor mig*, fol. 6*b*.

ference, all of them being feeling judgments. In pure sensation, however, or, in the wider sense of the word, in pure perception there are no judgments of any kind.

The 'Void' [*stong-pa*, Skt. *śūnya*(*tā*)] which together with the unchanging great bliss (*bde-ba-chen-po*, Skt. *mahāsukha*) in the experience called a unique kind of whole forms an indivisible unity (*zung-'jug*, Skt. *yuganaddha*) is the 'Śūnyatā endowed with all excellent occurrents'.[35] Although the literal meaning of the word Śūnyatā is 'void' and is used to point out the fact that it is impossible to speak in connection with it of either a physical or a mental substance, it would be erroneous to suppose that this term therefore refers to a vacuum. On the contrary, its constant epithet, besides that of 'being endowed with all excellent occurrents', is 'continuous', 'imperishable' (*'gag-pa-med*). This latter epithet is always used with the term which I translated by 'pure creativity' (*gdangs*) and which has the connotation of lustre. This term 'pure creativity', to be sure, does not denote something like a creation out of nothing, but is a pure descriptive term for what is going on in a certain experience and hence it is not a concept by postulation. This is clearly pointed out in the following quotation:[36]

> Creativity (*gdangs*) which is incessant (*'gag-pa-med*) is the capability of becoming everything (*thams-cad-du-rung*). Therefore it is said to be the foundation (or motive or cause, *gzhi*, Skt. *hetu*) of the manifold (of appearance). Further, since it only becomes a manifold when the conditions for its so becoming are present, from the intellect's point of view it is said to possess all occurrents (*rnam-pa-kun-ldan*).

The conditions are the residues of former experiences, in the narrower sense of the word, the belief we have about what we perceive, and these conditions do not obtain in pure sensation or pure perception to which the term 'the Śūnyatā endowed with all excellent occurrents' refers. This positive character of Śūnyatā is also insisted upon in the following passage:[37]

---

[35] *Phyag-chen snye-ma*, fol. 5*a*.
[36] *bSre-'pho'i lam-skor*, fol. 64*b*.
[37] *Ibid.*, fol. 60*b*.

> The śūnyatā with all excellent occurrents is not just the absence of the determination by a physical object or by processes in it of the sensum by which a certain physical object manifests itself as found out by a critical analysis of the situation.[38] For while this is found by critical analysis to be non-existent, this śūnyatā appears in direct perception.[39]

These quotations together with the statement that at this stage there is, from a philosophical point of view, only mind (*sems-tsam*, Skt. *cittamātra*) allows us to give an interpretation of the Buddhist technical terms in Western terminology. Since materiality is not a differentiating attribute and is at best delusive and what exists so far is only mind, noises, colors, fragrances and so on are literally mental events and as such are non-objective and non-referential. But since this Śūnyatā is said to be 'capable of becoming everything', it implies what C. D. Broad calls "epistemologically objectifiable" or "capable of corresponding to the epistemological object of some referential situation"[40] and "psychologically objectifiable" or "capable of being an objective constituent of some objective mental situation."[41] This is the case when a non-objective mental event (*rnam-pa*) becomes the objective constituent of a mental situation whenever it is sensed or used in perception. This is obviously intended by Padma-dkar-po's statement that "Cognition (*rig-pa*) is an inner cognition devoid of interpretative concepts and this is the Śūnyatā endowed with all occurrents."[42]

It is on this basis of an incessant creativity (*gdangs*, *stong-pa-nyid*) capable of becoming everything and its existentially given fact (*gshis*) which only to the analytical investigation appears as something different that the experience termed a unique kind of whole (*rtse-gcig*) is described as the bridging of the gap between the stationary (*gnas-pa*) and the fleeting (*'gyu-ba*)

---

[38]This passage contains a reference to Diṅnāga's *Ālambanaparīkṣā* where this problem has been dealt with in a more detailed manner.

[39]*mngon-sum*, Skt. *pratyakṣa*. *bSre-'pho'i-lam skor*, fol. 72*a*, *pratyakṣa* must be free from *kalpanā*. See above note 14.

[40]C. D. Broad, *The Mind and its Place in Nature*, p. 306.

[41]*Ibid.*, p. 307.

[42]*Phyag-chen gan-bdzod*, fol. 31*a*.

whereby the stationary obviously refers to the existentially given (*gshis*) and the fleeting to the incessant creativity (*gdangs*) with its immense richness of items (*rnam-pa*) experienced in pure sensation and pure perception. Thus the explanation of the unique kind of whole runs as follows:[43]

> At that time one knows the nature of the fleeting in the stationary and in the fleeting one holds the place of the stationary. Therefore it is called the bridging of the gap between the stationary and the fleeting and this is the understanding of the nature of the unique kind of whole.

Although it would be an oversimplification to say that the experience of this unique kind of whole is merely pure sensation and pure feeling, yet these items are characteristic of it. But what is more, they form the irremissible situation out of which the particularly Buddhist viewpoint and its philosophical premises emerge. This is the mode of knowing and understanding the things one apprehends before they are modified by our beliefs about them and before they are conceptualized and thereby become dead figures of our mental calculus. This mode of knowing I shall call 'pure intuition' (*rtogs*) and distinguish it from pure sensation and pure perception which I understand to refer to the 'sensuous' factor in knowledge. And just as pure sensation and pure feeling form an indivisible whole so also pure sensation and what is involved in it forms an indivisible whole with pure intuition, as may be seen from the following quotation:[44]

> Where the feeling, the transparency, and the absence of interpretative concepts of the situation known as indeterminate tranquillity and the intuition operating in an ampler vision coincide (*zung-'jug*, Skt. *yuganaddha*), the object is intuited as being in itself śūnyatā and the mind is experienced as light in itself.[45]

---

[43] *Phyag-chen-gyi zin-bris*, fol. 4*b*; *rNal-'byor mdzub-tshugs*, fol. 1.
[44] *rNal-'byor mdzub-tshugs*, fol. 4*b*.
[45] The translation of the term *yul-can* (Skt. *viṣayin*) by 'mind' is only tentative. Literally the term means 'owner of the object'.

However, one word of caution has to be added. 'Pure intuition', as it is understood in the Buddhist texts and as I use this term, has nothing to do with the Bergsonian concept of intuition which is at best 'empathy' and in connecting Bergson's intuition with empathy I am still rather charitable.[46] 'Pure intuition' in the Buddhist sense of the word is a function which gives knowledge which is at once penetrating and a gateway to a wider and richer world. Within the total of the developmental process it has a definite place inasmuch as it begins to function when all possibilities of conceptualization and verbalization have subsided[47] and when thereby the Path of Seeing Reality (*mthong-lam*, Skt. *darśanamārga*) has been made accessible.[48]

The realm into which one enters with the acquisition of the wider vision (*lhag-mthong*, Skt. *vipaśyanā*) and which, functionally speaking, is pure intuition, is the domain of the mystic. Yet this mystic knowledge is by no means speculative or is it marked by a lack of a specified criterion of verification. Actually the mystic knowledge is fundamentally empirical and realistic, taking into account the ineffability of the immediately given. Hence it must be experienced in order to be known and any description or definition is but a guidepost. The most remarkable feature which distinguishes this experience of vision from the antecedent experience of unity with its absorption in an ineffable feeling of bliss is the character of luminosity (*gsal*) and the suddenness in which all doubts and uncertainties are resolved. Therefore also the mystic intuitive vision is for all practical purposes the unique means to find a way out of a hopelessly entangled and blocked situation, and thus again the wider vision is beside being a function also a specific attitude which informs all other functions. This certainty of pure intuition, the positive

---

[46]As the critique by Jacques Maritain, *Bergsonian Philosophy and Thomism*, makes abundantly clear, Bergson's concept of intuition is a very muddled concept, "composed of quite diverse elements artificially gathered together" (p. 109).

[47]*Phyag-chen rnal-'byor mig*, fol. 7*a*; *Phyag-chen-gyi zin-bris*, fol. 7*a*.

[48]*Phyag-chen-bla-ma*, fol. 2*a*; *Phyag-chen rnal-'byor mig*, fol. 7*b*.

character of the newly found attitude in which freedom and impasse are no longer antagonistic, has been most clearly hinted at by Padma-dkar-po.[49]

> All conceptualizations and verbalizations such as origination and annihilation and so on as well as the categories of subject and object have subsided in their own place. Whatever rises is taken in its real nature and whatever has come to be born is intuited as being unborn. The fact that the object to be seen and the subject seeing the object are ultimately pure and forbid every formulation by concept or by speech (*spros-pa-med*, Skt. *niṣprapañca*) does not mean to be faced with a vacuum (*chad-pa'i stong-pa*); it is seeing the very nature of primordial knowledge (*tha-mal-gyi shes-pa*). By intuitively understanding (*rtogs-pas*) that error (*'khrul-pa*, Skt. *bhrānti*, *bhrama*) has no foundation and no root the gap between error and freedom (*grol*, Skt. *mukti*) is bridged. The fact that doubts have been dispelled from within means that the experience which forbids of any formulation by either concepts or speech (*spros-bral*, Skt. *niṣprapañca*) is born within one's self.

Similarly as the experience of the unique kind of whole was termed an absorption in which the feeling of bliss and the richness of śūnyatā form an indivisible unity, so the experience of pure intuition or mystic vision is called an "absorption in which luminosity and śūnyatā (*gsal-stong*) are the outstanding feature."[50] The intimate relation between the state of tranquility (*zhi-gnas*, Skt. *śamatha*) or the unique kind of whole (*rtse-gcig*, Skt. *ekāgratā*) and the ampler vision (*lhag-mthong*, Skt. *vipaśyanā*) or pure intuition with its ineffability (*spros-bral*, Skt. *niṣprapañca*), which I have pointed out above, is again displayed in the following discussion referring to the nature of the primordial knowledge (*tha-mal-gyi shes-pa*) mentioned in the preceding quotation. This knowledge is pointed at in the following way:[51]

---

[49] *Phyag-chen rnal-'byor mig*, fol. 4*b*; *rNal-'byor mdzub-tshugs*, fol. 1.
[50] *Phyag-chen rnal-'byor mig*, fol. 6*b*.
[51] *rNal-'byor mdzub-tshugs*, fol. 8*b*.

> Although it is permissible to speak of it as the conateness (*lhan-cig-skyes-pa*, Skt. *sahaja*) of the object as the śūnyatā and the mind (lit. the owner of the objects) as luminosity in itself (*rang-bzhin-'od-gsal*), in the actual experience it is a free-rising perception (*thol-skyes-kyi-rig*) of uninterrupted understanding in luminous knowledge. Not understanding this free-rising knowledge there is Saṃsāra, understanding it there is Nirvāṇa. But this knowledge itself does not belong to any side whatsoever. It is the coincidence (*zung-'jug*, Skt. *yuganaddha*) of great bliss as the essence *ngo-bo = gshis*) and the śūnyatā endowed with all excellent occurrents as the owner of the objects.

More aptly than this highly technical terminology, the description of the process by which this experience of luminosity and of richness is brought about, is able to convey something of this mystic vision and emotionally moving sustenance. Two stages are to be distinguished, the developmental stage (*bskyed-rim*, Skt. *utpannakrama*) and the consummate stage (*rdzogs-rim*, Skt. *sampannakrama*). The former begins when the object of contemplation is perceived in what approximates pure sensation and, devoid of all interpretative concepts and beliefs about its ontological nature, is viewed and felt as something divine in its own right. The character of light is not something attributed to it but something inherent in it. It is as if the object begins to glow from within and stands out sharply, with luminosity rather than clarity; where everything seen is felt, felt much more strongly than in any normal state of consciousness; and where the solidity of the outer world is lost and the belief in its absolute reality gives way to a mere vision of a phantom-like tableau (*sgyu-ma-lta-bu*, Skt. *māyopama*).[52] This is what Maitripa asserts with respect to this developmental stage:[53]

> Since there is only conditioned existence
> There is nothing real in it. śūnyatā, however,

---

[52]It must be observed that the Buddhists speak of the likeness with a phantasma but do not assert that the world or so is a phantasma.

[53]*Phyag-chen gan-mdzod*, fol. 36*a*. The translation is according to the Tibetan version which has the correct reading against the quotation of this verse in Advaya-vajrasamgraha, p. 51.

Though it is luminous and a divine occurrent,
Is the very nature of no nature.
In whatever way it may appear
It is the nature of śūnyatā.

And that this śūnyatā is not just a concept or idea one has reached by intellectually analyzing, moving in dichotomies is pointed out by Mañjughoṣa (*'jam-pa'i-dbyangs*):[54]

The śūnyatā arrived at by an intellectual analysis of the
of the psycho-physical constituents of man
Is like sea-weed and has no solidity;
But the śūnyatā with all excellent occurrents
Is not like this.

Seeing and feeling the object as divine in its own right is very often a stage beyond which many people, mystics and non-mystics, do not pass. In Buddhism, however, the consummate stage is still more necessary, since only with its realization a solid foundation for one's life has been built. This transition from one stage to the other and the consummatory experience of an all-pervasive luminosity Padma-dkar-po describes in the following words:[55]

> At the time when one attends to the development of tranquillity (*zhi-gnas*) one pays closest attention to the object of one's contemplation which has been made a deity and the divine appearance then becomes more and more radiant. At that time the whole tableau (*dkyil-'khor*, Skt. *maṇḍala*) which has been studied in its coarse form becomes as if it could be directly touched or directly seen. Due to this it is possible to discard the coarse appearance which possesses certain characteristics since these are accidental rather than essential. Although there is (at this instant) a profound and luminous vision, in reality it is a differentiated kind of tranquillity. Immediately thereafter, in the union with the consummate stage there is by the revelation of the symbolism of

[54] *Phyag-chen gan-mdzod*, fol. 36*a*. Only the first two lines are quoted in this text. I have given the two missing lines according to the oral explanation I got from my Lama friend bsTan-'dzin-rgyal-mtshan.

[55] *Phyag-chen gan-mdzod*, fol. 36*ab*.

> the divine form a self-finding and this profound and luminous experience in which there is only the appearance of phantoms after the belief in the concrete reality of the divine form has been given up is the (mystic experience of oneself being a) phantom-body (*sgyu-lus*). The more subtle it grows in its mere appearance it is resolved in the luminosity of the *sarvaśūnya*.[56]

This lengthy discussion of the two closely related experiences, the unique kind of whole and the intuitive mystic vision, which would have been still more lengthy if space had permitted to go into the details of their ramifications and implications, serves a double purpose. First of all, it shows plainly that the meditative process is not auto-suggestion but a spontaneous phenomenon, a release of hitherto unknown, or, maybe it is more correct to say, of hitherto disregarded factors which are just as necessary for the fulness of life as the commonly acknowledged operations of mind and which one cannot come into contact with in any other way but by meditation. Secondly, the mystic vision gives a specific note to one's outlook in life which in the Buddhist conception must be based on knowledge by acquaintance and not on knowledge by description. It is with the attainment of pure intuition and the mystic vision with its certitude that the foundation of philosophy in the Buddhist sense of the word is laid. This intuitive character of Eastern systems of philosophy[57] is evident from the very words used for what we designate by

---

[56]*sarvaśūnya* is a technical term referring to a particular kind of experience. It is the last and consummate experience, the preceding ones being called *śūnya* corresponding to *rtse-gcig*, *mahāśūnya* to *spros-bral*, *atiśūnya* to *ro-gcig*, and *sarvaśūnya* to (*b*)*sgom-med*. The last two kinds belong to the special (*thun-mong-ma-yin-pa*) form of meditation which realizes the sameness of Saṃsāra and Nirvāṇa as to their emotional feeling tone and goes beyond an object-bound meditation. The four terms *śūnya*, *mahāśūnya*, etc. are also met with in *Pañcakrama* III 4.

[57]F. S. C. Northrop, *The Meeting of East and West*, p. 315 *passim* is substantially correct in calling Eastern philosophies 'intuitive,' but he fails to note the differences that exist between the various systems. Except for this oversimplification his account of Eastern philosophies evinces a much better understanding than is found in most works on these philosophies which as a rule twist them into some Western philosophy or other, be this Hume or Kant.

philosophy, viz., 'seeing, view' (*lta-ba*, Skt. *dṛṣti, darśana*). Philosophy which thus is the Seeing of Reality is not the culmination of one's abilities but the very beginning of the arduous task of achieving spiritual maturity. In this way philosophy in the Eastern sense of the word only serves to clear the way and, quite literally, to open the student's eyes. What he then sees has to be closely attended to (*sgom-pa*, Skt. *bhāvanā*) and must be actually lived (*spyod-pa*, Skt. *caryā*).

Ever since its beginning Buddhism has insisted on avoiding the mutually contradictory extremes and on steering a middle course. Therefore also it calls its philosophy the 'Middle View' (*dbu-ma'i-lta-ba*, Skt. *madhyamakadṛṣti*). That this middle view is not discursive but is the mystic vision is clearly expressed in the following statement:[58]

> At the time of non-conceptualization and non-verbalization (*spros-bral*, Skt. *niṣprapañca*) the middle view (*dbu-ma'i-lta-ba*, Skt. *madhyamakadṛṣti*) has found its fulfilment. Devoid of all such conceptualization as existence and non-existence, origination and annihilation, coming and going, eternalism and nihilism, monism and pluralism, doubts have been dispelled.

The 'Middle View' is also the name of the most important school of Buddhism whose tenets have been rather baffling to most students who tried to approach them from the propositional method used in most philosophical systems. The middle view is given, as we have seen, when the Path of Seeing Reality has been realized. This has one important consequence. It makes the presentation of the essential points of Buddhist philosophy more than doubtful when their character of direct experience and of having been directly intuited instead of having been arrived at by the method of hypothesis and partial verification is not made clear. Padma dkar-po even goes so far as to declare that any such presentation has nothing to do with Buddhist philosophy. His words are:[59]

---

[58] *Phyag-chen rnal-'byor mig*, fol. 11*b*.

[59] *Phyag-chen gan-mdzod*, fol. 54*a*.

Since the Middle View is not realized before the Path of Seeing Reality has been attained, any other view before this stage falls under the opinion which a man of common-sense or a śrāvaka or a Vijñānavādin may hold, and it does not alter the fact even if he calls the tenets arrived at by hearing and thinking about 'The middle view'. The views of most people who nowadays advocate certain doctrines I consider as views of enlightened common-sense only. Also in the śāstra it has been said:

> The man of common-sense sees a concrete thing
> And conceives it as the ultimately real.
> Because he contends that it is not like a phantasma
> There is dissension between the man of common-sense
> and the critical philosopher.[60]

In conclusion then, there are three levels of understanding, but two of them are of major importance. First of all there is the level of common-sense in its naive and more enlightened form which gives knowledge by description. Then there is with the attainment of the Path of Seeing Reality the level of mystic insight and the first level of spirituality. It is from this level that after a prolonged practice the final level, Buddhahood or enlightenment, can be realized.

---

[60]This verse is taken from *Bodhicaryāvatāra* IX 5.

The Philosophical Background of Buddhist Tantrism

Buddhist philosophy is as varied a subject as can be. This is because the word 'philosophy' is a label for a set of problems and the varying answers to them. Two tendencies appear to be distinguishable in this large variety: the tendency seemingly to conceive of philosophy as essentially an intellectual discipline, and the tendency to consider it to be a way of living. On closer inspection, however, we find that the idea of philosophy as a way of conduct has been so predominant in Buddhism that even that which appears to be a merely intellectual procedure is only a means to further the paving of a way of life.[1] As a consequence no such philosophical systems have been developed which in C. D. Broad's words "only an inmate of a lunatic asylum would

---

[1]Due to this peculiar nature of Eastern thought, William S. Haas, *The Destiny of the Mind*, p. 133, says: "And thus comes the realization that the term philosophy is actually inapplicable—that it serves to obscure and to falsify the spirit of Eastern thought," and ". . . the East attempts to establish immediate contact with the Real." In coining the useful term 'philousia' he characterizes those Indian and Eastern 'philosophies' for which Essence or Isness is of decisive importance. However, 'philousia' is not applicable to Tantric thought, unless it be specified still more. It should be noted that 'essence' has become a rather confused term since its use in scholasticism; and it is a dangerous procedure to impose on Eastern texts a terminology which is hardly suited to elucidate the different structure of Eastern thought.

think of carrying into daily life."[2] Philosophy, in the Buddhist sense, becomes rather an expression of that which is most human in human beings, but it is not an automatic phenomenon. It is born or conditioned, so to speak, when man awakens to the fact that he is more than a specimen of an abstract class. When this happens he is instinctively philosophical (*rigs nges-pa*)[3]. Because of his humanness the philosopher ranks highest in the hierarchy of human beings, which is supposed to consist of three or four levels. On the lowest plane is the unregenerate man (*so-so-skye-bo*)[4] who has to be told at every step what to do and what

---

[2]C. D. Broad, *The Mind and its Place in Nature*, p. 5. Certain translations of Eastern texts seem to contradict my argument. The reason is that many translators are unable to grasp the distinction between the use of an expression and the analysis of its meaning, which is of utmost importance for philosophical considerations, as A. J. Ayer, *The Problem of Knowledge* (Pelican Book), pp. 8 *seq.*, has shown. Unless analytical and phenomenological methods are applied, Eastern, and in particular Buddhist, philosophy will not reveal its intrinsic value, but remain an oddity or sentimentality. The analytical method would coincide in many respects with what I. A. Richards has called 'Multiple Definition'. See his *Mencius on the Mind: Experiments in Multiple Definition.*

[3]Lit.: 'belonging to a definite family' (Skt. *niyatakula*). The above interpretation of this term is the one given by Padma dkar-po in his *Jo-bo Nā-ro-pa'i khyad-chos bsre-pho'i gzhung-'grel rdo-rje-'chang-gi dgongs-pa gsal-bar byed-pa*, fol. 6*a*. In the following this text will be quoted under its abbreviated title *gZhung-'grel rdo-rje-'chang-gi dgongs-pa gsal-bar byed-pa.* With the exception of the terms of the Pratītyasamutpāda ('Law of Interdependent Origination' or, more appropriately, 'Inductive Principle of Function Relation') I have refrained from giving the Sanskrit equivalents of the Tibetan terms. The reason is that I deal with indigenous Tibetan texts, not with translations from Sanskrit. Further, the Tibetan terms are more exact as to meaning than the Sanskrit ones and hence do not easily lead to confusion in a subject which by nature is abstruse and difficult. To give one example: everyone is familiar with the three terms *kāya*, *vāk*, *citta* in Sanskrit, usually translated by 'body', 'speech' and 'mind'. The Tibetan equivalents are *lus*, *ngag*, *yid*, although *yid* usually stands for Skt. *manas*. But there is another set of words in Tibetan for the same triad, viz., *sku*, *gsung*, *thugs*. Not only is the usage of this set different from that of *lus*, *ngag*, *yid*, it also has a different realm of meanings. Again A. J. Ayer's reference to the distinction between usage and meaning becomes important. The Sanskrit language has no such two sets. Any translation from Tibetan, which does not point out this marked difference and which merely interprets the text on the assumption of the inexact Sanskrit terminology, must necessarily be a distortion, if not a falsification.

[4]*Dags-po'i chos-bzhi'i rnam-bshad skyes-bu gsum-gyi lam nyin-mor byed-pa*, fol. 10*b*.

not. Then come those who follow a certain code of morals, especially those who have renounced a worldly life (*rab-tu byung-ba*, *dge-slong*),[5] but more often than not have turned escapists; and finally there is the philosopher (*rnal-'byor-pa*).[6] At his level two ways are open. The one is to pile up arguments, rebuttals, counter-arguments and rejoinders without end—it is this aspect which has become widely known and is dealt with in most works on Buddhist philosophy. The other, hardly touched upon as yet, is to absorb what has been said, be it in a book or by a person, into one's own life, to make it one's own and to return it to one's fellow-beings with a new and deeper sense. This is what sKye-med bde-chen understands by philosophy:

> Others explain by commentaries after (having read) the basic text;
> We, however, are tied down to the basic text after having been instructed by our Gurus.
> Since the philosophical enterprise of those who belong to the group that transmits its knowledge orally (bKa'-brgyud) is not completed by writing about it,
> I merely record the instruction by my Guru, not going beyond his permission.[7]

This way of philosophizing, which is characteristic for the mystic, is grounded in the firm conviction that experience alone provides a basis for philosophy and is able to make life healthier,

---

[5] *Ibid.*, fol. 15*b*. The *rab-tu byung-ba* is a man who has renounced life in a home (Skt. *pravrajita*); the *dge-slong* is a fully ordained monk or Bhikṣu.

[6] *Ibid.*, fol. 48*b seq.* This term is often given in its Sanskrit form as yogi in translations, which means 'a man who has to do with *yoga*'. According to the *Lam-zab-kyi rnam-par bshad-pa zab-lam-gyi snye-ma*, fol. 21*b*, *yoga* (*rnal-'byor*) is the non-duality of action and discriminating awareness (*thabs shes gnyis-su med-pa'i don-la rnal-'byor zhes btags-pa*). This non-duality of action and awareness is man's existential unity, both as starting point and goal of his endeavour.

[7] *Do-ha-mdzod ces-bya-ba spyod-pa'i glu'i 'grel-pa don-gyi sgron-ma* (*Dohākoṣa-nāma-caryāgīti-arthapradīpa-nāma-ṭīkā*), *bsTan-'gyur* (Derge ed.), *rgyud*, vol. zhi, fol. 34*a*. The same idea is expressed by gNyis-med-avadhūti in his *Do-ha mdzod-kyi snying-po don-gyi glu'i 'grel-pa* (*Dohākoṣa-hṛdaya-artha-gīti-ṭīkā*), *ibid.*, fol. 66*a*. A disciple is permitted to practice or engage in philosophical works only after having received his Guru's authorization (*lung*). In many cases the permission is identical in words with the text for study.

more beautiful, more complete and more satisfactory. The mystic understands experience in perhaps a still wider sense than does A. N. Whitehead in contemporary philosophy, and knowledge is for him more than the succession of momentary contents in consciousness. For he is constantly aware of the fact that it is possible to 'know' without having knowledge in the conscious sense which is often hardly more than a process of accretion. In experience, knowledge and reality are given together and cannot, without contradiction, be separated from each other. Since reality is not one thing among other things, but is everything, there can be no unknowable.[8] The failure to realize this fact is mainly due to our habit of confining ourselves to wholly pragmatic lines of conduct which for the most part remain on a low level of awareness. This confinement is equal to submitting ourselves, intellectually, to an absurdity which will bring forth many others of its kind, and emotionally, to a conflict–all of which is designated by the technical term *ma-rig-pa*, which may be variously translated by 'unawareness', 'unknowing', 'nescience' and even 'ignorance'. However, that which is designated by this term does not exclude knowledge in a general way. The difference between 'ignorance' (*ma-rig-pa*) and 'knowledge proper' (*rig-pa*) is that in the former case knowledge and emotion have not fused into understanding, because by habit the individual does not let them fuse or is even on guard against their doing so. In the latter case, however, the fusion has come about. Knowledge, in whatever sense we may take it, has a feeling tone, or as M. Oakeshott remarks: "Knowledge as something apart from that which affords satisfaction in experience is an idle fancy."[9] A further point to note here is that in the linkage of 'misery' (*sdug-bsngal*) with 'ignorance' (*ma-rig-pa*) and of 'bliss' (*bde-ba*) with 'knowledge proper' (*rig-pa*) the observable fact is brought out that pleasure marks furthered activity and pain unresolved conflicts, the thwarting of activity, and that the more coherent and unitary the world of our experience

---

[8]Michael Oakeshott, *Experience and its Modes*, p. 50 *seq.*

[9]*Ibid.*, p. 41.

becomes the more intense is the feeling of satisfaction. The uniqueness of experience comprising both knowledge and emotional appreciation, cannot be reduced to something already 'known' without losing its character of experience. It can only be pointed to by symbols which do not stand for anything as the symbol 'dog' does to that which it stands for, and which are guideposts, indices and, possibly, stimulants evoking within people who are ready to expand the range of their perception, the experience which those who have had it consider the most worthwhile one among all possible experiences. Thus "Everything, from the Buddha to an ordinary sentient being, becomes a gateway to the 'radiant mind' which is called the Ultimate."[10]

Although mysticism is not a philosophical school, but the perennial philosophy in the strictest sense of the word, certain mystics have figured preeminently in tradition and gathered a following. In Buddhism this mystic trend is said to derive from the Buddha himself and, in later times, is particularly associated with the mystic Tilopa (A.D. 988–1069) and his immediate followers. He sums up the philosophical quest in the words:

> Reality, the Way, and the Modes of Reality-Actualization.[11]

Each of these indices offers a number of problems. Here only the first will be discussed, in particular with reference to the symbol 'The Great Seal' (*phyag-rgya chen-po*, Skt. *mahāmudrā*), by which the followers of this mystic experience describe their approach to and conception of reality.

Although our world of experience is one world, not two, it may appear and disappear for us in two opposite perspectives: either as our plain self, our empirical existence and all that we perceive through it, or as transcendence which we arrive at as

---

[10] *gZhung-'grel rdo-rje-'chang-gi dgongs-pa gsal-bar byed-pa*, fol. 13*b*. 'Radiant mind' (*'od-gsal-ba'i sems, prabhāsvaracitta*) is to be understood as an index. It is not a mind as an entity.

[11] *bKa' yang-dag-pa'i tshad-ma zhes-bya-ba mkha'-'gro-ma'i man-ngag*, fol. 1. The authoritative version of this text of the bKa'-brgyud-pa school of Buddhism varies in the arrangement of ths subject matter from the version contained in the *bsTan-'gyur* (Derge ed.), *rgyud*, vol. zhi, fol. 271 *seq.*

the last thing, though not as an entitative object, and which nevertheless is in itself the first and present in all our queries. In a seemingly less technical language Tilopa says:

> Reality is twofold: the presence of the 'body' (*lus*) and that of the mind (*sems*).[12]

Such would be the literal, linguistically correct translation. Unfortunately, like most literal translations, it fails to convey anything of what is to be understood by this aphorism. The Tibetan term *lus*, which is usually translated by 'body' (as provisionally done here), does not mean the body-object described by biologists, but the body as lived in by the subject. It is a term for the plain self or our givenness (*gdags-pa'i gzhi*) as evident in bodily act, speech and thought. 'Body' (*lus*) thus refers to the whole man, body-mind, and is a name for the 'psycho-organismal individual'.[13] Similarly, the term *sems* which has been rendered by 'mind' does not signify what we usually understand by 'mind', which in Tibetan is termed *yid* and is included in the 'body' (*lus*) as a short term for the complex psycho-organismal patterns. But even *yid* is not merely 'consciousness' which we usually mean when we use the word 'mind', but it comprises the unconscious of modern psychology as well. In another sense, *yid* is a term for that which philosophers call the 'existential self', psychologists the 'self' (C. G. Jung), the 'super-ego' (S. Freud, J. C. Flugel), the 'psychic factor' (C. D. Broad), the 'metaphysical factor' or the 'called-in factor' (N. Jaquin), and biologists the 'Z-factor' (C. J. Herrick). In Buddhism another name for it is the 'subtle ego' (*phra-ba bdag*), and the texts make it abundantly clear that this is only an index, not an entity.[14] Finally, in the highly technical language of mystic philosophy it is called 'indestructible potential creativity' (*mi-*

---

[12] *Ibid.*

[13] I owe this term to G. E. Coghill and C. Judson Herrick, *The Evolution of Human Nature*, p. 274.

For the following analysis see in particular *gZhung-'grel rdo-rje-'chang-gi dgongs-pa gsal-bar byed-pa*, fol. 7*b seq.*

[14] *gZhung-'grel rdo-rje-'chang-gi dgongs-pa gsal-bar byed-pa*, fol. 6*b*.

shigs-pa'i thig-le). This cannot be said to be either physical or mental, it is irreducible to anything and prior to everything. It is not an entity; neither is it some 'stuff'. It is meaningful by its use. It may either refer itself to itself and thereby to its transcendence or, if we may say so, it may become 'distorted' by the carry-over of experience-traces (*bags-chags*) and under suitable conditions give rise to a new 'mind' which means a thinking organism.[15]

It is now evident that *sems* is not the same as *yid* or 'mind'. It encompasses 'body-mind'. Therefore, in order to distinguish it from 'mind' we shall render it by 'spirit' or 'spirituality'. But it will be necessary to be fully aware of the fact that our 'spirit' and the Tibetan *sems* are only indices which name without characterizing and so avoid the inane thesis of spiritualism. Another possible translation would be 'Mind' with a capital letter. In this case we also would have to be careful not to interpret this term as referring to some sort of mentalism. On the basis of this analysis of the two key-terms *lus* and *sems*, Tilopa's statement can now be rendered more adequately:

> Reality is twofold: the psycho-organismal individual and spirituality.

Spirituality is said to 'take its stand on', 'to ascend', the psycho-organism. 'Reality is twofold' therefore means that spirituality, as that which takes its stand on the psycho-organism as its basis, is present as that which encompasses the basis while leaving it intact. The relation is similar to that between the flower and its scent. Just as without being aware of the flower one cannot experience its fragrance so also without knowing the reality of the psycho-organism as the basis one cannot fully realize the reality of spirituality as that which takes its stand on the former. Hence in the beginning of our philosophical quest the nature of the psycho-organism has to be elucidated. As is stated in the *brTag-gnyis* (*Hevajra-mūla-tantrarāja*):

---

[15] *Ibid.*, fol. 14*b*.

How can there be bliss in the absence of the psycho-organism?
It is impossible to speak of bliss (in such a case).
According to the relation between the encompassed and the encompasser
Bliss encompasses a sentient being.
In the same way as the fragrance of a flower
Cannot be experienced in the absence of the flower,
Bliss is without meaning
In the absence of psycho-organismal patterns.

And in the *Sampuṭa:*

If one does not know the nature of the psycho-organism
Through the eighty-four thousand constituents of reality,
They all fail to bear their fruit.

"Since by being aware of the psycho-organism as the basis one becomes aware of the abode of that which takes its stand on it, spirituality, man's fulfilment is not an automatic process. It may be likened to the following: Although milk is present with the cow's existence, it does not spout forth when the horns of the cow are squeezed, but when the udder is pulled."[16]

The statement that spirituality takes its stand on the psycho-organism can only be understood in the light of the opening statement about the all-encompassing nature of reality. Spirituality is not something apart from and above reality; it becomes an actuality when man goes a certain way, which means if he strives for an enlargement and enrichment of life in every possible manner. Going-a-way begins with the given and ever-present, not with the postulation of a hypothesis. In stating that the Way leads from the psycho-organismal individual or the immediately given through its analysis to spirituality as the culmination of one's efforts, Padma dkar-po anticipates J. W. von Goethe's aphorism:

---

[16]*Ibid.*, fol. 7*b* See also *Jo-Bo Nā-ro-pa'i khyad-chos bsre-'pho'i khrid rdo-rje'i theg-par bgrod-pa'i shing-rta chen-po*, fol. 4*b*. In the following this text will be quoted under its abbreviated title *rDo-rje'i theg-par bgrod-pa'i shing-rta chen-po*.

If you want to approach the Infinite
Examine the finite on every side.[17]

When it is further stated that spirituality is 'action-born' (*thabs-byung*)[18] this shows that spirituality is evolved in the course of one's endeavor, not that it is produced like gastric juice by the stomach. Spirituality is not just a negligible by-product, hence the Tantric conception of it cannot be equated with epiphenomenalism. On the other hand, there is here in Tantrism also no search for explanation or causal theory. It is true that there is a 'forward reference' but that does not imply the metaphysical principle of teleological causation, rather there is here a kind of natural teleology which coincides with the progressive enhancement of values in the growth of man. Spirituality thus 'emerges' in course of evolution, because it is at the 'bottom' of it. Thus the statement that spirituality takes its stand on the psycho-organism as part of reality shows that, on the one hand, it is an acquisition and, on the other, there always occurs in human life something which gains ascendency and controls further behavior. This intimate relation between our plain self and spirituality serves another useful purpose in philosophy. It opens our eyes to reality and prevents us from allowing ourselves to be separated from it by believing ourselves to be either this or that and thereby ceasing to be real, or rather, remaining partly real.[19] It is certainly of no use and contrary to the conception of philosophy as a way of life to lose the ground under one's feet and to let oneself be swallowed up by an alleged Absolute which by definition can have nothing to do with man. The idea of an Absolute which received its apotheosis by Hegel creates more difficulties than it can bear and is as contradictory and nonsensical as the Kantian unknowableness of reality.[20]

---

[17]Willst Du ins Unendliche schreiten
Gehe im Endlichen nach allen Seiten.

[18]*rDo-rje'i theg-par bgrod-pa'i shing-rta chen-po*, fol. 4*b*.

[19]Buddhist Tantrism is opposed to the idea that Reality can be divided or that there are different layers of Reality with different degrees of Reality. See "The Concept of Mind in Buddhist Tantrism."

[20]A pertinent critique of the idea of an Absolute is contained in William S. Haas, *The Destiny of the Mind*, p. 155.

Since reality cannot be anything less than the whole, the way from partial reality to full reality also cannot be something apart, nor can there be any essential difference between the part and the whole.[21] Therefore the starting point must not be considered in aloofness from the goal and the way to it. This is evident from the interpretation of the term Mahāmudrā (*phyag-rgya chen-po*) which is used to denote the whole of reality. Literally translated it means the 'Great Seal' and is explained as " 'Seal' has the double meaning of 'imprinting' and 'not going beyond', while 'great' means that 'nothing superior is possible'."[22]

Logical analysis has shown that language has often created problems which on closer inspection turned out to be pseudo-problems.[23] So in order not to be accused of having succumbed to a pseudo-problem or having created one, let us see what is the real meaning of 'seal' in this term 'Great Seal' (*mahā-mudrā*).

---

[21]*bSre-'pho'i lam-skor-gyi thog-mar lam-dbye-bsdu*, fol. 66*b*. See also *ibid.*, fol. 55*a*.

[22]*Phyag-rgya-chen-po'i man-ngag-gi bshad-sbyar rgyal-ba'i gan-mdzod*, fol. 26*a*; *gZhung-'grel rdo-rje-'chang-gi dgongs-pa gsal-bar byed-pa*, fol. 87*a*; *bSre-'pho'i lam-skor-gyi thog-mar lam-dbye-bsdu*, fol. 19*b*.

[23]In *The Tibetan Book of the Great Liberation*, ed. by W. Y. Evans-Wentz, the technical term 'Mahāmudrā' is rendered as 'The Great Symbol'. Apart from the fact that this translation is not supported by the original texts and that the editor's comments have nothing to do with the term in question, C. G. Jung adduces this wrong rendering as proof for the correctness of his interpretation of mind as a symbol. His 'Psychological Commentary' is thus a comment on the usage of the English word 'symbol', but not on what the text indicates by 'Mahāmudrā'. Since most translations of Eastern texts fail to give an analysis of the meaning of the terms used, commentaries on them, psychological or otherwise, are hardly able to elucidate the philosophical ideas. Anyone who engages in comparative studies should be mindful of I. A. Richards' words in his *Mencius on the Mind*, pp. 91 *seq.*: "The danger to be guarded against is our tendency to force a structure, which our special kind of Western training (idealist, realist, positivist, Marxist, etc.) makes easiest for us to work with, upon modes of thinking which may very well not have any such structure at all—and which may not be capable of being analysed by means of this kind of logical machinery. As we do so all chance of genuine comparative studies is wiped out." Valuable attempts in the direction indicated by I. A. Richards, are F. S. C. Northrop, *The Meeting of East and West: An Inquiry concerning World Understanding*, New York: 1946, and William S. Haas, *The Destiny of the Mind: East and West*, New York: 1956.

With the idea of 'seal' we tend to connect the idea of causation. The proposition 'a seal leaves an impression' may be rephrased as 'a seal causes a certain material to bear an impression'. In asserting such a proposition the plain man would say that the material under consideration would not bear an impression unless a seal had been pressed on it. He would regard the cause as relevant to the effect. He would also assume that since the cause and the effect are determined with equal precision, the relation will be one-one, so that given the effect, the cause is thereby determined, and *vice versa*. This distinction between cause and effect further means that the cause precedes the effect. The relation holding between cause and effect is thus asymmetrical, that is, if xRy, then never yRx.

This idea of causation does not attach to the Tantric ideal of 'seal'. The relation expressed here is symmetrical, so that if xRy, then always yRx. This is evident from Saraha's statement:

> Nothingness is sealed by appearance
> And appearance by nothingness.[24]

The same symmetrical relation with reference to cause and effect, which, if the distinction between cause and effect were so sharp as common sense assumes it to be, would give rise to the awkward statement that the effect precedes the cause, is stated in the *Kālacakra-mūla-tantra*:[25]

> The semblance risen from nothingness is the cause,
> The pleasure born from invariableness is the effect:
> The effect is to be sealed by the cause,
> But also the cause by the effect.

The last part of this quotation is already found in the *Guhyasamājatantra*[26] and therefore the idea of 'seal' as a symmetrical relation is a very old one. It seems that here we have

---

[24] *sKu'i mdzod 'chi-med rdo-rje'i glu* (*Kāyakoṣāmṛtavajragīti*), *bsTan-'gyur* (Derge ed.), *rgyud*, vol. zhi, fol. 112*b*.

[25] Quoted in *Phyag-rgya-chen-po'i man-ngag-gi bshad-sbyar rgyal-ba'i gan-mdzod*, fol. 27*a*. See also Sekoddeśaṭīkā, p. 70.

[26] *Guhyasamājatantra* XVIII, p. 157.

the principle of circular causation which can best be illustrated by the device by which a guided missile is directed towards a moving target by sound waves, light rays or other emanations from the target. There is a sort of 'feed-back' from the goal and the end does control the means. The action, however, is here and now, although the goal to be reached is in a future time as yet undetermined.[27]

The second meaning of 'seal' as 'not going beyond' indicates that, if everything bears the seal of reality, there is no way away from reality and this is a kind of commitment.[28]

The inseparableness of cognition and emotional appreciation in experience, the index character of all the technical terms used in the process of philosophizing and the principle of circular causation are met with again in greater detail in the elucidation of the meaning of 'spirituality' (*sems-kyi gnas-lugs*). Here in particular it will become evident that all that is being said is a stimulus to that which K. Jaspers seems to have divined by speaking of 'transcending the object within the object thinking'[29] and which William S. Haas more succinctly terms 'withdrawing from or shedding what there is of objective constructions'.[30] Such a procedure is facilitated by the use of mantric syllables which hardly ever become objectifying concepts and therefore, instead of freezing life, are better suited

---

[27]The question is whether under such circumstances the term causality is to be retained. Bertrand Russell is in favor of excluding the word from the philosophical vocabulary. William S. Haas, *loc. cit.*, p. 209, plainly states: "Not even the law of causality can be said to bear the meaning it has in Western philosophy and science," and with reference to Karma he says on the same page pertinently: "The relation between the karmatic tendencies or the cravings which survive death and their concurrent appearances as rebirth cannot be conceived under the image of cause and effect. The only adequate kind of relation is that prevailing in the magic world. This has been formulated as 'if or when there is *a*, there is *b*'. Such a relation is foreign to and beyond time and is therefore incompatible with causality though certainly it is no less effective." It seems the 'primitive' magic world is more akin to the 'advanced' modern mind than any other rational system.

[28]*bSre-'pho'i lam-skor-gyi thog-mar lam-dbye-bsdu*, fol. 19*b*.

[29]Karl Jaspers, *The Perennial Scope of Philosophy*, p. 22.

[30]William S. Haas, *The Destiny of the Mind*, p. 181.

to an exploration of its realm of possibilities. This mantric element we find in a passage by Padma dkar-po:[31]

> By giving the ending of the seventh case (locative) to the letter A elucidating nothingness (*stong-pa nyid*) we obtain the letter E. By this designation we refer to 'discriminating awareness' (*shes-rab*) having the property of nothingness endowed with all causal characteristics, otherwise symbolized by spaciousness and the ground of all and everything. By the letter VAṂ we refer to 'action' (*thabs*) having the property of compassion and unchanging great bliss. The combination E-VAM is to indicate that to the extent that there is discriminating awareness there is also action and *vice versa*.

This short passage contains a number of highly technical terms and suggestive ideas, all of which need some explanation and analysis. The locative case is indicative of the terminus of the noetic act and corresponds to what we would call the content of consciousness. However, the content is not of primary importance; it is utterly contingent and may be absent without consciousness thereby losing its validity. This is the reverse of what most Western philosophies would assert, namely that in the absence of content there can be no consciousness. One may even go so far as to say that in Tantrism consciousness is ontologically prior to content, in which case the terms 'consciousness' and 'ontological' would have to be re-defined. Discriminating awareness' (*shes-rab*) is essentially a manifesting and illumining function, not a creation of a new object, and in order to perform this function it must in itself be as nothing (*stong-pa*, *stong-pa-nyid*). This nothing, of course, is no absolute nothing which would mean an object that just is not. As Padma dkar-po observes:

> 'Nothingness endowed with all causal characteristics' is not something which the investigating intellect does not perceive. This simply is not. The nothingness in question is actually experienceable.[32]

---

[31] *gZhung-'grel rdo-rje-'chang-gi dgongs-pa gsal-bar byed-pa*, fol. 58*b*.
[32] *bSre-'pho'i lam-skor-gyi thog-mar lam-dbye-bsdu*, fol. 60*a*.

It is the almost imperceptible moment which one may experience between sleep and full awakening; the moment which is so full of lucidity and awareness only to become instantaneously eclipsed by the sundry contents of 'normal' consciousness. In the more technical language of existentialist philosophy it is an "outstretched nothingness ready to be filled with any structure, but in itself not determined at all."[33] To this meaning of 'nothingness' corresponds the index 'spaciousness' in the above quotation. As a matter of fact, there is room for everything because there are no *a priori* limits to the scope of experience. Moreover, since awareness is not the bringing forth of some new entity, because awareness itself is not a thing, least of all a container of some sort, the phenomenon can unfold and present itself as it is[34] without fear of being distorted by conceptual interference and hence we are entitled to say with Padma dkar-po that awareness is the stable 'ground' on which all that we may experience, can rest securely. In view of the fact that, as the terms 'nothingness', 'spaciousness' and others imply, there can be awareness without anything of which awareness is aware, the statement that this nothingness is 'endowed with all causal characteristics' demands an interpretation different from the one we usually tend to give to endowment. Certainly, it does not mean possession. This would, as William S. Haas points out, presuppose "an instrument to seize what it wishes to bring in to its forum. And this instrument is the concept. Going to and fro between subject and object in the process of knowledge it links both together and at the same time keeps them apart."[35] There is here no concept to distort the pure 'being-there' of any phenomenon. And thus the 'endowment' is more of the nature of a possibility to become terminated in a definite content rather than the content itself which by way of conceptualizing thought

---

33 John Wild, *The Challenge of Existentialism*, p. 222.

34 This is referred to in the texts by the term *rang-snang*. See *rTen-'brel kho-bo lugs-kyi khrid chos thams-cad-kyi snying-po len-pa*, fol. 2*b*; 4*a*; *The Concept of Mind in Buddhist Tantrism.*

35 William S. Haas, *The Destiny of the Mind*, p. 182.

may be split up into causal and non-causal aspects. This qualifying term again is an index to awareness as a process manifesting itself in every possible mode and content.

Unlike conceptual thought which forever consists in the effort to discover, invent or create a new and 'objective' reality which for some time even may be considered as indisputable (although this indisputableness is mere wishful thinking), awareness. It is nothing in itself, and is, so to speak, at rest and self-contented. This accounts for the fact that pure awareness is said to be linked with unchanging blissfulness which in a more tangible sense is compassion (*snying-rje*). It is, as the text points out, co-extensive with awareness. Again it will be necessary to clarify the meaning of this term. Compassion must not be confused with sentimentality which is a passing mood and linked with a definite content in consciousness.[36] It will change as quickly as the content is replaced by another one. Compassion has a thoroughly stabilizing character and remains the same with itself. This again has nothing to do with staticness which so often is ascribed to Eastern mentality. The text itself declares that it is 'action' (*thabs*) which we, to put it bluntly, usually tend to identify with 'doing things', 'busy-bodying', and creating wants instead of feeling contentment with the present. The co-extensiveness of awareness and compassion can be clarified in still another way. Inasmuch as awareness is nothing in itself its terminal content or its continuing phenomena can also be viewed as emp-

[36]One has to distinguish between compassion as a constitutive mode of human existence, which is often termed Great Compassion and equated with unchanging great bliss, and compassion in the ordinary sense of the word as a sentiment. The latter has its root in hatred. See *Bar-do'i chos-bshad mi-rtag sgyu-ma'i bang-chen dang-po*, fol. 8*b seq.*; *dPal mtshungs-med rgyal-dbang chos-rjes mdzad-pa'i bar-do gsol-'debs-kyi dgongs-don mdo-tsam bkral-ba myur-lam zab-mo'i them-skas*, fol. 12*a seq.*; *gZhung-'grel rdo-rje-'chang-gi dgongs-pa gsal-bar byed-pa*, fol. 187*a*. In this respect one is reminded of Max Scheler's analysis of altruism and similar forms of modern sentimentality which are based on resentment, on hatred of higher values. According to him an attitude of hatred and envy leads to egalitarian and humanitarian ideals as the fundamental denial of love. Altruism based upon resentment, on the one hand, and compassion as a form of hatred, on the other, may well become the subject matter of a comparative study.

ty frames which in their emptiness, paradoxically speaking, are filled with a feeling tone remaining always the same. The reason is that the phenomena do not affect this pure awareness and hence are unable to change the inherent feeling tone or emotional value.

Padma dkar-po gives still another account of what is to be understood by 'presence of spirituality' (*sems-kyi gnas-lugs*). He says:

> Discriminating awareness (*shes-rab*) which is 'commonly accepted truth' (*kun-rdzob-kyi bden-pa*) because of its lucidity (*gsal*) or because of its being nothingness endowed with all causal characteristics or its having a certain reference, is factually (*ngo-bo-nyid-kyis*) present as twelve 'truth-indices' (*bden-don*). Action (*thabs*) which is either unchanging great bliss because all changeability has come to an end, or 'ultimately significant truth' (*don-dam-pa'i bden-pa*) because of its profoundness (*zab*) or the fact that it does not proceed by concept, is the factual completeness of sixteen degrees of compassion. Both discriminating awareness and compassion enter factually into the relation of coincidence (*zung-'jug*) or a sevenfold union (*kha-sbyor bdun*)[37] because they do not exist as and cannot be split up into two separate entities. As E-VAṂ they are present in the psycho-organismal individual (*lus*) by taking their stand on the indestructible potential creativity (*mi-shigs-pa'i thig-le*) in the six focal points of possible experience. However, since both the basis and that which takes its stand on it are known to be beyond conceptuality, they are not 'body-born' and hence do not disintegrate with the decay of the body. Therefore one speaks of 'natural co-emergence' (*rang-bzhin lhan-cig-skyes-pa*).[38]

This passage again contains a number of concepts and terms, essentially as a means and to the extent that they are use-

---

[37]'Sevenfold union' is the name for the various aspects of the satisfaction inherent in the experience of non-duality. They are the non-duality of the two kinds of truth, relative and ultimate; the fusion with the bliss therein; the incorruptibleness of this bliss; the non-entitative character of this; its great compassionateness that transcends every dichotomy; its continuity, and unendingness. See *gZhung-'grel rdo-rje-'chang-gi dgongs-pa gsal-bar byed-pa*, fol. 132*ab*; *bSre-'pho'i lam-skor-gyi thog-mar lam-dbye-bsdu*, fol. 6*b*.

[38]*rDo-rje'i theg-par bgrod-pa'i shing-rta chen-po*, fol. 8*b seq.*

ful for the preparation of realization, not for the purpose of exteriorizations with an apparent objective existence. Special emphasis is laid on the factuality (*Tatsächlichkeit*, *ngo-bo-nyid*) of the topics under consideration. This term is often translated by 'essence', although no evidence is found for it. The usage of this term in Tibetan corresponds to our word 'factuality'. There is here no problem as to the 'essence of' a thing, because in Buddhism the essence of a thing is the thing itself. Apart from the fact that the term 'essence' is a rather muddle-headed concept even in Western philosophies, there is no reason to introduce into Eastern philosophies something which is not there. In addition one should be on guard against committing what Bertrand Russell calls "a transference to metaphysics of what is only a linguistic convenience."[39]

Lucidity (*gsal*) indicates that by transcending the realm of object thinking one arrives at a new dimension which carries more insight and hence is symbolically referred to by terms denoting light. The new dimension is a more enlightened state of cognition than the relative darkness of the ordinary three-dimensional situation or 'ignorance' (*ma-rig-pa*). At the same time this more enlightened cognition is supported by and reaches deeper down into a feeling of satisfaction. Similarly we too speak of 'feeling deeply'. The overcoming of the shallowness of a passing sentiment coincides with the growing perspicacity of the cognitive process. Hence lucidity and profoundness are co-emergent (*zab-gsal lhan-cig-skyes-pa*).[40] Being a unitary

---

[39]Bertrand Russell, *History of Western Philosophy*, p. 224.

[40]*gZhung-'grel rdo-rje-'chang-gi dgongs-pa gsal-bar byed-pa*, fol. 129*b*. 'Co-emergence' is one of the key-notes of Buddhist Tantrism. The term *lhan-cig-skyes-pa* means literally 'born together' and corresponds to Skt. *saha-ja*. In *The Concept of Mind in Buddhist Tantrism*, I translated this term by 'co-nascence'. Afterwards I found that this English rendering was also used in connection with one of Buddhaghosa's conditions (*sahaja-paccaya*) which, however, is different from the Tantric conception. It is therefore advisable to have another term. 'Co-emergence' is one of the leitmotifs of Saraha's *Dohākoṣa* of which an English translation, full of grammatical mistakes and serious misunderstandings of the significance of the verses, is found in E. Conze's *Buddhist Texts Through the Ages*. This translation ignores the Tibetan text and the commentaries thereon. In it the important term

process, co-emergence is not the manifestation of two juxtaposed entities. Juxtaposition belongs to the realm of things, i.e. isolable entities, but here there is no such realm.[41] This is expressed by stating that there is natural co-emergence (*rang-bzhin lhan-cig-skyes-pa*). Or as Padma dkar-po points out elsewhere, 'Because profoundness and lucidity are such that their

---

lhan-cig-skyes-pa (sahaja) is rendered by 'Innate' for which the translator can adduce as only authority the wrong French translation of this term by 'l'Inné'. Texts like the *Phyag-rgya-chen-po'i man-ngag-gi bshad-sbyar rgyal-ba'i gan-mdzod*, fol. 39*a seq.*; the *gZhung-'grel rdo-rje-'chang-gi dgongs-pa gsal-bar byed-pa*, fol. 60*b*, 129*a*, and others make it abundantly clear that there is nothing of innatism in Tantric philosophy. One example may suffice to show that by ignoring the Tibetan tradition the *Dohās*, which are at the core of Tantric thought, fail to reveal their significance. The beginning of *Dohā* no. 38 (36) means according to the Pañjikā in P. C. Bagchi's edition, Dohākoṣa (=Calcutta Sanskrit Series, No. 25c):

> The root of mind is not demonstrable,
> In co-emergence three topics are false.

According to M. Shahidulla's edition, *Les Chants mystiques de Saraha et de Kāṇha*, the same verse is given as

> The root of mind is not demonstrable,
> In co-emergence three topics are true.

D. L. Snellgrove translates the *Apabhraṃśa* version as follows:

> They do not perceive the true basis of mind,
> For upon the Innate they impose a threefold falsification.
> Where thought arises and where it dissolves,
> There you should abide, O my son.

In the *Apabhraṃśa* text there is no equivalent for the translator's 'thought'. But what does the Tibetan tradition say? Together with the commentary by *gNyis-med-avadhūti*, *Do-ha-mdzod-kyi snying-po don-gyi glu'i 'grel-pa* (Dohākoṣa-hṛdaya-arthagīti-ṭīkā), *bsTan-'gyur* (Derge ed.), *rgyud*, vol. zhi, fol. 76*a seq.*, this verse means:

"The root of all entities is mind, but since mind is not found as something existing by itself as the root of everything it is undemonstrable. Hence (Saraha says): 'The root of mind is undemonstrable'. Appearance or mental events rise from non-memory, remain in it and fade into it, therefore the co-emergence of appearance (with non-memory) is experienceable in/through non-memory. Mind, in the absence of conditions for its appearance as mental events is non-memory or nothingness (*stong-pa-nyid*, Śūnyatā). This nothingness rises from unoriginatedness, stays therein and fades back into it. Hence the co-emergence of nothingness (with unoriginatedness) is experienceable in/through unoriginatedness. Mind as such (*sems-nyid*), in the absence of the origination of either memory or non-memory, is beyond origination and

actuality cannot be divided, they are co-emergent'. Viewed from another angle this co-emergence is the logical relation of coincidence (*zung-'jug*).[42]

Lucidity (E) and profoundness (VAṂ) take their stand on, i.e. control, what is termed 'indestructible potential creativity' (*mi-shigs-pa'i thig-le*). This may either point beyond itself to its transcendence referred to in other texts as 'radiant light' (*'od-gsal*), or under the control of lucidity and profoundness it becomes the seminal root of a psycho-organism (*lus*), the cradle of which is motility (*rlung*) proceeding along structural pathways (*rtsa*). It is important to note that this 'taking its stand on' does not mean the interaction of two entities. Actually 'lucidity' and 'profoundness' as determinants of spirituality (*sems*) are not different from potential creativity. They are this potential creativity viewed from its controlling (gaining ascendency) or value aspect. Padma dkar-po is quite explicit on this point. He says that "in view of the basis (structure)-forming aspect one speaks of pathways (*rtsa*); in view of the dynamic process, of motility (*rlung*); in view of the control or value, of potential creativity (*thig-le*)."[43] Due to the fact that there are

---

destruction, it is beyond the realm of the intellect. Since the ultimate of all entities rises, stays in and fades into this reality stretching across time (i.e. not being a content in time), by the co-emergence of unoriginatedness (with that which is beyond the intellect, transcendence) one understands the inconceivable (or transcendence). Hence when one understands mind (as Saraha implies by his words): 'Through the three modes of co-emergence', then, because appearance, nothingness and unoriginatedness disappear where they originate, (or as Saraha puts it): 'Where they originate and where they vanish', it is impossible to find the ultimate of all entities even if one seeks for it and (so Saraha concludes): 'One does not really know where they stay'."

[41] *gZhung-'grel rdo-rje-'chang-gi dgongs-pa gsal-bar byed-pa*, fol. 5*b*; 60*b*.

[42] The interpretation of this term as 'coincidence' is the one given by the bKa'-brgyud-pa school of Buddhism, which follows the one given in *Pañcakrama* VI. They have criticized Tsong-kha-pa for interpreting this term as 'harmonious juxtaposition'.

[43] *rtsa*, *rlung* and *thig-le* are terms used exclusively in mysticism. Attempts to reduce what they signify to physiological processes have failed. The *rtsa* has nothing to do with the veins or arteries or the physical body, the *rlung* is not vital air, and the *thig-le* is not a seminal drop. They may mean all this, but then, as my Lama teachers and friends told me, we move in a world of distortions.

many focal points of possible experience one can speak of several instances of potential creativity. The numerical account is of subordinate importance, because it refers to the most outstanding focal points; of paramount importance is the dynamic character, and so Padma dkar-po declares that 'the six (instances of) potential creativity are non-dichotomic motility or enlightenment-motility'.[44] In this context 'enlightenment' is another term for 'value' or 'control' and reflects the conviction that awareness is at the bottom of human nature. This awareness is not some static entity, a container of some sort, but 'motility' which refers to the noetic act which in turn in its end-state reveals a certain structure. 'Non-dichotomic' is not to be understood merely as of epistemological significance. It is a term which comprises every split, be it of subject-object or body-mind and so on. In meditation literature the basic meaning of the term 'dichotomy' (*rnam-rtog*) is rather what we would circumscribe by stating that man is divided against himself. 'Non-dichotomic' therefore refers to an experience before the split in the individual has occurred.

The formativeness of potential creativity, designated by the term 'motility', is present in that which has been formed in so far as the formed is the record of the formative process. Again we see here that there is no sharp division between the formed and the forming. This aspect is compared in the Tantric texts with water turning into ice and since ice can become water again through a process of unfreezing, we have to consider every technical term as a two-way process-product word. Another important point to note is that a new structure can only be formed when the old one is dead, not only in the realm of matter but also in that of ideas which Max Planck so admirably pointed out by saying that new ideas conquer by the death of their

---

These terms again point out the necessity of analytical considerations. The failure to do so has resulted in what Noel Jaquin, *The Theory of Metaphysical Influence*, p. 29, puts so admirably: "In many cases the repeated attempts to explain certain symbols in three-dimensional terms has merely succeeded in creating an entirely false concept, and one that often has no relation to the actual meaning of the symbolic representation."

[44] *rDo-rje'i theg-par bgrod-pa'i shing-rta chen-po*, fol. 7*b*.

opponents. However, there are many kinds of death. In any case, death is something more than the objective biological stoppage which can be observed from the outside. It is also an inner experience. Existentialist thinkers have directed our attention to the phenomenon of personal death, but their interpretation is more often than not linked with certain dogmas that have been taken over uncritically. The problem of death which is raised by the statement that formativeness does not come to an end when its formed frame breaks up, needs special examination and falls outside the scope of the present essay.

The twelve 'truth-indices' (*bden-don*) resemble in name the twelve members of the so-called Law of Interdependent Origination (Pratītyasamutpāda). The latter are rather abstractions created by analysis, while the former are peculiar structural modes which are not so much fixed properties of a finished thing but relational phases of man's being.[45] Nāgārjuna is credited with having pointed out the structural nature of this 'Law', which is no 'law' at all but is a heuristic principle. He declared that the first ('ignorance', *ma-rig-pa*, *avidyā*), eighth (desire, *sred-pa*, *tṛṣṇā*) and ninth members (ascription-organization, *len-pa*, *upādāna*) represented 'emotionality' (*nyon-mongs-pa*, *kleśa*); the second (motivation-configuration, *'du-byed*, *saṃskāraḥ*) and tenth (existence, *srid-pa*, *bhava*) 'action' (*las*, *karman*); and the remaining third (consciousness, *rnam-par shes-pa*, *vijñāna*), fourth (name and form, *ming-gzugs*, *nāma-rūpa*), fifth (six sensory fields, *skye-mched drug*, *ṣaḍāyatana*), sixth (total pattern, 'contact', *reg-pa*, *sparśa*), seventh (feeling, *tshor-ba*, *vedanā*), eleventh (birth, *skye-ba*, *jāti*) and twelfth (old age and death, *rga-shi*, *jarāmaraṇa*) 'misery' (*sdug-bsngal*, *duḥkha*). The three topics of emotionality, action and misery are always found together so that in the absence of one the others also do not obtain. Hence they are likened to a trivet.[46] This anal-

[45]In the *rDo-rje'i theg-par bgrod-pa'i shing-rta chen-po*, fol. 8*b* it is stated that the twelve members of the Pratītyasamutpāda belong to the 'impure aspect' of reality (*ma-dag-pa'i cha-nas*), while the twelve truth-indices represent the 'pure aspect' (*dag-pa'i cha-nas*).

[46]*bSre-'pho'i lam-skor-gyi thog-mar lam-dbye-bsdu*, fol. 51*b seq.*

ysis by Nāgārjuna shows that the Law of Interdependent Origination has nothing to do with causality as we understand this term. While the members of the 'Law' may be said to "proceed out of each other just as do the consecutive states of an organism–say childhood, adolescence, mature age and old age,"[47] they all refer to the human situation. This situation may now be viewed from another angle. Emotionality, action and misery cover the whole of human existence and it is here that various phases of man's being can be distinguished. The first three members of the 'Law', ignorance, motivation-configuration and consciousness refer to the cognitive aspect of human life. Ignorance, as has been shown, is not absence of knowledge, it is rather the dim light of object thinking in its incipience which as a formative act finds its final form in consciousness, the discriminating activity usually moving in the subject-object dichotomy. The three topics, ignorance, motivation-configuration and consciousness, form a unity viewed under the aspects of quality (ignorance), act (motivation-configuration) and actuality (consciousness). This unitary feature is termed *ye-shes rdo-rje* (jñānavajra) which may be rendered by 'cognitive being'. It is, as Padma dkar-po points out, a status of least conflict. What he means by this remark will become clear through the relation of this mode of being to the other modes.

The next three members, name and form, the six sensory fields and the total pattern of 'contact', clearly point to the phase of man's being-in-the-world or being-in-contact-with others. It is important to note here that name and form refer to the total individual; 'name' comprises the perceptual and instinctive powers and 'form' is above all the epistemological object of a perceptual situation out of which the corporeality of things is established in co-operation with the tactile sense. It is this sense that through its experience of resistance points to something beyond the body. However, we must not assume that 'contact' relates to the tactile sense exclusively. The term 'contact' is found with other sensory perceptions as well, it even relates to

[47]William S. Haas, *The Destiny of the Mind*, p. 254.

the ideational. Actually we move in a world in which our distinction between body and mind, physical and mental, material and ideal, does not obtain in such marked contrast. Moreover, while in our world-experience the sense of touch is regarded as mere receptiveness, in Tantrism the same sense interlaces man with his environment and with the physiological side of his being. Thus the triad of name and form, six sensory fields and 'contact' refer to both the inner and outer world of man. Technically this is known as *sku rdo-rje* (*kāyavajra*), which may be rendered as 'environmental being', where environment must be understood as both internal and external. The internal environment may then be likened to Cannon's principle of homeostasis. 'Environmental being' is, according to Padma dkar-po, a status of mediocre conflict.

The next triad of feeling, desire (positive as adience and negative as avoidance) and ascription, as the fitting of the experience into the total pattern of human life, is technically called *gsung rdo-rje* (vāgvajra) and may be rendered as 'communicative being'. Feeling is a kind of judgment; it declares that something is pleasant or unpleasant or indifferent. Naturally the tendency is to seek pleasant experiences and to avoid unpleasant ones. In this seeking man 'communicates' with his fellow beings and with the objects that surround him. He addresses them, and language as the most polished tool of communication is thus both expressive and evocative. This phase of man's being is a status of deep conflict.

The last triad of (i) existence as the realm of possibilities taking shape in (ii) the birth of a new complex phenomenon of experience which in course of time will (iii) age and die, is known as *thugs rdo-rje* (*cittavajra*). It clearly indicates man's 'situational being'. As the existentialist thinkers have shown, man is always in a situation. This being-in-a-situation is what in the Buddhist texts is termed 'existence' (*srid-pa*, *bhava*). But this is not all: man tries to solve the situation in which he finds himself, only to become involved in another one that has to be solved after solving the former in some way or other. The solution of any situation depends on man's decision which is implied in the term *thugs* (*citta*). In most cases however, he is unaware of the decisions that have brought about his being in a situation and hence his situational being is a status of deepest conflict.[48]

There is, however, another way of facing this status of conflict. Conflict and its attending pain and suffering exists as long as 'ignorance' prevails. But once man has made up his mind what he wants, he is hard to bewilder; he realizes that the situation is his and he acts in whatever situation he may find himself in the light of his possibilities and interprets the events of his life in relation to his ultimate end. In brief, he uses 'discrimination' (*shes-rab*) which reflects authentic awareness (*ye-shes*), permeating every phase of his being. On the other hand, as long as he postpones his decision and works under the spell of ignorance the more he becomes involved in conflict situations. Misery as a constitutive phase of his being increases.

While 'discriminating awareness' (*shes-rab*) is essentially an act by which mind stretches out to meet its object or, as the text says 'has a certain reference' (*dmigs-pa dang bcas-pa*),[49] it does not feel the situation in which man may find himself at the moment. And yet the feeling tone or the mood of a situation is as revealing as the cognitive aspect involved in it. This feeling tone is referred to by the 'sixteen degrees of compassion' of the text, each degree gaining in intensity and being concerned with itself rather than being a succession of events proceeding within the soul of man. As John Wild says: "It discloses the naked facticity of this situation into which I have already been thrown. But this facticity is not that of an object from which I am detached, and at which I can stare. It is an existential facticity concerned with itself and either turning back to take over its factuality, or turning away from this as a burden and a chain. For the most part, it is the latter type of feeling that predominates."[50]

According to the Tantric texts, feeling, which is generally one of joy, is least intense as long as there is ordinary object think-

---

[48]The above analysis is found in *gZhung-'grel rdo-rje-'chang-gi dgongs-pa gsal-bar byed-pa*, fol. 21*ab*.

[49]*rDo-rje'i theg-par bgrod-pa'i shing-rta chen-po*, fol. 8*b*. See also *ibid.*, fol. 57*b*.

[50]John Wild, *The Challenge of Existentialism*, p. 87.

ing. It grows in intensity with the gradual process of de-objectification. This process is illustrated by the sexual syndrome. The first type of joy (*dga'-ba*) which comprises five degrees and is linked with the objective reference, is said to be 'small bliss'. It is present in the amorous exploration of the partner. The next type of intense joy (*mchog-dga'*) which also comprises five degrees is marked by a decrease in the intensity of the objective reference. In it the division into an I and You fades into a feeling of communion and hence is said to be 'mediocre bliss'. The third type of joy is termed variously, either as a 'special joy' (*khyad-dga'*) or as 'joylessness' (*dga'-bral*). It is a special joy because in it the division into the I and You has, as it were, completely disappeared, and it is a joyless joy, because the ordinary judgments as to the varying intensity do not apply any more. Nevertheless, this joy is said also to comprise five degrees. But since in these three types of joy there is still a latent trace of the division into an I and You, they are indices of and pointers to true joy, rather than the actual consummation which is reserved to what is called the sixteenth degree. Its name is 'co-emergence joy' (*lhan-cig-skyes-pa'i dga'-ba*), because here thought and feeling have fused into a unitary experience. This last intensity degree is rarely realized in its purity because of the presence of 'ignorance'.

With the exception of the sixteenth degree the preceding fifteen ones are related to certain focal points of experience in such a way that the first five degrees or joy (*dga'-ba*) belong to the 'head' focal point, the second five or intense joy (*mchog-dga'*) to the region between the 'throat' and 'heart' focal points, and the remaining five or special joy (*khyad-dga'*) to that between the 'heart' and 'navel' or 'sex' focal points.[51] In so far as the various joys are related to the sexual syndrome and sex is, in spite of the haters of love, of paramount importance in the life of man, the following may be given as a sort of explanation. The 'head' focal point is the ordinary object thinking situation in which we take stock of the erotic possibilities the partner may have to offer or, as the texts point out, where one engages in kissing and

---

[51] *gZhung-'grel rdo-rje-'chang-gi dgongs-pa gsal-bar byed-pa*, fol. 54*b seq.*

embracing or other amatory practices.[52] Gradually the object character disappears and we find ourselves in a communicatory situation in which we put 'all our heart'. This then culminates in the convulsions after the peak of orgasm has been reached, and since it is rather difficult to differentiate between the orgasm and the subsequent convulsions one experiences either the special joy of what is considered to be the ultimate consummation or, what is the same, a state of joylessness in the sense that this joy is different from and devoid of the preceding and common types of joy.[53]

Although the highest or sixteenth degree of intensity is realized only by him who has gone beyond 'ignorance' or objectifying thought, this does not mean that it is something utterly alien. It is present in the structure of each type of joy. Padma dkar-po says: "By dividing the four types of joy into four aspects each, one obtains sixteen degrees of joy. In this way there is the sixteenth degree, co-emergence joy, present in every joy in a subtle way. Ordinary people are unable to realize this and hence do not penetrate to its experience. The philosophers by virtue of the instruction by their Gurus realize this sixteenth degree immediately and make it the way of their philosophical quest."[54] This again emphasizes the index character of everything that we may experience in life. And it is in the immediate experience that there is co-emergence of discrimination and feeling transcending every limit of content and intensity. It has to

---

[52] *Ibid.*, fol. 156*b seq.*

[53] The elucidation of the various degrees of joy (*dga'-ba*) in connection with the sexual syndrome and the process of de-objectification is given in *bSre-'pho'i lam-skor-gyi thog-mar lam-dbye-bsdu*, fol. 44*b seq.* The distinction between orgasm as the peak of sexual activity and the spasms and convulsions as the after-effect, which A. C. Kinsey, Wardell B. Pomeroy, Clyde E. Martin and Paul H. Gebhard have made in their *Sexual Behavior in the Human Female*, p. 627, is also elaborated in gNyis-med-rdo-rje's *Phyag-rgya bzhi'i man-ngag* (*Caturmudrā-upadeśa*), *bsTan-'gyur* (Derge ed.), *rgyud*, vol. zhi, fol. 213*ab*. This text is not identical with the *Caturmudrā* in *Advaya-vajrasangraha*, pp. 32 *seq.* The text contained in this collection has the title *Caturmudrāniścaya* according to its Tibetan translation. Its author is Nāgārjuna(sāra).

[54] *gZhung-'grel rdo-rje-'chang-gi dgongs-pa gsal-bar byed-pa*, fol. 157*a*.

be noted that this feeling is not an absorption in a static and absolutized bliss, even if the texts speak of 'unchanging great bliss' (*mi-'gyur-ba bde-ba chen-po*), but the sustaining value in man's situation in the world. As compassion (*snying-rje*) it acts (*thabs*), although this action is not of the hit-and-miss type of 'ignorance'.

Finally we have to refer to the relation of coincidence (*zung-'jug*) between 'discriminating awareness' (*shes-rab*) and 'compassion' (*snying-rje*), between 'lucidity' (*gsal*) and 'profoundness' (*zab*), or whatever other symbol may be used.[55] Coincidence having the formal property of identity as a relation always involves an aspect of duality, which is nevertheless transcended in some way. It seems that this relation cannot be analyzed further. It belongs to our being to be thus disclosed to ourselves. For in actual life feeling and discrimination, sense and reason, never work separately, but always in combination.

Discrimination and feeling–to mention only the most outstanding aspects–form an existential unity, which is presupposed by all later action and theoretical reflection. This existential unity is designated by the term 'foundation-Mahāmudrā' (*gzhi phyag-rgya chen-po*).[56] Because of the unity of reality this foundation is also the path (*lam*) and the goal (*'bras-bu*) which, as we have seen, in a certain way determines and controls the foundation and the action built on it. In other words, the successive incidental differences of a continuous process are transcended by its essential unity. Therefore we can refer to its unity from beginning to end. To preserve this unity at every stage of one's life becomes the philosopher's task.

---

[55] *Ibid.*, fol. 188*a*. See also *rNal-'byor-bzhi'i bshad-pa don-dam mdzub tshugs-su bstan-pa*, fol. 10*b*.

[56] *gZhung-'grel rdo-rje 'chang-gi dgongs-pa gsal-bar byed-pa*, fol. 58*b*; *rDo-rje'i theg-par bgrod-pa'i shing-rta chen-po*, fol. 8*b*; *Phyag-rgya chen-po rnal-'byor bzhi'i bshad-pa nges-don lta-ba'i mig*, fol. 2*a*.

Indian Buddhist Thought in Tibetan Perspective:

Infinite Transcendence Versus Finiteness

Buddhism in Tibet owes much of what it was to become to the genius of three persons, each of whom distinguished himself in his own field by his specific capacities, but all of whom are unanimously acclaimed to be alike in being the spiritual ancestors of the rNying-ma-pa school of thought, which is one of the four major Buddhist traditions in Tibet.[1]

From a purely intellectual point of view, foremost among them ranks the Indian pandit Śāntirakṣita, revered as a veritable Bodhisattva, a benefactor of mankind. He may be called the theoretical founder of Tibetan Buddhism. He was a representative of the Yogācāra-mādhyamika-svātantrika line of thinking, a rather late product of the Buddhist philosophical movement. As a Mādhyamika, Śāntirakṣita rejected the idea that a thing, be it a natural object or an introspected self, could claim any existence of its own and as such apart from our engaging in what, in

[1]The other three are the bKa'-brgyud-pa, the Sa-skya-pa, and the dGe-lugs-pa (also called dGa-ldan-pa) who are the continuation of the earlier bKa'-gdams-pa.

modern times and terms, L. Wittgenstein has called the 'language game'. That is, we do use the name 'dog' to refer to something, and though we need to recognize what the thing is like to make sure that we use the appropriate name of it, if it has one, the name is logically independent of the characteristics of the thing which is given a name. The Mādhyamikas thus recognized a (grammatical) noun as a name that could be given a use regardless of whether it stands for a thing whose existence we are prepared to admit.

As a Svātantrika, Śāntirakṣita retained the idea of an essence, though not so much in the sense of a principle by which a thing is what it is or of the possibility of being, but in that of the given or actual before a mind.

Lastly, as a Yogācāra he denied the existence of an external world as independent of our experiencing it. This does not mean that there is 'only mind' and that, as a consequence, physical objects–trees, houses, rocks, tables, chairs, and the like, all of which everybody will admit to be genuine objects of knowledge by human beings–are mind, as lexical translations of Buddhist texts want to make us believe. The so-called 'only mind' (*sems-tsam*, Skt. *cittamātra*) thesis means that there must be a mind to experience and know things and that things in order to be known must appear before a mind. Appearance, however, does not commit us to much. It does not commit us to the belief that it is mental, nor yet that it is physical.[2]

Apart from many other subtleties the Yogācāra-mādhyamika-svātantrikas claimed that the belief in a self was wishfulness and emotivity, setting up all the other emotively toned action and

---

[2]Tshul-khrims blo-gros (otherwise known as Klong-chen rab-'byams-pa) most emphatically argues against the mentalistic thesis that everything is mind, in his *Theg-pa chen-po'i man-ngag-gi bstan-bcos yid-bzhin rin-po-che'i mdzod*, fols. 2*b* ff, and in his own commentary to this work, the *Theg-pa chen-po'i man-ngag-gi bstan-bcos yid-bzhin rin-po-che'i mdzod-kyi 'grel-pa padma dkar-po*, fols. 8*a* ff. So also does Kun-mkhyen 'Jam-dbyangs bzhad-pa in his *Grub-mtha'i rnam-bshad rang gzhas grub-mtha kun dang zab-don mchog-lu gsal-ba kun-bzang zhing-gi nyi-ma lung rigs rgya-mtsho skye-dgu'i re-ba kun skongs*, part iv, fol. 77*a*.

reaction patterns in a human being, while the belief in things other than the self, as existing as such, was intellectual opacity.[3]

It may have been the difficulty of this type of philosophy that prevented Buddhism from making any headway in Tibet after its introduction. It is also likely that as a profound scholar Śāntarakṣita had his own personal contact difficulties. It remains a historical fact that because of his failure to make Buddhism acceptable to a larger public he suggested that Guru Padmasambhava be invited to Tibet.

Padmasambhava, who is credited with having been a representative of the Prāsangika mode of reasoning, dispensing with the idea of the given or actual as such as well, has been much maligned by writers on Tibetan Buddhism. The account of his activities, when divested of the mythological accessories, clearly shows that he did precisely that which nowadays we consider to be the activities of a public relations man. In this capacity Padmasambhava certainly succeeded in creating a more favorable climate for the spread of Buddhism so that Śāntirakṣita's ideas could develop.

Quite different from these personalities is Vimalamitra,[4] who may be called the founder of living Buddhism in Tibet. His philosophical outlook was basically that of the Yogācāra-mādhyamika-svātantrikas, but he was not primarily concerned with the elaboration of a philosophical system. He is essentially an expounder of the Tantras, particularly of the *gSang-ba snying-po*,[5] which has remained the most authoritative work for the rNying-ma-pas. The word 'Tantra', which has become

---

[3]For the Prāsangikas any belief in something, whether a natural object or an introspected self, is wishfulness, while the tendency toward such a belief is intellectual opacity. The difference between the two sections among the Mādhyamikas has been clearly stated in dKon-mchog 'Jigs-med dbang-po's *Grub-pa'i mtha'i rnam-par bzhag-pa rin-po-che'i phreng-ba*, fols. 13*a* and 15*b*.

[4]He was of Indian origin but spent much of his life in China. Biographical notes are found in *Bi-ma snying-tig*, Vol. IX, and in the *bLa-ma yang-tig*, Vol. E, part I, fols. 11*a* ff.

[5]The full title is *rDo-rje sems-dpa' sgyu-'phrul dra-ba gsang-ba snying-po de-kho-na-nyid nges-pa'i rgyud-kyi rgyal-po chen-po*. There exists a vast commentary literature on this Tantra; some of them have been utilized in the following notes.

part of the English language, is in Buddhism a term referring to one's individual spiritual growth, and only secondarily is it made to cover the literature which deals with this developmental process.[6] The words used in the Tantra literature are symbols for the experiences that are being lived through as the process of growth and maturation unfolds. They are not so much labels for things as, for instance, the label 'dog' is, rather are they incentives to lead people to, and finally to evoke within them, those experiences which those who have had them consider to be of vital importance and which they try to communicate by those peculiar verbal expressions which do not seem to stand literally for anything. This is important to note, because one will not do justice to the rNying-ma-pas by reducing their statements to pre-existing philosophical systems and then proceeding to show that they have mixed the categories.

By deriving their origin from so seemingly different personalities like Śāntirakṣita and Vimalamitra, the rNying-ma-pas plainly prove that a deeply religious nature, a capacity for the most exalted religious experience, and the most abstract and systematic philosophical thinking are quite compatible. As a matter of fact, the mystics have always been better reasoners than the desiccated rationalists.

The realm of experience, whose formulation is contained within the intellectual horizon of an age and a society, in many respects does not fit the language of everyday thought, and its range is wider than the world of the 'practical', 'matter-of-fact' concerns. Yet, man as a communicative being has to use this language when he wants to express something of his experiences to others. Although language is an indispensable, and even highly polished, instrument, it has limitations that must clearly be understood. Since words, the stock of trade in every

[6]The rNying-ma-pa texts clearly distinguish between *tshig-gyi rgyud*, Tantra as literature, and *don-gyi rgyud*, Tantra as the spiritual development of man as it proceeds from a starting point or ground to the goal. See for instance the *rGyud-rgyal gsang-ba snying-po'i 'grel-pa Rong-zom chos-bzang-gis mdzod-pa*, fols. 14*a* ff., by Rong-zom chos-kyi bzang-po, whose life and work is detailed in George N. Roerich, *The Blue Annals*, part I, pp. 160 ff. Or, Klong-chen rab-'byams-pa's *Theg-pa'i mchog rin-po-che'i mdzod*, fols. 84*a* ff.

language, merely label things and have no closer relationship to the things they label than the labels on bottles, and since there are just too many things (whether physical objects, mental processes, qualities, actions) we would get quickly into difficulty if we were to try to give a name or stick a label on each thing. Only to a certain extent is it possible to make up a new word and use it to refer to something that has not yet been given a name in one's language before. This, then, is a new arbitrary symbol which, when it is accepted by others, will have become a conventional symbol. The other way to overcome the limitation of a language is to stipulate a new use for a word already in common use. One would then have two (or more) meanings, and this may often be very confusing.

Both procedures are found in the Buddhist texts when they deal with the exploration of the inner world of experience. There are many new terms, not found in any other context, but there are still more old terms which have been given a new use and so, by stipulation, have been taken out of the hazy area of reference they had in common usage, and given a more precise application. These latter terms are the death-trap for all lexical translators who, unaware of (and more often willfully ignoring) the context and indulging in some irrelevant etymologies, produce pathetically ridiculous, if not utterly nonsensical, cribs.[7]

---

[7]There is no harm when cribs do not claim to be more than cribs, but they become a menace when they want to be understood as contributions to philosophy. An instance of ridiculousness is the translation of the technical terms *anāsrava* and *sāsrava* by 'without an outflow' and 'with an outflow'. (E. Conze). There is nothing in the Buddhist texts to show that this alleged outflow is gaseous, liquid, or otherwise. The context makes it abundantly clear that this term refers to factors which arouse emotive responses. What factors do so depends on whether the treatise in which these terms occur is written from the Vaibhāṣika, Sautrāntika, Vijñānavāda, or Mādhyamika point of view. An instance of utter disregard of what the Buddhist texts understand by using a certain term is the current translation of *prajñā* by 'wisdom'. *Prajñā* is a selective discriminative function bearing on a definite object of cognition. When properly used it becomes a transcending function freeing the observer from his naïve belief in the concrete existence of things. Within the structure of mind, consisting of a responsiveness (*citta*) and specific functions (*caitta*), *prajñā* is one of the five object-determined (*niyataviṣaya*) ones and is always defined as 'discrimination'.While the structure of mind, as already detailed in

As an illustration of the rNying-ma-pas' emphasis on experience as a means of cultivating and refining the personality and of realizing spiritual maturity and freedom of the mind, as well as of their claim that spiritual meaning and the understanding of value are, as with the other Buddhist traditions in Tibet, on a higher rung of knowledge than the analytical ratio which for them is a straying away from the eternal home of the mind, I shall give the translation of a small text by Kun-mkhyen 'Jigs-med gling-pa. I shall then compare it with the traditional system of the Vijñānavādins with which it seems to have a certain similarity, although this similarity is only one of terms. The comparison also will show that the philosophical spirit has been kept alive among the rNying-ma-pas and that 'Jigs-med gling-pa must be counted as a true philosopher, rather than as a recorder of philosophy in tradition.

The text is called "The Tantra of the Reality of Transcendent Awareness [symbolically referred to as] Kun-tu bzang-po, the Quintessence of Fulfilment and Completion."[8] Its five chapters cover the whole of the Buddhist path of spiritual development: the starting point or the ground, the path or the unfolding of transcendent thought, and the goal or the attainment of freedom as a mode of being.

I

Salutation to the potentiality of Buddhahood, victoriously transcendent:[9]

---

the *Abhidharmakośa* and the *Abhidharmasamuccaya*, has been recognized by all schools of Buddhism, there has been merely a difference of opinion concerning its ontological status. The wide range of application of this discriminative function has been fully discussed in the *Shes-rab bsdus-pa'i sgron-ma* in the *Bi-ma snying-tig*, Vol. IV, fols. 97*b* ff.

[8]*rDzogs-pa chen-po kun-tu bzang-po ye-shes klong-gi rgyud.* This work belongs to the eighteenth century. Its author wrote another work, the *Thun-mong-gi sngon-'gro sems-sbyong rnam-pa bdun-gyi don-khrid thar-pa'i them-skas*, which he dated as A.D. 1761.

[9]The translation of *bcom-ldan-'das* by 'victoriously transcendent' attempts to convey something of what is understood by this term: *bcom* relates to the conquest of the four Māras (boundary situations) of organismic being, emotionality, overvalued ideas, and death; *ldan* indicates the possession of tran-

In the Great Akaniṣṭha realm which is the immediate evidence of the field of reality where no errancy[10] obtains, Kun-tu bzang-po who is. the cognitive mode that is for ever in the process of awakening to Buddhahood, resides in the company of the five spiritual rulers who (on the level of the analytical ratio are known as) the physical, feeling, ideation, motivation, and cognition; of their five consorts (who on a lower level are) the dynamics of solidification, cohestion, temperature, movement, and spatiality; of their (eight) sons (who otherwise) are immanent and transitive sensory processes; and of their (eight) daughters who ordinarily are reified as) objects and temporal phases.

Then and there the great spiritual being rTog-pa'i rdo-rje rose from his seat and spoke the following words:

O Teacher, you have repeatedly declared that there occurs a split into the different and mutually opposing entities of Saṃsāra and Nirvāṇa, owing to the specific differences between an all-ground and a supreme transcendent awareness. What are their distinctive characteristics, and of what nature is that which is labeled mentality and spirituality and how is their modality or facticity?

Kun-tu bzang-po replied:

"All-ground" (*kun-gzhi*) is the common comprehensive foundation of both Saṃsāra and Nirvāṇa; it may be likened to the situation when the senses have not yet waked up to their objects. Its capacity for serving as the requisite for and the use of mentality and spirituality is latently present even in the five

---

scendent awareness; and *'das* indicates the passage beyond the turmoil of worldliness. See, e.g., *Bi-ma snying-tig*, Vol. III, fol. 14*b*; Rong-zom chos-yi bzang-po's commentary on the *gSang-ba snying-po*, fol. 41*a*; and gYung-ston rdo-rje dpal-bzang's commentary on this work, the *dPal gsang-ba snying-po'i rgyud don gsal-byed me-long*, fols. 11*b* ff.

[10] *'Khrul-pa*, Skt. *bhrānti*. The above translation has been suggested by modern existentialist thought, particularly by M. Heidegger's conception of '*das Irren*', the straying away from the Real. However, this straying away does not contain the idea of culpability. This distinguishes Buddhist reasoning from existentialist thought with which it often has a certain affinity. The most marked difference, however, is that Buddhism is based on 'joy', 'bliss' (*bde-ba chen-po*), while the common presupposition of Western existentialist thought is the fundamental mood of despair (*Angst*).

unconscious states.[11] In those works which address themselves to people of lesser intellectual acumen, it is stated to be the very potentiality of Buddhahood,[12] but this is meant only to attract the simpletons who harbor some doubts about the existence of a pure reality. Therefore, since in this all-ground there is present in an intellectually unfathomable, directly unobservable, and dormant manner both a pure modality which is the gateway of transcending awareness and which comprises (i) the path to Nirvāṇa, (ii) the manifestation of pure reality before this awareness, and (iii) the goal-realization which is as vast as the ocean, and an impure modality which is the gateway to Saṃsāra and which comprises (i) karmic actions, (ii) emotively toned action and reaction patterns, and (iii) the mass of interpretative constructs and judgments; therefore it is itself neither the status of a sentient being nor that of a Buddha, neither the awareness operating during the period of traversing the path of spiritual development nor spirituality itself; but being the vessel for all this or the ground on which all this comes to pass, it is spoken of as the 'all-ground'.

It may be viewed under four aspects: as the all-ground of the initial ground of Saṃsāra; as the all-ground providing the link with either Saṃsāra or Nirvāṇa; as the all-ground of our physical existence; and as the all-ground of experientially initiated potentialities of experience.[13]

Their modality is in brief: As a pervasive medium (*kun-*

---

[11] I.e., the absence of any ideas, the two kinds of cessation of all mental activity, swoon, and deep sleep.

[12] This statement contains a critique of the bKa'-brgyud-pas for whom the potentiality of Buddhahood is of a mixed character and only in the course of the person's spiritual development becomes pure and finds its climax in Buddhahood. For the rNying-ma-pas the distinction between that which is pure and impure or, in existentialist terms, between that which is authentic and unauthentic, must be made at the very beginning of the path.

[13] This fourfold aspect is already detailed in Klong-chen rab-'byams-pa's *Theg-pa'i mchog rin-po-che'i mdzod*, fol. 304*a*. The dGe-lugs-pas' objection against this classification is that in the last aspect there is a confusion between the 'all-ground' and the 'experientially initiated potentialities of experience' which are not identical with the all-ground. See in particular Tsong-kha-pa's *Yid dang kun-gzhi'i dka-gnas rgya-cher 'grel-pa legs-bshad rgya-mtsho* (*Collected Works*, Tashilhunpo ed., Vol. XVIII, part 3).

gzhi'i khams) in which the intentionality of a mind does not yet operate,[14] it is like an egg. Its dynamic which manifests itself as the reason for or the ground on which many things come into existence, is a cognitive mode and termed 'all-ground cognitiveness' (*kun-gzhi'i rnam-par shes-pa*). Out of it motility (*rlung*), present in the analytic and synthetic functions of a mind and activated by the traces of positive and negative actions and of the emotively toned patterns of attraction, antipathy, and indifference (all of which have been produced by past experiences and serve as cause-factors in producing later experiences), begins to stir; this is the distinct feature of mentality (*sems*). In this way the activity of the six senses awakening to their objects marks the emergence of the subjective mind operating in the subject-object dichotomy (*yid*). In favoring the emotively toned and constituted aspect of mind (*nyon-mongs-pa'i yid*), which is the egocentricness of conscious life, it occasions the five basic emotively toned action and reaction patterns, the twenty subsidiary ones, the fifty mental events, and the eighty-four thousand interpretations and judgments, so that everything without exception[15] is set for the origination of Saṃsāra.

Listen, rTog-pa'i rdo-rje! Although the transcending awareness which knows reality as it is in reality, is, in view of its continuity, not a different substance from the pervasive medium of the all-ground, it is said to be a change in its modality. It is like the awakening from deep sleep. But although here the senses wake up to their objects they are not affected by the appearance of these objects (in the sense that the principles of interpretation which we apply to the data of sense perception remain inactivated). This transcending awareness does not fall into either

---

[14]Buddhist texts clearly distinguish between the intention (*dmigs*) and the intended object (*yul*) of the mind. It is the very nature of mind to 'intend' something or to be 'responsive to'. Where this is not there is also no mind in the proper sense of the word.

[15]*ma-lus shing-lus-pa med-pa* is short for *ma-lus mi-lus lus-pa-med-pa* which in the rNying-ma-pa diction has a specific connotation inasmuch as each term refers to one aspect of the triple division of reality. See gYung ston rdo-rje dpal-bzang's commentary on the *Gsang-ba snying-po* (see above n. 9), fols. 18*a* f.

chasm of the two kinds of unknowing, the one co-emergent with mentality and the other the diffusive one of mentality.[16] Although, in the actuality of the mere absence of any dichotomic activity, mentality and spirituality seem to be alike, mentality retains its intentional character and enters into a specific relation to the mnemic consequences of the apprehended sensum in a non-observable (and hence unanalyzable) manner (which gives the perceptual situation the specific external reference). Spirituality, however, as far as its facticity (*ngo-bo*) is concerned, remains free from any projectibility into words and their inherent externalization; its givenness (*rang-bzhin*) or actuality is a free unimpeded movement; and its observable quality (*rnam-pa*) is an analytic-appreciative capacity that can take in everything. Inasmuch as this capacity cannot be thwarted by reification into external objects and by avidity and listlessness, everything is set for the origination of Nirvāṇa.

The First Chapter, explaining the Ground and the Gates to Saṃsāra and Nirvāṇa.

II

Again Rtog-pa'i rdo-rje asked:

Is it possible or not to point to an earlier and later phase concerning the split into Saṃsāra and Nirvāṇa and to indicate the exact moment of the occurrence of this split? Further, O teacher Kun-tu bzang-po, does your projected and externalized appearance happen to be in the manner of an apparition to those who are prepared for your vision by good deeds, or are you a concrete, truly existing, entity as are other living beings? Kindly explain this problem.

Kun-tu bzang-po replied:

While the predicates of past, future, and present can be applied to the appearance of my manifested existence, my very being is time itself (rather than an event in time) because it is

[16] *lHan-cig skyes-pa'i ma-rig-pa* provides the general pattern of Saṃsāra, while *kun-tu btags-pa'i ma-rig-pa* provides the detailed one. The former is, as it were, constitutional, the latter, moving in the subject-object division, institutional.

beyond the range of fragmentizing and temporalizing words. To call me the Primordial Lord by assigning a beginning in time to me, is merely to put a convenient label on me. For this reason, the very moment the analytic function of mind, differentiating between and thinking about Samsāra and Nirvāṇa, begins to operate, the split into these two aspects has occurred, because on the one ground two ways have opened.

Listen, rTog-pa'i rdo-rje! If you think that that which is labeled that exalted and auspicious Kun-tu bzang-po, the Primordial Lord who embodies the potentiality of all Buddhahood, is some entity apart from the psychological makeup of the sentient beings, which is as vast as the ocean, the very chance of Saṃsāra and Nirvāṇa separating in their togetherness has been eliminated and, since (on such an assumption as yours) the living beings are without the possibility of realizing Buddhahood, all the teaching about the two prerequisites of merits and knowledge, as vast as the ocean, is meaningless. Therefore, since my givenness which is fulfilment and completion, by its very nature comprises both a path of freedom and one of errancy, you must know what the ground is. When in this way you come to know that, in view of it being free from all impurities or in view of it being sullied by karmic actions and emotively toned action and reaction patterns, that which constitutes Buddhahood, on the one hand, and that which marks the status of a sentient being are self-emergent qualities, you will stop seeing and expecting me, Kun-tu bzang-po, to be a separately existing being or an artificially contrived Buddha who manifests himself like an apparition.[17]

The Second Chapter, explaining the Split into Samsāra and Nirvāṇa.

---

[17]An apparition (*sgyu-ma*) belongs to the world of the dichotomizing intellect (*rtog-pa*) and as such partakes in errancy (*'khrul-pa*). It may be mentioned in passing that the Buddhists clearly distinguish between an illusion and a hallucination (which for us is mostly restricted to the notion of psychic derangement). The Buddhists also have been careful not to pass judgment to the effect that the world is but an illusion. Lacking any existence as such it may on closer inspection appear *like* an apparition (*sgyu-ma lta-bu*, Skt. *māyopama*).

III

Again rTog-pa'i rdo-rje asked:

How does the differentiation into sensory cognition, mentation, and emotively toned mentation occur?

The answer was:

When the noetic capacity by its inherent dynamic has stirred from the all-ground and is about the meet its object, the 'all-ground cognitiveness' (*kun-gzhi'i rnam-par shes-pa*) has risen; it is as if the (indeterminate) psychological makeup (or the pervasive medium which makes a mind, in the strict sense of the word, possible) has been roused from its deep sleep. The concrete objects of the five senses are not yet really present; but a very subtle cognitive capacity which tends to grasp its objects has risen and makes itself ready in every respect to receive the impressions of the objects of the discursive mind, like a mirror. This receptivity is confronted with the objects by the five senses operating according to their structure (*rtsa*) and their specific motor activity (*rlung*) so that the eyes see color-shapes, the ears hear sounds, the nose smells fragrances, the tongue tastes flavors, and the body sense has kinesthetic sensations. Then through emotionality and mentation it arranges the action and reaction patterns of attraction, antipathy, and indifference and so sets up the cause and effect of Saṃsāra in a total manner, the cause being the triad of unknowing, karmic action, and emotive patterns of response. In brief, one speaks of an 'all-ground cognitiveness' because of its responsiveness; of the 'five senses' because of it looking outward and waking up to the sense objects; of 'emotionality' because of it becoming emotively toned in itself and organizing the emotive patterns of action and reaction; and of 'mentation' because of it differentiating between manifold things. Thus there are eight group-patterns of the mind.

Again rTog-pa'i rdo-rje asked:

How is it that since the whole field of appearance is errancy, such genuine objects of knowledge as houses and the like appear to sentient beings as houses and so on?

Kun-tu bzang-po replied:

Concerning appearance as it exists for those who understand

reality, there has never been any errancy-appearance; but for those who do not there is a difference in appearance according to the six forms of life in which these people find themselves, as a rule,[18] so that (what we humans consider to be) water appears for the gods as nectar, for the denizens of hell as glowing embers, and for the spirits as dark blood. This is so because their psychological makeup, the sensory equipment, and their mental operations, all of which are the manifestation of their karmic activity and the shaping of the noetic dynamic of the beings according to their situation and status, participate in the errancy-appearance which is roughly the same (for each group). However, this does not apply to the understanding or non-understanding itself, even if there be such appearance. For instance, for a yogi who rests in the contemplation of reality, rocks, houses, palaces, and the like will continue to appear, but on the part of his cognition there will not occur any reification. It is out of such a situation in which appearance and mentation are of the same nature and value, that such phenomena as rising into the sky like an eagle or floating on the water like a swan or passing straight through rocks will occur, because there is no reification of appearance.[19]

Therefore, I, Kun-tu bzang-po, have become a Buddha as the prototype of all Buddhas by not doing any good deed that in any way is connected with emotively toned responses, because I know that the existentiality of mind, the all-creating king, resides in the infinitude of the all-ground in an invisible and hidden manner as the substrate of that which is called Saṃsāra and Nirvāṇa; that although it is from this ground that the

---

[18] I.e., men, gods, demigods, animals, spirits, and denizens of hell.

[19] Klong-chen rab-'byams-pa, in his *Theg-pa chen-po'i man-ngag-gi bstan-chos yid-bzhin rin-po-che'i mdzod-kyi 'grel-pa padma dkar-po*, fol. 9*b*, expressly states that "it is extremely important to distinguish between appearance and the apparent object." What he wants to imply is that the notion of a physical object has not been abstracted from the data of sense but is something that answers certain postulates. On this problem see in particular C. D. Broad, *The Mind and Its Place in Nature*, 6th impression, London: Routledge & Kegan Paul, 1951, p. 217 ff.

boundless light of the magnificent appearance of the ground[20] will shine forth, it will not become mixed up with an object (which is a construction of mentation), but will remain pellucid in its own realm, will not falsify itself by reification, will not be fettered by the reified, and, discarding all formal cognition and the intellectual opacity that goes with it, will become the enlightened realization of the value sphere which is the realm of reality in the highest sense; and that moving away from the ground as formal cognition it is bound to become mentation and, associating with the formidable demon of the subject-object division, will perform its evil working of providing the requisites of karmic activity and emotional responses.

The Third Chapter, explaining the eight group-patterns of the mind.

IV

At that time Ye-shes rdo-rje, who is one with all Buddhas, rose from his seat and, in a spiritual mood where each being listens to his own teacher and transmits what he has heard to his environment, he asked:

Exalted One, is the no-thing-ness (*stong-cha*)[21] of pure

---

[20]The various ways in which this experience may come about have been detailed in the *Bla-ma yang-tig*, Vol. VAṂ, part I, fols. 1 ff.

[21]Skt. *śūnya*. This is one of the most controversial terms even in Buddhist philosophies. For the dGe-lugs-pa it means the fact that things do not exist in truth as such. It is understood by them as absolute negation (*med-dgag*). See, e.g., *Byang-chub lam-gyi rim-pa chung-ngu'i zin-bris blo-gsal rgya-mtsho'i 'jugs-ngogs*, fol. 187*b*. The rNying-ma-pas distinguished between *stong-cha* and *gsal-cha*. The former term is used to show that the knowing power arises from a completely indeterminate foundation that does not restrict its terms in any way. That is to say, the knowing power must be as nothing in order to unite with its intended object, but this being nothing is not sheer nothingness. Rather it is an intensive mode of existing. The second term is used to show that cognition does not consist in bringing forth some new entity but that it is revealing and manifesting. When the texts speak of 'mind as a creator' this never means that something new is created; it refers to what may be considered a hierarchy in the cognitive process. First there is the nothingness (*stong-cha*) ready to be filled with any structure and its activity is revealing and manifesting (*gsal-cha*), after that the postulates that define a 'physical object' are brought to that which has been revealed whereby the 'thing' has been 'created'.

knowing, which is free from all projectibility and which is referred to by the label 'initially pure' (*ka-dag*), all that is? Or, apart from this, what and how is the givenness of the radiant light symbolized as mother and child? Kindly explain this.

Kun-tu bzang-po replied:

'Initially pure' is a convenient label for the fact that in the sphere of transcending awareness where no errancy has ever occurred and which is not improved by the status of a Buddha as being something positive and also not vitiated by that of a sentient being as something negative, everything that makes its appearance is on the level of Buddhahood. This is what my message wants to impart. Since the modality of that which is labeled 'initially pure' is such as not to fall into either appearance or no-thing-ness, do not try to find Buddhahood in the creation of something which as something created is confined to the cause-effect relationship. Why? In my spiritual course which is beyond all toil and purposiveness, I speak of the light of the ground and the light of the path as one light; the division of it into a mother and child aspect is not the primary concern. On the contrary, the division into two of that which is not two is for the purpose of guiding the spiritually minded. In this respect the reality of the primordial ground, the sublime place of ultimate freedom, as vast as the sky, may well be called the Mother(-like) light. Only now, during the period of traversing the path of spiritual growth, the process of becoming acquainted with the potentiality of Buddhahood, which is of the nature of genuine light and which, like the air inclosed in a covered jar, is present in the midst of the psychophysical constituents, biotic forces, and fields of interaction, as well as the group-patterns of the mind, is given the designation 'child'. And when these aspects are felt as if the mother is really outside and around and the child huddled up inside, I speak of this experience as a meditative concentration in which the unexperienced approach Buddhahood.

Listen, Ye-shes rdo-rje! The infinitude of my transcending awareness is such that it is not something existing eternally, because its facticity (*ngo-bo*) has no determinate traits; and that it is also not something that has ceased to exist, because its actuality (*rang-bzhin*) is a light that is not dimmed in any way; and that it has neither bounds nor limits, because its observable quality (*rnam-pa*), compassion, does not know of any partiality.[22] Even when it is ultimate no-thing-ness it cannot be compared by something which is empty and nothing. It is like the luster of the sun and moon, revealing in its cognitiveness. My appearance is an outer no-thing-ness because in it there is no reified object, and my no-thing-ness is an inner no-thing-ness because in it no reifying mind is found, and the infinitude of cognitiveness is an inalienable no-thing-ness because the transcending awareness has not suffered a rift. In brief, since all entities which one admits to exist have found their fulfilment and *raison d'être* in a modality where no substance obtains, the ground is a great initial purity, the path a great self-authentication, and the goal a great self-freedom. By meditation Buddhahood is not attained, and by not meditating one does not stray into Saṃsāra. This great transcending awareness, pure from the very beginning and possessing the five properties of freshness, freedom, ease, encompassment, and settledness, does not change throughout the three aspects of time. Out of its realm the radiant light of the magnificent appearance of the ground, representing a pattern of communication in the highest perfection,[23] comes as a

---

[22]This is a critique of the conception of Being as held by the dGe-lugs-pa. Being (*yod-pa*) according to them is twofold: substance (*dngos-pa*) and non-substance (*dngos-med*). The former, consisting of the physical (*gzugs*), mind (*sems*), mental events (*sems-byung*), and a group which cannot be classified as either (*ldan-min 'du-byed*), is transitory, while that which makes up the category of non-substance is eternal. To give an example: The Buddha (*sangs-rgyas*) as an individual (*gang-zag*, listed in the group of the *ldan-min 'du-byed*) is transitory, but as Buddhahood he is eternal. Now, the term *dngos-med* 'non-substance' also can be interpreted as meaning a nonentity, something which has no existence at all. The actuality of transcending awareness is beyond all categories of existence which by definition would turn it into something finite. These subtle points have been elucidated in such rNying-ma-pa works as the *Don rnam-par nges-pa shes-rab ral-gri* by Mi-pham 'Jam-dbyangs rgya-mtsho (who died in the late 1920's), the *lTa grub shan-'byed gnad-kyi sgron-me* by mDo-sngags bstan-pa'i nyi-ma, and others.

[23]*longs-sku*, Skt. *sambhogakāya*. The communicative character of this pattern is evident from the fact that according to the rNying-ma-pas the Tantras have been communicated from the Sambhogakāya of the Buddhas and not by the historical Buddha as the dGe-lugs-pas claim.

self-rising appearance where the light shed by the lamp of self-risen analytical awareness marks the beginning, that of the lamp of distant vision marks the gates through which the ground appears, that of the lamp of pure value reveals the beauty of the ground that has appeared, and that of the lamp of glittering colors illumines the distinct features of the ground that has appeared.[24] When in this way the great pellucidity of pure knowing, which is an ultimate continuity, using the four lamps (just mentioned) (i) meets the light of reality in its directness, then (ii) the felt knowledge of reality becomes more and more intense, (iii) cognition attains its fullest measure, and (iv) reality reigns alone.[25] This fact that the goal is perfectly present in the light of the path because the four lucidity experiences are ultimate experiences, is the intellectually unfathomable mystery of Kun-tu bzang-po.

The Fourth Chapter, explaining the Path of the Magnificent Appearance of the Ground.

V

Again Ye-shes rdo-rje, who is one with all Buddhas, asked:

O Teacher, kindly explain the difference between communicating existence as true existence and communicated existence as the true perspective of reality.[26]

Kun-tu bzang-po replied:

The starting-point of communicating existence is the materialization of the dynamics of spiritual existence. Its distinctive characteristic is that it is nothing and yet everything.[27] Its

---

[24]The names of these four lamps resist any attempt to translate them in a lexical manner. Their significance has been detailed in the *Theg-pa'i mchog rin-po-che'i mdzod*, fols. 288*a* ff.

[25]See also *Bla-ma yang-tig*, Vol. VAṂ, part I, fols. 18*a* ff.

[26]The terms *ngo-bo-nyid-kyi sku 'bras-bu'i longs-sku chen-po* and *ngo-bo-nyid-kyi snang-ba chos-nyid-kyi longs-sku*, which defy any lexical translation, are peculiar to 'Jigs-med gling-pa.

[27]*rNam-pa thams-cad-pa'i mchog dang ldan-pa* = *rnam-kun mchog ldan-gyi stong-nyid*, *sarvākāravaropetā śūnyatā* (*Ratnagotravibhāga Mahāyānottaratantraśāstra* I, 92) has found various interpretations in Tibetan literature. The dGe-lugs-pa conception of it as absolute negation (*med-dgag*) has been severely criticized by Mi-pham 'Jam-dbyangs rgya-mtsho (also known as

modality is that it does not move away from actuality of spiritual existence. The term 'communicating existence' itself means the presence of the spiritual level of utter radiance, which is the eleventh (in the hierarchy of spiritual levels), because there is continual communication concerning the message of Buddhism by virtue of the fact that everything without exception constituting the cause-and-effect relationship of the three existential patterns[28] and their seven properties is in view.

Out of this communicating existence, having five determinate features,[29] the communicator is seen, like one's face in a mirror, according to the temperature of the aspirant, and it is through the compassion of the teacher rDo-rje-'chang (Vajradhara) that the Buddha-realms of the ten regions of the compass, such as mNgon-par dga'-ba, dPal-ldan brtsegs-pa, Padma brtsegs-pa, Las rab grub-pa, Me-ri 'bar-ba, and others, are manifested. This experience is spoken of as a mode of existence which is halfway between communicating and communicated existence because Buddha-realms and all that pertains to them have become manifested (and projected), while in the immediate evidence they are not different from the communicating existence. This is so because the light of the potentiality of Buddhahood, which as the radiant light of the magnificent appearance of the primordial ground shining in one's heart marks the beginning of the five kinds of transcendent awareness (i.e., the awareness of reality as such, the mirror-like awareness, the

---

Mi-pham 'Jam-dbyangs rnam-rgyal rgya-mtsho and 'Jam-dpal dgyes-pa'i rdo-rje) in his *gNyug-sems zur-dpyad skor-gyi gsung-sgros thor-bu-rnams phyogs-gcig-tu bsdus-pa rdo-rje rin-po-che'i phreng-ba*, part III, fols. 61*a*, 68*a* etc.

[28]*sku, gsung-thugs*, Skt. *kāya, vāk, citta*. As distinct from *lus, ngag, yid*, these terms refer to that which in existentialist thought is considered as authentic being-in-the-world, authentic communication, and an unbiased perspective. *sku* has many features in common with K. Jaspers' concept of *Existenz*.

[29]I.e., the spiritual teacher, his realm of residence, his entourage, time (as time itself, rather than as an event in time), and the teacher's message. See Rong-zom chos-kyi bzang-po's commentary quoted above, fols. 20*a* ff., and, in particular also the *dPal-ldan gSang-ba snying-po'i spyi-don-gyi bshad-pa'i zin-bris bla-ma'i man-ngag don gsal snying-po legs-bshad rol-mtsho*, fols. 24*a* ff. (MS.) by 'Gyur-med tshe-dbang mchog-grub.

awareness of the equality [of all entities of reality], the awareness of the specific nature of all that is [as being nothing in itself], and the effortless awareness of reality realization) becoming established in their own function sphere, now brings about the signs of cognition reaching its maximum clarity, and as communicated existence serves the needs of the sentient beings as in a dream, even during the period of the intermediate state between death and rebirth. It does so even if those who have seen the gate through which one passes into the spiritual development within this sublime mystic course, and who strive to abide by this great commitment, do not experience the four kinds of felt knowledge in their highest intensity during this life.[30] Therefore the difference between the two kinds of existence is as follows: Those who live in these Buddha-realms are Bodhisattvas who will become Buddhas in their next life; the communicating existence, however, which is the pure no-thing-ness of the presence of Buddhahood, is not seen by the beings on the ten spiritual levels participating in this continual communication.

When this explanation had been given, the attending Buddhas and Bodhisattvas in their joy of participating in immediate evidence through this immediate evidence, asked:

O Teacher Kun-tu bzang-po, since in your spiritual being there is neither identity nor difference, kindly explain the existential mode of the inner light of reality[31] which is the ultimate knowledge of ultimate reality in ultimate reality.

Then the exalted primordial Lord by the mere thought of the inconceivable reality became silent and when he had answered the question by way of being silent, his face, hands, and other limbs and marks, all of which are the unchanging indestructibility of reality, faded in the process of awakening to Buddhahood (as infinite transcendence). Then Ye-shes rdo-rje who is one

[30]I.e., reality experienced directly, the knowledge of reality becoming more and more intense, cognition attaining its maximum clarity, and reality reigning alone.

[31]Technically known as *gzhon-nu bum-pa'i sku*.

with all Buddhas, exhorted by the compassion of the inconceivable mystery of Kun-tu bzang-po and having opened the great treasure of wisdom revealing the existence of an ultimate reality, expressed his feelings in thse words:

> Indeed!
> The Buddha-existence of true reality awareness
> Which is a unitary existence to which
> Neither cognitive existence, being transitory,
> Nor radiancy, being continuous, apply separately,
> Is the ever young inner light;
> It is the essence of the five Buddhas and their awareness
> In the vastness of radiant reality
> As infinite as the sky which has neither end nor center.
> It is ever young because it does not age nor ever become frail,
> And it is an inner light because its cognitive nature is radiant within.
> It is a subtle existence which is not inert although
> The very essence and specific character of the activity
> Of unchanging transcending awareness
> And discriminative acumen in incessant work
> Have subsided in the vastness of reality.
> All the qualities of the two perceptible patterns of being,[32]
> Residing in it, thought not shining outward,
> Like the new moon in the sky,
> Appear differently to the spiritual aspirants, (and in so doing)
> They yet remain one with the vastness of ultimate spiritual being,
> Are perfect in all major and minor characteristics by way of authentic communication
> And through authentic being-in-the-world guide countless aspirants.
> In brief, that which is the great transcending awareness

---

[32]I.e., Sambhogakāya and Nirmāṇakāya. These terms which are usually left untranslated reveal their meaning in the light of the Tantras. They are grounded in noetic existence (Jñānadharmakāya) and are manifested as authentic communication and authentic being. In other words, the mind (Jñānadharmakāya) can be fulfilled only in the human person which points to transcendence (Nirmāṇakaya) by authentic communication (Sambhogakāya), not by becoming dissolved in a frozen Absolute.

Of the intellectually inconceivable mystery of
The Buddha's
Existence, communication, spirituality, culturedness, and activity[33]
Is in union with the realm of the Real.

The Fifth Chapter, explaining the Great Level of Freedom as goal attainment; the clear statement concerning Existence and Knowledge.

Here, as is the case with other Tibetan texts, the preamble is of particular significance, because it outlines the whole philosophical-religious background of the writer. There is no doubt that 'Jigs-med gling-pa has been deeply influenced by the *gSang-ba snying-po*, especially in his view of human awareness. The philosophical tradition of the rNying-ma-pas, discussed in the introduction, made them realize at an early stage that awareness is not a kind of *thing*, but a mode of being, manifesting itself in various levels. As the union of the noetic power with subjective being it may present itself as the relative knowledge of things in relation to man's projects in a world of ego-centered existence and practical action. Or it may detach itself from such frameworks and attain an unrestricted perspective from which reality can be known as it is without inner warpings. This latter mode of knowledge is achieved only after a long process of intensive inner discipline. But inasmuch as in ordinary life practical considerations have always reigned supreme such detached knowledge is commonly held to be 'merely subjective,' if not utterly incommunicable, although it lends itself to communication by symbols which can be recognized 'objectively'. There is, however, the danger that in stating the problem in this way we may misrepresent it and misunderstand what it is all about by taking symbols as dead counters to be manipulated like any other thing and by

---

[33] *sku, gsung, thugs, yon-tan, 'phrin-las.* Skt. *kāya, vāk, citta, guṇa, karma.* This quintuple division shows that the spiritual development process does not lead into some quietistic state but that it enables man to act in the light of his infinite possibilities.

overlooking the communicative value of them, stimulating him to whom this knowledge is communicated, to find access to similar experiences.

A symbol of inner spiritual growth and detached knowledge is Kun-tu bzang-po who, residing in the Akaniṣṭha heaven in the company of spiritual beings, points beyond himself toward transcendence, which is the main theme of 'Jigs-med gling-pa. More specifically, Kun-tu bzang-po is the symbol for that which in the technical language of philosophy is known as 'self-knowledge' (*rang-rig*). It has been as much a point of controversy in Buddhism as it has been in Western philosophies. The rNying-ma-pas, however, did not for a moment interpret this term as meaning that a mind knows itself by way of a 'privileged access to its own doings',[34] being its own target, as which it has been criticized by the Prāsangikas, but merely as meaning that we know we are doing certain things and are feeling somehow while we are doing these things and feeling in certain ways.

Knowledge, in Buddhist philosophy, is always intentional in structure. That is to say, we cannot know without knowing something. As a matter of fact, if there were any knowledge without being knowledge of something it could not deserve the name "knowledge" and would be indistinguishable from inertness. That which Kun-tu bzang-po knows in knowing that he knows, is the Akaniṣṭha-heaven. Just as man is *in* the world, knowing it by being in cognitive union with it, so Kun-tu bzang-po resides *in* the Akaniṣṭha-heaven, knowing it in the same way. Sometimes this knowledge is depicted in the well-known images of a God being in conjugal embrace with his consort. Far from illustrating some sexual episode, such representations indicate a total relationship in which there is a blend of opposites. The various postures also represent the different phases in the cognitive process.[35] Here, as in all other

[34]Gilbert Ryle, *The Concept of Mind*, New York: Barnes & Noble, 1949, pp. 154, 197.

[35]See gYung-ston rdo-rje dpal-bzang's commentary, quoted above, fol. 86*a*.

instances where the problem of knowledge is discussed in Buddhism, we must be careful not to confuse this terminal union, which may be called 'noetic identity', with the mere reception of a causal impulse or with complete existential identity. Nothing of what in other mystic philosophies is called the merging of an individual soul in an all-soul, is found in the whole of Tibetan Buddhism. Knowledge always remains intentional in structure.

While Kun-tu bzang-po may further be said to symbolize the integrative aspect of knowing, the five spiritual rulers represent the analytic function of knowledge within a total pattern of knowing. Both aspects, the integrative and the analytical ones, are inseparables and their classification as such can never be understood as being rigidly established. Thus, the spiritual 'rulers', each of them representing a partial structure within a total one, participate in the integrative function by being 'Gods' (*lha*), that is, ciphers of transcendence, while they are analytic by lending themselves to being projected outward as the five psycho-physical constituents which by virtue of being 'projects' (*rtog-pa*) lend themselves to further analysis.[36]

---

[36]According to Rong-zom chos-kyi bzang-po, *loc. cit.*, fols. 56*a* ff., and gYung-ston rdo-rje dpal-bzang, *loc. cit.*, fols. 26*a* ff., and 'Gyur-med tshe-dbang mchog grub, *loc. cit.*, fols. 24*b* ff., we have the following correspondences:

Projects	*Ciphers of Transcendence*	*Existential Patterns*
Consciousness	Aksobhya	Spirituality
The physical (color-shape)	Vairocana	Existence
Feeling	Ratnasambhava	Culturedness
Ideation	Amitābha	Communication
Motivation	Amoghasiddhi	Activity

The female consorts in this order are:

Spatiality	Dhātvīśvarī	Spirituality
Solidification	Buddhalocanā	Existence
Cohesion	Māmakī	Culturedness
Temperature	Pāṇḍaravāsinī	Communication
Movement	(Karma-) Tārā	Activity

The action sphere of knowledge is primarily the senses, which again are both integrative and analytic. As the integrative or immanent action the senses of seeing, hearing, smelling, and tasting are in cognitive union with their 'objects' or color-shape, sound, fragrance, and flavor, and as the analytic or transitive action these senses are in union with the time projections of a past, a present, an as yet undetermined time aspect, and a future. Each set again represents a specific structure.[37]

In arranging his subject matter according to the triple division into the starting point, the path, and the goal, 'Jigs-med gling-pa follows the traditional method of presenting the essence of Buddhism. The underlying assumption is the psychologically verifiable fact that man is capable of ascending to the highest levels of spiritual awareness and also of falling into the deepest abyss of misery and suffering. This division is furthermore linked to three questions. The first is a metaphysical one: What is that from which these alternatives are possible? It is obvious that such a question can be asked only in view of a possible path, where 'path' is synonymous with a possible developmental process. This leads to the second question: Of what kind is that which inspires us and sustains our highest aspirations? The last question is epistemological and genetic: How do we come to know?

---

[37]According to the same sources we have

Immanent Sensory Processes		and their *Objective References* as	
Projects	*Ciphers*	*Projects*	*Ciphers*
To see	Kṣitigarbha	Color-form	Lāsyā (La-sya-ma)
To hear	Vajrapāṇi	Sound	Gītā (Ghir-ti-ma)
To smell	Gaganagarbha	Fragrance	Mālā (Mā-le-ma)
To taste	Avalokiteśvara	Flavor	Nṛtyā (Nir-ti-ma)

Transitive Sensory Processes		*Objective References*	
Projects	*Ciphers*	*Projects*	*Ciphers*
Seeing	Maitreya	Past	Dhu-pe-ma
Hearing	Nirvaraṇaviṣkambhin	Present	Puṣpe-ma
Smelling	Samantabhadra	Indeterminateness	A-lo-ke-ma
Tasting	Mañjuśrī	Future	Gandhe-ma

'Jigs-med gling-pa answers the first question by pointing to an 'all-ground' (*kun-gzhi*), a substrate that underlies the passage from a more or less private superstrate to the end phase of the developmental process, termed Saṃsāra and Nirvāṇa, respectively. Saṃsāra is basically a descriptive term for the observable fact that man in ignorance of his real being is driven by his actions and emotions, while Nirvāṇa refers to the experienceable passage beyond suffering.

The superstrate seems to be a pervasive medium of which the incipient mind is a modification insofar as its cognitive quality becomes predominant over the indeterminate character of the pervasive medium itself. This distinction between a superstrate which exhibits indeterminate as well as cognitive traits, and an 'all-ground' or substrate is, in a sense, a piecemeal mode of apprehension of the ground, which, however, does not lead to any destruction because the distinct modes are united in the unitary 'all-ground'. Yet there is the danger that in this piecemeal apprehension we may center all our attention on the developmental phase and lose sight of the 'all-ground', or even identify the 'all-ground' with the ground underlying one particular direction of the development. This actually has happened and the tendency has been to conceive the 'all-ground' as the ground leading to Saṃsāra.[38] The rNying-ma-pas never lost sight of the 'all-ground' and in order to counter the tendency to move away from transcendence into finiteness coined a new term, 'the initially pure' (*ka-dag*), which, with the exception of a few authors, is identical with the 'all-ground' (*kun-gzhi*) in the sense of infinite transcendence.

Although the terminology used by 'Jigs-med gling-pa is intriguingly similar to the one employed in the Vijñānavāda system of philosophy, where an 'all-ground cognitiveness' (*kun-gzhi rnam-par shes-pa*, Skt. *ālayavijñāna*) figures promi-

[38]A critique of this tendency is found in Rang-byung rdo-rje's auto-commentary to his *Zab-mo nang-don*, which is reproduced and enlarged upon by Blo-gros mtha-yas in his *rNal-'byor bla-na-med-pa'i rgyud-sde rgya-mtsho'i snying-po bsdus-pa zab-mo nang-gi don nyung-ngu'i tshig-gis rnam-par 'grol-ba zab-don snang-byed*, fol. 12*a*.

nently, there is a marked difference. For the Vijñānavādins the 'all-ground cognitiveness' is an indeterminate cognition, a subjective responsiveness and readiness, which tends to be filled by a concrete content of that which makes up the finite world. For 'Jigs-med gling-pa this 'all-ground cognitiveness' is merely a one-sided development out of a pervasive medium or superstrate on a substrate, that might as well have developed into another direction. That is to say, in the former case cognition develops into the theoretic cognition of things other than they are because this cognition becomes tainted and colored by some bias or other, in the latter it remains true to itself and becomes the cognition of reality as it is. Both possibilities derive from the superstrate or pervasive medium (*kun-gzhi khams*) which for the Vijñānavādins is identical with the 'all-ground' as long as the cognition tends to become involved in the world of finite things, while for them in the cognition of reality as it is, the all-ground no longer figures inasmuch as it has turned into the so-called 'mirror-like awareness'. 'Jigs-med gling-pa agrees with the Vijñānavādins insofar as the cognition of reality as it is is a change in perspective, but for him this new perspective exists only in a certain closeness to transcendence. We are thus presented with two outlooks. In the one case the inferior formal intellect is confronted with dead things incapable of offering deliverance and deeper meaning, while in the other there reigns the freedom of the spirit moving in a realm of values which alone can give meaning to life. In this way also two basic paths are open. Man may give himself over to the world and its ultimately futile aims, or he may see the fleeting character of the world and give himself over to his existential possibilities in the face of transcendence. In this connection the tradition that derives from Vimalamitra expressly speaks of a path upward to and being a path of freedom and a path going downward and getting lost in a maze of bewilderment, in the flickering appearances distorted by subjective aims and biases. It here so happens that man strays away from 'existence' (*sku*) into mere 'organismic being' (*lus*), from the vividness of pure awareness (*rig-pa*) into the toilsomeness of mentation (*sems*), and from a sphere of values (*dbyings*) into the world of constructed objects (*yul*).[39] Decisive choice occurs at a moment, and when decisive action in the present moment is directed to the future in the light of one's ultimate possibilities, the short span which we call a human life can be filled with a consistent and even timeless content. The two basic paths, which are the constant theme of the Tantras, evince a certain similarity to the unauthentic and authentic pathways in modern existentialist thought. The main difference, however, is that in Buddhism even the unauthentic path into the world is not tainted with guilt. Guilt can apply only to a specific act and when it is finished. The straying into the world, however, is never a finished act and hence is neither guilty nor non-guilty.

In his conception of infinite transcendence, 'Jigs-med gling-pa goes far beyond the arguments of classical philosophy for it. Transcendence (*ka-dag*) is wholly other, although unlike the first cause of change in classical realistic philosophy, it does not exist by itself in separation from all finite entities that make up what we call the world. Moreover, it is neither personal nor omnipotent, for that which we associate with creation and a creator is the working of our own ignorance[40] which in a certain way is connected with transcendence and in its connection with it is termed 'the given' (*lhun-grub*). The question as to whether transcendence is all that is, reflects a certain tendency among the rNying-ma-pas to center attention on merely one feature, either on transcendence or on the given. Both views are, to speak with Karl Jaspers, too 'ontological' and 'objective'. The fallacies involved in such a procedure have been detailed by gYung-ston rdo-rje dpal bzang-po. According to him,[41] transcendence (*ka-dag*) can be taken entitatively (*dbyings*), in which case there would never be any errancy because transcendence cannot be the sustaining cause of unknowing; or it can be taken operationally

---

[39]*Man-ngag dum-dum khrigs dum-bu bdun-cu rtsa bzhi-pa* (=*Bi-ma snying-tig*, Vol. VIII, fols. 1 ff.).

[40]So gYung-ston rdo-rje dpal-bzang, *loc. cit.*, fols. 43*a*–43*b*.

[41]*Loc. cit.*, fol. 45*b*.

(*ye-shes*), in which case our projects (*rtog-pa*) would be one thing and the ciphers of transcendence (*lha*) another because with the realization of true existence (*sku*) and its pure awareness (*ye-shes*) all unknowing with its projects has been abolished. Transcendence also does not imply that, conceived along Neo-Platonic and pantheistic lines, the world is an inescapable emanation from the divine nature of the first cause. If this were the case, the world, which again may be viewed under the aspects of Reality (*chos-nyid*) and the Real (*chos-can*), would in the first case be so intimately entwined and fused with the divine being that it would be impossible to overcome unknowing, and every attempt to do so by setting out on a path of spiritual development would be meaningless. In the latter case even the attainment of Buddhahood would be something futile because it would not differ from the actuality of unknowing.[42] Hence, if the world is everything then there is no transcendence, but if there is then there must be in the world something that points to it. 'Jigs-med gling-pa here refers to the experience which is called the magnificent appearance of the ground in which transcendence is poignantly revealed through certain symbols of which the religious image of Kun-tu bzang-po is the most stimulating. Kun-tu bzang-po is not a person, for a person is an individual substance of a rational nature, a being existing in himself. Nor is he the immanent power of the world; he is beyond and above all Gods. This gives us the clue to understanding the answer to the second question bearing on the religious aspect. Intimately related to the philosophical or metaphysical problem of infinite transcendence, the religious implications neither favor a sort of theism nor can they be interpreted as being of a pantheistic character. Kun-tu bzang-po is a cipher through which transcendence shines forth, but is not transcendence itself, and as a cipher Kun-tu bzang-po is not a sign which is always distinct from the *signatum* that can be known independently.

'Jigs-med gling-pa's unique theory of infinite transcendence becomes most conspicuous in the goal realization by his dis-

---

[42] *Loc. cit.*, fol. 46*b*.

tinction between communicated existence, which is a true cipher, and communicating existence, which is beyond all form and change and, similar to Jaspers' 'ultimate *Umgreifende*' is never seen, although it is possessed by every being as the 'inner light' which is man's very self. It too cannot be known as an object, and it also cannot be grasped as a subject behind the phenomena of world and man. Rather it is the awareness of the transcendent which remains inaccessible except through this awareness, illustrated by the simile, frequently found in Tantric literature, of the child coming to its mother.

'Jigs-med gling-pa's view of the origination of human awareness in its finiteness very rarely strays from the conceptions of the Vijñānavādins insofar as they accepted eight group-patterns of consciousness.[43]

From this short analysis of the basic ideas of 'Jigs-med gling-pa it becomes obvious that his way of philosophizing is much more akin to modern trends in philosophy than to the classical ideas. The elucidation of Buddhist philosophy and religion in relation to, or as counterpart of, Western modes of thought will be the task of the future and such comparative studies may well help in gaining a clearer picture of the working of the human mind in realizing the problem of being and value which is beyond formal intellectualism and its fetters of finiteness.

---

[43]According to the *Grub-pa'i mtha'i rnam-par bzhag-pa rin-po-che'i phreng-ba*, fol. 12*a*, only those Vijñānavādins who followed the Five Divisions of the *Yogācārabhūmi* recognized eight group patterns; all others accepted the traditional six, leaving out the 'emotively toned mentation' and the 'all-ground cognitiveness'.

Some Aspects of Tibetan Religious Thought

It generally has been recognized that true religion, as distinct from the comfortable religiosity of the sham article, overarches the whole of human culture and the whole of life; that it inspires, sustains, and guards man's highest aspirations. In recognizing the importance of religion it is, of course, dangerous to conceive of 'religion' in terms of one particular religion or creed which is but the end formulation (and often ossification) of a certain aspect of religion, not religion itself. It is equally disastrous to make religion mean everything, and so nothing. Every attempt to define religion in terms of man's 'feeling' or 'sense' or 'attitude', all of which emphasize what is better called 'religious experience', must fail in spite of the fact that such definitions are valuable in a given context, which always means to have singled out a certain aspect. Religion, and more exactly religious knowledge, includes and transcends all these aspects. This transcendence certainly has a mystic character, but it is not *eo ipso* mysticism, which, like a creed, may be said to be a systematization, and hence a loss of the vividness and richness of religion. Transcendence must be understood as a dynamic movement, not as a static entity, and therefore by its very nature it transcends the idea that "all the *different* things in the world become *one*, become identical with one another."[1] It is true that

---

[1]W. T. Stace, *Religion and the Modern Mind*, New York: J. B. Lippincott Co., 1960, p. 258.

in the writings of the mystics 'oneness' is emphasized, but it is wrong to conclude that this is an existential or ontological oneness; rather, it is a noetic oneness.

Although religion always implies acceptance and commitment, it is more than that as it is also the desire to understand more fully and clearly that to which one has committed oneself or is about to commit oneself. Here, mind does not and must not cease to inquire; thus what is found by such a critical and constructive scrutiny becomes the cornerstone of a more secure and enlightened reconstruction.

Such an attitude of enquiry and commitment is found most markedly with the rNying-ma-pas, whose contribution to the development of Buddhism in Tibet, both as a religion and a philosophy, is still little known. The rNying-ma-pas are unique in the sense that, unlike the other great schools of thought, the bKa'-brgyud-pas, Sa-skya-pas, and dGe-lugs-pa in particular, who all give preference to the Indian habit of emphasizing epistemology and logic as the main objectives of the philosophical and religious quest, they also recognize the importance of metaphysics and psychology. They also openly acknowledge the contribution of the Chinese teachers who must be considered the forerunners of Zen Buddhism.[2] It is because of this

---

[2]On the whole, all schools of Buddhism in Tibet are unanimous in rejecting the teaching of the Chinese Hva-shang. However, as Padma dkar-po (in his *Phyag-rgya chen-po'i man-ngag-gi bshad-sbyar rgyal-ba'i gan-mdzod*, fol. 107*a*), points out, we have to distinguish between the *ston-min* and *rtsen-min* lines of thought. The former is to be rejected, while the latter is acceptable. Failure to distinguish between these two sections of Chinese Buddhist thought has been the reason to cast aspersions on the bKa'-brgyud-pas and rNying-ma-pas by the Sa-skya-pas and dGe-lugs-pas. Klong-chen rab-'byams-pa (in his *sDe-gsum snying-po'i don-'grel gnas-lugs rin-po-che'i mdzod ces-bya-ba'i grel-pa*, fol. 31*a*), after quoting from the *Khyung-chen*, makes the remarkable statement: "Although it did not enter the minds of those with an inferior kind of intelligence, what the great teacher Hva-shang said at the time (of the alleged debate at bSam-yas) was a factual statement." In his *Kun-mkhyen zhal-lung bdud-rtsi'i thigs-pa*, which is a commentary on the *Gnas-lugs rdo-rje'i tshig-rkang*, 'Jigs-med gling-pa openly defends the Hva-shang and declares (fol. 6*b*) that what is alleged to be the defect of the Hva-shang's teaching is actually the quintessence of the *Prajñāpāramitā*

broader outlook of the rNying-ma-pas that among them we find the largest number of "philosophers in tradition"—to use a term coined by Karl Jaspers—as distinct from mere traditionalists. While the details of the rNying-ma-pas' conception of Buddhism will have to be worked out in future studies, at the present state of our knowledge it can be stated plainly that their treatment of Buddhism is the outcome both of an intensely philosophical spirit, discontent with the mere rationality of philosophical systems[3] and convinced that it is possible to know reality by direct acquaintance rather than by description, and of an intensely religious spirit, discontent with mere dogmatism and shallow sentimentality. Their penetrating insights also come as a corrective of what is commonly held to be the nature of mysticism, a deliberate cult of alienation from this world and the realization of absolute Being and absolute Good, which by definition must remain a postulate rather than become a living reality. As a matter of fact, the rNying-ma-pas' kind of mysticism, if ever this be the correct term for their line of thought, is concerned with the unity of the phenomenal and noumenal; it avoids the ideas of an absolute One and an absolute

---

works. As they are the words of the Buddha, only the Buddha himself can decide whether the Hva-shang is correct or not in having understood the Buddha's words. In his *Grub-mtha' thams-cad-kyi khungs dang 'dod-tshul ston-pa legs-bshad shel-gyi me-long*, section *rGya-nag-gi yul-du nang-pa sangs-rgyas-pa'i grub-mtha' byung-tshul*, fol. 13*b*, Blo-bzang chos-kyi nyi-ma dpal bzang-po (A.D. 1737–1803) distinguishes between the Hva-shang Mahāyāna proper and the *tsung-men* line of thought within Chinese Buddhism in Tibet and concludes with the significant statement that "because the teaching of one Hva-shang is wrong it is not proper to hold all Hva-shang views to be erroneous." There can be no doubt that the rNying-ma-pas had close contacts with Chinese Buddhist teachings. gYung-ston rdo-rje dpal-bzang's conception of three truths instead of the ordinary two truths (*dPal gsang-ba snying-po'i rgyud-don gsal-byed me-long*, fols. 27*b*–28*a*) clearly indicates T'ien-t'ai thought. All quotations are from block prints or their microfilms in the author's possession.

[3]The discontent with philosophy as the establishment of a rigid system has found its expression in the *Kun-tu bzang-po'i dgongs-nyams* by 'Jigs-med gling-pa. It has been forcefully elaborated in the *'Od-gsal rdzogs-pa chen-po yang-gsang bla-na-med-pa spyi'i khyad-par-gyi khrid-yig lam-bzang ye-shes snying-po* by A-'dzoms 'Brug-pa Rig-'dzin sNa-tshogs rang-grol.

Many, pivots of traditional idealistic and realistic thought. They recognize the unity of reality and the supreme value of this unity in the sense that it is an act of decision, just as the fragmentation of reality and the accompanying loss of value and its inherent feeling of frustration and suffering is an act of decision, which in relation to and contradistinction to the former is considered to be a straying away from the possibility of authentic being.[4]

In substantiation of these characteristics I shall give the translation of a short text by 'Jigs-med gling-pa (A.D. 1729–98) and then analyze the essential points with reference to other texts.[5]

THE ANALYSIS OF THE THREE ESSENTIAL POINTS IN THE ABSOLUTE-PERFECTION DOCTRINE[6]

Salutation to Kun-tu bzang-po's vastness![7]

Inasmuch as those who in this degenerate age meditate on (the meaning of) Absolute Perfection have no clear ideas about

---

[4]See, e.g., the *Kun-tu bzang-po'i dgongs-pa zang-thal-las Bi-ma-mi-tra'i snyan-brgyud chen-mo rgyal-po-la gdams-pa yang-gsang bla-na-med-pa rdzogs-pa chen-po'i 'grel-pa ye-shes rang-gsal* = Vol. *Hri*, section *Ce* of the *Dgongs-pa zang-thal* by Rig-'dzin rGod-kyi ldem-'phru-can), fol. 27*a* and *b* (hereinafter cited as "*Ce*").

[5]I am deeply indebted to the Incarnate Lama of Dar-thang monastery, Kun-dga' dge-legs, who made this text and the other rNying-ma-pa works from which I quote available to me and with whom I was able to discuss every point relating to the meaning of the texts.

[6]"rDzogs-pa chen-po'i gnad gsum shan-'byed." This essay forms part of the *Klong-chen snying-gi thig-le.*

[7]*Kun-tu bzang-po*, in Sanskrit *Samantabhadra*, must be sharply distinguished from the Bodhisattva of the same name. Here, the word *Kun-tu bzang-po* is synonymous with *rig-pa*, the cognition of being *qua* being, or a value-sustained cognition having a strongly aesthetic character. Its transcendental character is explained in Klong-chen rab-'byams-pa's *Chos-dbyings rin-po-che'i mdzod* (Gangtok, ed., 1964; published by Dodrup Chen Rinpoche and distributed by Tarthang Tulku of Sanskrit University, Varanasi), fol. 3, and in the commentary on this passage in his own commentary, *Chos-dbyings rin-po'che'i mdzod-kyi 'grel-pa lung-gi gter-mdzod*, and in gYung-ston rdo-rje dpal bzang, *op. cit.*, fol. 12*b*.

the nature of the ground, the path, and the goal, among these partisans of wishful thinking and meditational exercises, those who will become free from the fetters of their intellectualism are as rare as a star at noon. Therefore I shall give the analysis of three essential points, which is [like] the perfect majesty of a lion:[8] the distinction between mentation and value awareness. *Samaya.*

The all-ground[9] is the foundation of all that is, Saṃsāra and Nirvāṇa. It is not different from turbid water. When delusion, lying latent in it, has started its deceptive work, the clarity of value-awareness in transcendent knowledge has gone into hiding.

Decisive existence[10] is like water when the mud has settled.

---

[8]This seems to be an allusion to the Tantra of the same name, *Seng-ge rtsal rdzogs gnad-kyi don*, the title of which is explained in the *Dung-yig-can rgyud-kyi klong don bsdus-pa sgron-ma snang-byed*, fol. 14*b* (= *Bi-ma snying-tig*, Vol. V) as follows: "A lion is not frightened by others [because he is superior to other animals as is this Tantra to other doctrines]; coming forward in the majesty of overpowering the appearance of error (because through the self-majesty of the proper viewpoint error is resolved and freedom as freedom is established); perfect because the three essential points are complete and perfect (i.e., the body is the eye, the object space and transcending awareness is the lamp of spirituality whereby the three essentials of viewpoint, contemplation, and action are an integral presence)." What has been given in parentheses is contained in the text as notes.

[9]*kun-gzhi*, in Sanskrit *ālaya*. The rNying-ma-pas distinguish between the *kun-gzhi*, 'all-ground', and the *kun-gzhi'i rnam-shes* (in Sanskrit, *ālaya-vijñāna*), which is a cognitive potency within the all-ground and which represents the whole apperceptive mass. There are subtle, but nevertheless important, differences in opinion about the nature of the all-ground cognitiveness among the various Buddhist schools of Tibet. None of their interpretations, however, justifies the current lexical translation of 'storehouse consciousness'.

[10]*chos-sku*, in Sanskrit *dharmakāya*. Lexical translations usually leave this word untranslated. This is the reason why the importance of Eastern thought is far from being recognized. Throughout this article I have tried to give a translation of each term, however difficult such an enterprise may be. There is no harm in using a foreign term, provided it has been adequately defined, and once this has been done the foreign term has its proper place in a footnote. There is a big difference between a translation that is readable and an edition of an oriental text. The Tibetan language facilitates the task of 'translating' because it is more precise than Sanskrit and clarifies the meaning of Buddhist Sanskrit terms. Thus, the use of *sku* and *lus*, both of which are said to

Its nature is the removal of incidental impurities [due to mentation]. It is the facticity of freedom and of everything positive. It is the transcendent knowledge which henceforth knows no erring.

Therefore, just as water and mud have separated, so decisive existence has parted from a nondescript state of being.

Be firmly settled in the openness of decisive existence which is a self-revealing value-awareness; witness [the world] as a play from the domain of values accessible through unsullied transcendent knowledge!

The all-ground cognitiveness is like ice on water. It comes about as the activity of grasping [as an object] the felt presence of ultimate being[11] and, becoming attached to the object so grasped, it is generally mistaken.

Therefore, the essential point is to become translated into decisive existence which is a value-awareness in the transcendent knowledge of appearance manifesting itself as external objects, feelings, ideas, and so on, being nothing in itself.[12]

Those who do not understand it in this way and take the all-ground for decisive existence are like blind men without a guide, erring about in a desert. As they are deluded about the nature of the ground and the goal, the path by which Bud-

---

mean 'body' in a dictionary, is that *sku* expresses the idea of existence in an almost Parmenidian sense and that *lus* refers to the physical organism. See in particular Klong-chen rab-'byams-pa's *Theg-pa mchog-gi mdzod*, fols. 265*a*–269*b*.

[11]*ngo-bo'i gshis*. This term is peculiar to the rNying-ma-pa and bKa'-brgyud-pa diction. Usually the rNying-ma-pas use *ngo-bo* and the bKa'-brgyud-pas *gshis*. The combination of the two terms introduces a very subtle shade of meaning. Infinite transcendence or the facticity of being (*ngo-bo*) may shine forth suddenly, only to vanish before it can be clearly fixed. It is this dynamic phenomenon (*gshis*) which the discursive mind attempts to grasp, and in so grasping it distorts it into a *thing*-object.

[12]'Jigs-med gling-pa adds in a note that this does not mean that it is a judgmental cognition to the effect that the external objects are stated to be nothing as such but, rather, that the whole process of appearing is nothing intangible.

dhahood can be realized in one lifetime has been blocked. *Samaya*.

Mentation and value awareness are like the wind and the sky.[13] Mentation is determined by the fleeting images of objects; it is like a blown-up bubble staying glittering for a while or like a whirlwind coming suddenly to blow; and it provides the basis for sundry feelings about that which appears before the mind.

Value awareness needs no such props; it is all-encompassing. Being as nothing, it opens up to understanding like the sky [letting things appear in and against it as background];[14] and being translucent and without thought-constructions, it is like a pure crystal.

Therefore the essential point is to become firmly settled in genuine existence[15] which is the vastness of value awareness freed from the constructs of mentation.

---

[13]This simile is elaborated by Zhabs-gar tshogs-drug rang-grol (who calls himself Bya-btang tshogs-drug rang-grol) in his *'Od-gsal rdzogs-pa chen-po'i khregs-chod lta-ba'i glu-dbyangs lam ma-lus myur-du bgrod-pa'i rtsal-ldan mkha'-lding gshog-rlabs*, fol. 19*b*, where he uses *sems-nyid* instead of *rig-pa*. The rNying-ma-pas distinguish between *sems*, 'emanation' or 'mind' in the sense in which we usually use it, and *sems-nyid* which refers to the cognition of being *qua* being. Zhabs-gar tshogs-drug rang-grol's words are:

Although the sky is used as an illustration of the cognition of being *qua* being,
It is only a simile to indicate an utter openness.
The cognition of being *qua* being is a live process; it is nothing that may appear as some thing.
The sky is nothing cognitive, it is sheer nothingness,
Therefore the sky is not an explanation of Mind.

In contemporary philosophical language this means that awareness is not a passive container of subjective impressions which are immediately known because they are contained. Awareness is an unlimited openness that may be filled with any content.

[14]So also *gZhi-snang ye-shes sgron-me*, fol. 2*a* (=*Bla-ma yang-tig*, Vol. *VAṂ*).

[15]*Gnas-lugs* is supposed to be the translation of the Sanskrit *tathatā* which, however, is usually rendered by *de-bzhin-nyid* in Tibetan. *gnas-lugs* is always distinguished from *yin-lugs*, which means 'being this or that'.

In his *Khregs-chod-kyi rgyab-yig nam-mkha' dri-med* (=*Bla-ma yang-tig*, Vol. *E*, part IV), fol. 41*a* and *b*, Klong-chen rab-'byams-pa illustrates the nature of becoming firmly established in genuine existence as follows:

"*a*) Unchangingness as when the king is seated on his throne: When a great

Those who do not understand this and, in their ignorance about the nature of mind being such that its being or not being affected by the appearances of objects is like water or quicksilver falling to the ground, declare that everything is mind, are deluded about the place where freedom can be found immediately through this (Absolute-Perfection Doctrine which is the) climax of Vajrayāna, making the goal the path. *Samaya.*

Quiescence is like a man who is not in the possession of all his faculties. It has an objective reference for its inspection in which the noetic capacity is gathered [to the exclusion of everything else] in a clear, distinct, elated, and speedy manner.

The wider perspective of insight is like a man having the five senses in full. In knowing the nature of mind it sees its being and intellectually pursues its objects and other topics through intensive discursive reasoning.

Therefore, the essential point is to become composed throughout the three aspects of time in the reality of genuine existence which simply is and which is no fiction of the mind, needs no props and has no postulational being, and in which [actuality or the phenomenal and facticity or the noumenal] remain in primordial unity.

The followers of the intellectual courses who do not understand this arrive at a dense state in which all mental activity due to the functioning of motility seems to have ceased

---

and powerful king ascends the throne all his subjects live in peace, the king himself living in his palace and not leaving his throne. Similarly, when one knows that the authentic king of value awareness resides in one's heart, then the all-ground cognitiveness with its eight group patterns and endowed with sundry experientially initiated possibilities of experience returns to its original purity, there being neither hope nor fear concerning whatever something may be.

"*b*) Unchangingness as when a minister is taken prisoner: When a new dignitary takes over, the king must be consulted. Similarly, when the straying of thought has been stopped, the king of value awareness alone is obeyed. It is grounded in facticity.

"*c*) Unchangingness as when the inspection tour is over: When the king has completed his tour of inspection whatever he says must be followed. Similarly, when the five sensory cognitions have become empty [of their preoccupation with *thing*-objects], the name of Saṃsāra is no more."

by a process in which being and non-being are 'sealed'[16] by nothingness. They run after the objects into which they reify and then dereify the images of insight, analyzed according to the dictates of scriptures and reason.

Those who make their wishful thinking the path of spiritual development, apart from evincing some interest in this spiritual course, have no chance of apprehending it as it really is. *Samaya.*

Since future beings will possess merits of a low standard, it will be very difficult for them to find a real guru; having little intelligence they will not understand the meaning of tantra; having little faith, only a few of them will (be suited to) receive the transmission; and their mental capacity being weak, they will not comprehend the essence of instruction.

But to those fortunate beings who through former practices have waked up and have firmly grasped the significance [of Buddhahood], even if they have heard and studied but a little here and there and with few longings have spent a lifetime of hardship in mountain solitudes, the Ḍāka will reveal through symbols the vastness [of true existence].

May the fortunate beings grow spiritually through this treatise which is very profound and in which the deepest meaning is expressed in but a few words. *Samaya. rGya rgya rgya.*

This short essay, about which its author rightly says that its profound meaning is condensed in a few words, is important for the history of ideas because, on the one hand, it contains a critique of the indeterminacy of certain trends among the bKa'-brgyud-pas, of the mentalism of the Sa-skya-pas, and of

[16]This is one of the four pitfalls against which a person has to guard himself in meditation. It is the intellectualistic disruption of a unity of an experience into the content of the experience as one aspect and the fact of its being nothing tangible as another aspect. This 'seal' has been discussed in very concise terms by 'Jigs-med gling-pa in his *Gol-shor tshar-gcod seng-ge'i nga-ro* (forming part of the *Klong-chen snying-tig*). 'Jigs-med gling-pa here criticizes the dGe-lugs-pa conception of nothingness and openness (*stong-pa nyid*, in Sanskrit *śūnyatā*) as absolute negation (*med-dgag*). Absolute negation cannot account for the noetic nothingness and openness that makes all cognition possible.

the intellectualism of the dGe-lugs-pas, and, on the other, it deals with problems which, under the impact of existentialist thought, have come to the foreground in modern philosophical and religious thought.

When 'Jigs-med gling-pa compares the all-ground (*kun-gzhi*) with turbid water, he has in mind not so much the ground of being itself, which as infinite transcendence is possessed by all beings and things whatsoever and is itself wholly beyond any determination and cannot be defined or characterized in any way because even to conceive of it as a vast continuum out of which all specific entities are somehow formed is already to misconceive it. Rather, he has in mind the complex phenomenon to which we refer by such words as 'choice' and 'decision', though not in the sense of a supposed arbitrariness of choice between things determined as good or evil beforehand but, rather, in the sense of decision being something that lies at the very center of man's being and from there determines the texture and meaningfulness or meaninglessness of his existence. This is to say that as human beings we have access to something through which we become true to ourselves and which, in a sense, is our very self, although it must not for a moment be assumed that this something or self can be known as an object or grasped as a subject behind the phenomena. Other texts specify this phrase as 'existential dynamics' (*rtsal*) and speak of the 'ground serving as the origin of either Saṃsāra or Nirvāṇa'.[17] In the light of 'Jigs-med gling-pa's distinction between a nondescript state of being and decisive existence as well as in the view of the importance of cognitive being, which is the pivot of Buddhist thought, this description clearly shows that Saṃsāra and Nirvāṇa are not to be approached as a kind of thing or as the end state of change but are ways of existing which affect every other aspect of man's being.

'Decisive existence' (*chos-sku*)[18] is said to be a self-revealing

---

[17]See, e.g., *Zab-don rgya-mtsho'i sprin*, fol. 42*b* (= *mKha'-'gro yang-tig*, Vol. II, Part I).

[18]Sanskrit, *dharmakāya*. See n. 10, above.

awareness.[19] Such self-awareness as a process of revealing and disclosure makes little sense without the assumption that we exist in a world whose facets we may know as they really are. It is important to note that self-revealing is understood by the rNying-ma-pas in the sense that the act of becoming aware reveals itself, not in the sense that cognition becomes its own object. Such self-revealing awareness is not a different kind of thing which can be added to or subtracted from existence. As cognitive being it is more like a pervasive existential category that affects every phase of man's being in all its modes and levels. This cognitive being, which is known technically as "existence and transcendent knowledge not to be joined or separated,"[20] has certain traits which, in their entirety, clearly mark it off from any *thing*-being which is the stock and trade of ordinary [non-reflective] thinking. Cognitive being, like any other experience, is relational in structure: I cannot be aware without being aware of something; and while it is true that in order to know a thing I must be it, it is not true that I must be it without qualifications. Only formal identity is involved. In the words of John Wild this means that "the noetic relation terminates in a distinct existence with which formal identity is achieved. We may call this terminal union a noetic identity, which must be sharply distinguished both from the mere reception of a causal impulse, and from complete existential identity."[21] Since identity as a relation always involves an aspect of duality which is somehow transcended, this self-revealing awareness "includes

---

[19]*rang-rig*, in Sanskrit *svasaṃvitti*. This term does not mean, as the Prāsangikas maintained, that the cognition cognizes itself. It seems that such an interpretation was a deliberate misrepresentation by the Prāsangikas. It only means that the act of knowing reveals itself as this act. See Mi-pham 'Jam-dbyangs rgya-mtsho in his *Yid-bzhin-mdzod-kyi grub-mtha' bsdus-pa* (Sarnath edition), fol. 15*a*.

[20]See, e.g., *Man-ngag snying-gi dgongs-pa'i rgyud rdo-rje-sems-dpas gsungs-pa* (= *dGongs-pa zang-thal*, Vol. *Hri*, section *Ke*), fol. 2*a* (hereinafter cited as "*Ke*"); *dNgos-gzhi 'od-gsal snying-po'i don-khrid* (= *Bla-ma yang-tig*, Vol. *E*, part IV), fol. 19*a*.

[21]John Wild, *The Challenge of Existentialism* (Bloomington: Indiana University Press, 1955), p. 226.

an aspect of formal identity, and an aspect of existential difference which is responsible for the objective nature of knowledge. This object is known. Formal identity is involved. But it is always known as something other that retains its existential diversity. This fusion of sameness with difference is properly referred to as noetic union or identity."[22]

Moreover, the knowing power arises from a completely indeterminate foundation which does not restrict its terms in any way. It is an utter emptiness which may be filled with any structure. However, this emptiness is not the emptiness of a container, which as sheer nothingness has no power of any kind, cannot and does not unite with being, and simply is not.[23] Rather, is it an intensive mode of being, ready to identify itself with anything as it really is. Just as this noetic capacity, grounded in (subjective) existence, is as nothing (because if it were something determinate and permanently tainted by some bias or other, it could not properly perform its function of revealing and manifesting), so the 'objective' pole also is not something fixed and determined and narrowly circumscribed but, rather, being *qua* being. Since the discernment of being is of primary importance for man's decisive existence, and since even pure awareness has its mood of detached concentration and blissful excitement, in order to convey something of what is implied by the perception of being we may refer to the 'objective' pole, being *qua* being, as 'value' and to the 'subjective' pole, the self-revealing awareness, as 'value-[sustained] cognition', because 'value' is sufficiently objective to be perceived by a subject and sufficiently subjective to sustain interest and action.

---

[22]*Ibid.*

[23]This point is clearly brought out in Mi-pham 'Jam-dbyangs rgya-mtsho's *gNyug-sems skor gsum*, comprising the three works *gNyug-sems 'od-gsal-gyi don rgyal-ba rig-'dzin brgyud-pa'i lung bzhin brjod-pa rdo-rje snying-po*, *gNyug-sems 'od-gsal-gyi don-la spyad-pa rdzogs-pa chen-po gzhi lam 'bras-bu'i shan-'byed blo-gros snang-ba*, and *gNyug-sems zur-dpyad skor-gyi gsung-sgros thor-bu phyogs-gcig-tu bsdus-pa rdo-rje rin-po-che'i phreng-ba*. See, e.g., the first work, fol. 3*a* and *b*.

All these points are clearly brought out by the rNying-ma-pa texts speaking of the complex phenomenon of decisive existence.

> The translucency of one's noeticness, which is nothing in the sense that it cannot be found as a thing or an essence, is the [value] reality Kun-tu bzang-mo. The (same) translucency of one's noeticness, though being nothing yet not turning into sheer nothingness, is the [value] awareness Kun-tu bzang-po. Its facticity being nothing and its cognitiveness being brilliantly revealing, and its presence as the indivisibility of revealingness and nothingness, is decisive existence, Buddhahood.[24]
>
> Being *qua* being, decisive existence, and transcendent knowledge may be discussed as separate topics, but actually they form an indivisible unit. To give an example, the stars in the sky, their glittering reflection in the sea, and the water of the sea are indivisible in their lustrousness, the one coinciding with the other. An illustration of the indivisibility of decisive existence and transcendent knowledge is afforded by water and salt, the one enhancing the nature of the other.[25]

Decisive existence as a distinct mode of cognitive being is an act of decision[26] in the light of infinite transcendence which is allowed to shine forth in all aspects of being, holding them together in an integrated structure. In this way decisive existence

---

[24]*Ke*, fol. 2*b*.

[25]*rDzogs-pa chen-po kun-tu bzang-po'i dgongs-pa zang-thal-gyi rgyud-chen mthong-ba dang thos-pa dang btags-pa dang smon-lam btab-pa tsam-gyis sangs-rgya-ba'i rgyud* (= *dGongs-pa zang-thal*, Vol. *Hri*, section *Nge*), fol. 13*a* and *b* (hereinafter cited as "*Nge*").

[26]Decision is the act of a moment in which my whole being may be changed; it is not a gradual buildup, although it may have gone on unconsciously. The rNying-ma-pas distinguish between two types of man, he who decides (*khregs-chod*) and he who arrives at a decision gradually (*thod-rgal*). For the former the distinction between mentation (*sems*) and value awareness (*rig-pa*) is the essential point. The latter is taught by pointing out the metaphysical background, the paths leading to Saṃsāra or Nirvāṇa, the 'gates' through which transcendence may shine forth, the objective references of the cognitive process, the means of pursuing the path of self-development, the important points to be noted, and so on. See Tse-le rig-'dzin sNa-thogs rang-grol's *Theg-pa thams-cad-kyi mchog rab gsang-ba bla-na-med-pa 'od-gsal rdo-rje snying-po'i don rnam-par bshad-pa nyi-ma'i snying-po*, fol. 10*a*; and A-'dzoms 'Brug-pa rig-'dzin sNa-tshogs rang-grol, *op. cit.*, fol. 93*a*.

is superior to mere transcendence, which, unless it becomes embodied in existence, remains a lifeless abstraction. Cognitive being, which always involves an aspect of noetic union, is symbolized by and represented in works of art as a male and female deity in conjugal embrace. Thus, Kun-tu bzang-mo as the [female and 'objective'] being *qua* being or 'value' pole in this union inspires and sustains Kun-tu bzang-po as the [male and 'subjective'] act of value cognition, their union being grounded in and constituting decisive existence or Buddhahood as pure bliss. Inasmuch as every awareness is relational in structure or, to use the concrete symbols employed in the fine arts, comprises a male and female component, awareness in whatever aspect it may function tends to become expressed in male-female union shining forth in specific colors, each of which symbolizes a certain aspect of awareness.[27] But, although the noetic union is represented in male-female form, this personalistic created form must not be confused with the formative dynamics underlying it.[28]

As contrasted with decisive existence, the nondescript state of being (*lung-ma-bstan*) also is not a kind of thing but a mode of unknowing, confusion, and indecisiveness. It is a perpetuation of indeterminateness, a growing alienation from transcendence. This is admirably brought out in the following passage:[29]

> Before there is error and the status of a sentient being[30] and before there is freedom and Buddhahood, there is the primordial

---

[27]*Nge*, fol. 13*a*.

[28]*Ce*, fol. 21*b*.

[29]A-'dzoms 'Brug-pa rig-'dzin sNa-tshogs rang-grol, *op. cit.*, fols. 91*a*–92*b*.

[30]*sems-can*. This word stands for the Sanskrit *sattva*, which emphasizes the aspect of being (*sat*) and has a more or less static connotation. If *sems-can* had been a lexical translation, its prototype should have been **cittavant*. This is one of many other instances that prove the Tibetans interpreted what they translated. The Tibetan word points to the fact that man possesses and releases the powers which involve him in the world with all its attendant suffering and that, through an act of decision, he can make these powers ineffective. In his *Khregs-chod-kyi rgyab-yig nam-mkha' dri-med*, *op. cit.*, fol. 40*b*, Klong-chen rab-'byams-pa gives the following definition of *sems-can*: "Although we may speak of a primordial place of freedom because, just as in the case of the disk of the sun, there has never been any impurity, it is through the veiling power of

ground of infinite transcendence. Its apparent disposition is one of indeterminateness, and it may be likened to an egg. Since the act of being free through knowing that infinite transcendence is the self-existing triune reality of acticity, actuality, and sensibility means that the primordial Buddha Kun-tu bzang-po and all the other Buddhas (following his example) have awakened to Buddhahood from the all-ground of infinite transcendence, this all-ground serves as the link with the higher forms of decisive existence. But when the motility of unknowing, making an intellectual analysis of appearance believed to constitute a duality, has started to operate, the all-ground forms the link with suffering in error or the status of a sentient being, and this straying away from the ground of infinite transcendence is as follows: (1) Being *qua* being (*chos-nyid*) serves as the basis for it becoming mistaken for a *thing*-object (*yul*); (2) the five-colored hue of transcendent knowledge (*ye-shes*) serves as the basis for it becoming mistaken for a container world and the living beings in it (*snod-bcud*); and (3) value-(sustained) awareness (*rig-pa*) serves as the basis for erring into mentation (*sems*). This process which generates the misery of the world and its being develops in the following manner: At the beginning of the straying into the subject-object dichotomy, (*i*) being *qua* being which has been utterly pure from the very beginning, which is beyond all propositions, initially pure and an utter nothingness, is not recognized (as what it is), but by the very fact that one asks oneself what this nothing which is not some thing or other might be, being *qua* being becomes the basis for it becoming mistaken for a *thing*-object. (*ii*) The effulgence of the five colors of transcendent knowledge, which in its indivisibility of facticity and actuality is like the light refracted in a crystal or like the glittering hue of the eyes in a peacock's tail, is dualized, and by the very fact that one asks oneself whether this effulgence comes from me and is projected away from me or whether it comes from yonder to me here,[31] it becomes the basis for it

---

various conditions which are like clouds and, lastly through our organismic being, our talk, and our mentation [that the primordial luster is not seen]. As long as we are not delivered from them we speak of a sentient being (*sems-can*) because he is in possession of the veiling powers of mentation (*sems*) in the worlds."

[31]So also *Thod-rgal-gyi rgyab-yig nyi zla gza'-skar* (= *Bla-ma yang-tig*, Vol. *E*, part IV), fol. 48*b*; *Nge*, fol. 8*a* and *b*.

> becoming mistaken for a container world and the beings in it. (*iii*) Although in self-existing value awareness no impurity as (exemplified by) error can be found, it is vitiated by the impurities of unknowing, the belief in external things as such, emotionality, motility, and mentation, and so serves as the basis for the error of sentient beings.
>
> The first aspect (1, *i*) brings about the appearance of the fragmentation into *thing*-objects and the belief in them. The influence of the second aspect (2, *ii*) brings about the idea of (*a*) duration, since the experientially initiated possibilities of experience through which the outer world—constituted by the elements of earth [solidity], water [cohesion], fire [temperature], wind [movement], and so on—appears to come into existence, to last [for some time], to dissolve, and to become nothing in this order are fairly reliable, and the idea of (*b*) the body of sentient beings belonging to four categories of birth, being constituted by the assembly of the five derivative elements to exist. All this (*a* and *b*) is technically known as the all-ground or organismic being experientially initiated. The third aspect (3, *iii*) serves as the foundation of the 84,000 constitutive factors making up the psychophysical constituents, their constitutional varieties, their interactional fields, and so on, as well as the thoughts and emotions arising from mind and mental events. This is known as the all-ground of sundry experientially initiated possibilities of experience.

Since the most important factor among these topics set up by the experientially initiated possibilities of experience is mind (*sems*), it may be analyzed into a (dormant) apperceptive mass,[32] the rise of thought,[33] the emotionally toned response,[34] and the sensory cognitions.[35] The apperceptive mass is like deep sleep or unknowing which possesses (potential) cognitiveness, but as long as it is not roused from its sleep and made to face its objects, it is simple and solitary unknowing (*bdag-nyid gcig-pa ma-rig-pa*) as cause factor [for all cognitions to occur within

---

[32]*kun-gzhi'i rnam-shes*, in Sanskrit *ālayavijñāna*.

[33]*yid-kyi rnam-shes*, in Sanskrit *manovijñāna*.

[34]*nyon-mongs-pa'i rnam-shes*, in Sanskrit *kliṣṭa*(*mano*)*vijñāna*.

[35]*sgo lnga'i rnam-shes*, in Sanskrit *cakṣur-ādi-vijñāna*.

the framework of unknowing]. When it stirs from its sleep and faces its objects it is the rise of thought or [as it is technically known] a co-emergent unknowing (*lhan-cig skyes-pa'i ma-rig-pa*). Insofar as it responds to each individual object, it is emotively toned responsiveness or [as it is technically known] an unknowing bearing on every thing (*kun-tu brtags-pa'i ma-rig-pa*).[36] The five sensory cognitions, united with these three aspects of unknowing, err into the direction of the subject-object dichotomy. And since there is no end to the suffering of the six kinds of beings who move from birth to birth, without beginning or end, like the chain of a waterwheel, one speaks of Unknowing Wandering about Mentation possessed.[37]

When 'Jigs-med gling-pa distinguishes between decisive existence and a nondescript state of being and declares that in decisive existence the integrity of man's being is preserved within an ultimate horizon and that in the nondescript state of being he loses this integrity, becomes involved in a world which he considers to be a vast collection of things, and is lost in his own artifacts which lack all intrinsic value and real being, he reopens the problem commonly known as ontology which has had a peculiar history in the past because Being itself has been confused with some kind of being. 'Jigs-med gling-pa, who closely follows his spiritual master, Klong-chen rab-'byams-pa, who in turn is greatly indebted to the teaching of Vimalamitra, is quite explicit that Being is not the kind of existence possessed by physical objects and also that to exist is not the same as to be perceived. In this respect the rNying-ma-pa philosophers are very much akin to Karl Jaspers, Gabriel Marcel, and Jean-Paul Sartre, who openly reject both materialism and [traditional] idealism. But they differ from these existentialist thinkers in their conception of the transcendental structure of Being as a

---

[36]This threefold structure of unknowing (*ma-rig-pa*, in Sanskrit *avidyā*) corresponds to the triune structure of transcendence of which unknowing is its existential dynamics tending to become involved in the world. It is dealt with in all rNying-ma-pa works.

[37]I have tried to imitate the Tibetan diction, *ma-rig-pa 'gro-ba sems-can*, which deals with concrete existence from a multitude of aspects.

triunity of facticity, actuality, and sensibility.[38] The analysis of this structure is outside the scope of the present essay, which is primarily concerned with the distinction between decisive existence and the nondescript state of being. It is the contention of the rNying-ma-pas that such a distinction and the accompanying discrimination between the two is the very beginning of man's spiritual development enacted by decision.

Knowledge belongs to the being of man, and just as his being may reveal itself as decisive existence or as a nondescript state, so also knowledge has a double nature. The one is the cognition (*rig-pa*) of being *qua* being. It provides and safeguards man's integrity because the most inclusive perspective of being is gained. It is a cognition which has the intangible flavor of what we may call 'value', although this word is likely to create certain misconceptions because under the influence of scientism value is considered to be merely subjective.[39] Above all, it is a cognition whose mood is one of unchanging bliss because the fragmentation into a past I may mourn because it is gone, into a future I may dread, and into a present in which I am involved instead of making a decisive choice has been transcended.[40] It is also an aesthetic apprehension of reality which, if the attempt is made to

---

[38]The three Tibetan terms are *ngo-bo*, *rang-bzhin*, and *thugs-rje*, which often correspond to Sanskrit *vastu*, *svabhāva*, and *karuṇā*. The first is defined as an utter openness and as nothing as such (*stong-pa*), the second is irradiative (*gsal-ba*), and the third as emotively moving awareness (*rig-pa*). Although we have to be extremely cautious in applying Western philosophical terminology, we may say that *ngo-bo* refers to the ontological aspect of Being, *rang-bzhin* to its factual function, and *thugs-rje* to the mood of cognitive being. This shows that the translation of *thugs-rje* (or *karuṇā*) by 'compassion' is both right and wrong. It is wrong when it is used in the sense of an emotion or a sentiment; it is right when it is used as indicating the mood of a situation. For an analysis of the triune structure of transcendence see *Tshig-don bcu-gcig-pa* (= *Bi-ma snying-tig*, Vol. *Da*), fols. 3*a*–4*b*, among other rNying-ma-pa works.

[39]Values cannot be separated from facts. Where man is concerned the ultimate issue is whether he is really to be or not to be. Therefore existence and value go together, and to choose a life lived more abundantly in ordered activity is a choice or decision made in a world of facts.

[40]See, e.g., *Ce*, fol. 61*b*; Mi-pham 'Jam-dbyangs rgya-mtsho, *gNyug-sems 'od-gsal-gyi don-la dpyad-pa rdzogs-pa chen-po gzhi lam 'bras-bu'i shan-'byed blo-gros snang-ba*, *op. cit.*, fol. 67*b*.

communicate something of it to others, cannot but utilize the deeply moving symbols of art and religion. The other is termed 'mentation' (*sems*). I have chosen this translation against the current one of 'mind' in order to convey something of the dynamics that is understood when this word is used in a Buddhist context and in order to avoid the current association of mind being a 'container of ideas'. Mind or mentation, as understood in Buddhist texts, is not walled up within itself but is transmissive. Only the objects of thought may be static and fixed, but mind is tendential and works in a field of shifting forces. It is, as it were, a surface phenomenon that strays away from its home. Such at least is its explanation in the original texts. "It is a superficial impurity."[41] "It is (a straying away) from its abode and a becoming involved, involvement is all of it."[42] "Where does mentation operate? Within the field of Saṃsāra and Nirvāṇa. What does it effect? Different thought flashes and various ideas. Why does it operate? Because of the presence of Saṃsāra and Nirvāṇa."[43]

Mentation is thus characterized by its horizon being restricted and its point of view being biased; it is not concerned with being *qua* being but with being of some kind. It is dominated by a *thing*-object at which I may gaze with but little clear consciousness of the noetic act. What the senses reveal is assumed to be facts, *objects* such as visual patterns, sounds, flavors, and fragrances; and although in this framework of 'unknowing' (*ma-rig-pa*) man believes that his senses reveal 'real' things and that his thoughts have to do with hard facts in a way believed to be a detached mode of reasoning, it is and tends to become increasingly disturbed by emotive responses which serve as diffusive action patterns. To the extent of mentation straying from its source the whole cognitive atmosphere becomes poisoned.

---

[41]Tse-le rig-'dzin sNa-tshogs rang-grol, *op. cit.*, fol. 12*a*.

[42]*Sems-kyi dmigs drug-gi rnam-par bshad-pa* (= *Bi-ma snying-tig*, Vol. *Nya*), fol. 34*b*.

[43]*Ibid.*

Co-emergent unknowing represents an additional cause to the nondescript aspect of the all-ground, while the unknowing that bears on everything lets the tendency of believing in this become inveterate so that all the sentient beings in saṃsāra pertaining to the three realms[44] are erring. 'Mind' (*sems*) means that if a thought is to stay it will not settle, and if a thought is to be dismissed it will not go; it is [like] a sudden gush of wind; it goes by fits and starts; it is [like] a whirlwind, [like] fog becoming denser and denser. If it gets a chance it rushes into the five kinds of poison, the five emotively toned responses; and if it does not it just rests for a while in its eagerness to rush along. Birth, old age, illness, death , and change of abode belong to mind; it is incessantly stirring and moving. It is similar to wind, clouds, mist, and waves. A cold breeze refreshes and is gone; clouds and mist gather and disperse; waves come and go, and there is no cessation to it. When anger is born in the mind it is as if a fierce winter storm has come; when desire is born it is as if a stream is rushing downward; when bewilderment is born it is as if fog has come to stay; if pride is born it is as if the wind is fighting against a rock; and when envy is born it is as if a stream of water falls into a ravine. The result of this is the misery of the three evil forms of life.[45] Every physical body, as the embodiment of unknowing (which characterizes) a sentient being, is a mentation-born body. This is born and dies in uninterrupted succession. All the teachings contained in the nine courses[46] do not understand the meaning of birthlessness and deathlessness. The fault lies in the fact that they do not distinguish

---

[44]The worlds of desire, form, and formlessness.

[45]Animals, spirits, and denizens of hell.

[46]Against the traditional divison of Buddhism into three *yānas* or courses of spiritual growth and development, the rNying-ma-pas accept a ninefold one: Śrāvakayāna, Pratyekabuddhayāna, Bodhisattvayāna, Kriyā, Upa, Yoga, Mahā, Anu, and Ati. The last six belong to Tantrism and roughly correspond to the more commonly known classification of the Tantras into Kriyātantra, Caryātantra, and Yogatantra with its division into 'Father' Tantras, 'Mother' Tantras, and 'Non-dual' Tantras. In translating *yāna* by 'spiritual course' instead of by the customary 'vehicle' I try to express what the Tibetans think when they hear or use this term. *Theg-pa* (in Sanskrit *yāna*) is synonymous with *lam* (in Sanskrit *mārga*), which in turn is synonymous with *ye-shes* (in Sanskrit *jñāna*). The process indicated by these terms is not travel in a certain 'vehicle' along a certain 'path' from one point to another but is the unfolding of an a priori transcendent awareness.

between mentation (*sems*) and the cognition of being *qua* being (*rig-pa*).[47]

This distinction between two types of awareness is a recurrent theme in rNying-ma-pa literature. While one is tempted to relate these two types to the division into a practical and a theoretical awareness as elaborated in existentialist literature, which often reveals a contempt for the latter, the one being concerned with active tendencies, fused with appetition and having a restricted horizon, the other affording the widest perspective of being, the rNying-ma-pas differ from the line of thought presented by Martin Heidegger in claiming that there is no original mode of awareness which is neither the one nor the other; all knowledge is either one or the other.[48] Inasmuch as man possesses and releases the powers of unknowing which then overwhelm and hold him prisoner in a world of his own artifacts, and inasmuch as these powers are the existential dynamics (*rtsal*) containing, as it were, the seeds of decision and knowledge as well as the continuation of undecisiveness, it is only through hard practice that knowledge is gained. Just as decisive existence is a parting from a nondescript state of being, knowledge may be said to be a parting from mentation or unknowing, a liberation from the power to fetter. "The moment mentation and knowledge part, real knowledge shines forth in the awareness of being, and in that very moment when this great transcendent knowledge has appeared Buddhahood is won."[49] Or, as Tse-le Rig-'dzin sNa-tshogs rang-grol says:[50] "That which really has to be felt in experience is the transcendent knowledge in the

---

[47]*Nge*, fols. 18*b*–19*b*. A long discussion of the difference between mentation (*sems*) and cognition of being *qua* being (*rig-pa*) is found in Klong-chen rab-'byams-pa, *Khregs-chod-kyi rgyab-yig nam-mkha' dri-med*, *op. cit.*, fols. 40*b*–42*a*.

[48]This is quite clear from such statements as in *Nge*, fols. 5*b*–6*a*: "In the remote past when there was no knowledge there also did not exist the name 'Buddha,' and when there was no unknowing the name 'sentient being' also did not exist."

[49]*Nge*, fol. 26*a*.

[50]*Op. cit.*, fol. 14*a*.

awareness of being *qua* being. Since mentation is its exterior luster or its dynamics, it is powerless to embark on its course of error when the awareness of being *qua* being has been grasped firmly. For instance, if a king is taken prisoner his subjects are automatically conquered."

From what has been culled from the rNying-ma-pa texts it is obvious that neither existence nor knowledge are to be found in an absorption in an absolute. Such a negativistic and quietistic conception runs counter to the idea of decisive existence being something positive and affirmative and of knowledge being given us in order to act. But to act is not the same as to be busy, with which action is very often confused. Moreover, in the human context action must take into account man's existence, which is quite different from the existence of a thing. It is a well-known fact that the more I understand myself and others as a thing, a complex aggregate of matter, the more degraded my action becomes. This shows that awareness and action as phases of man's being are closely fused and interdependent. The problem of awareness and action is the very essence of Tantrism, which aims at making us see our fellowmen in the world around us transfigured so that in seeing every man as a god and every woman as a goddess man may be able to do justice to his being.

The relation between action and awareness is so intimate that one often wonders how action enters into the picture at all. Actually, it is our preoccupation with action in the sense of busyness that prevents us from connecting quiescence with action. As 'Jigs-med gling-pa points out, it is wrong to conceive of quiescence as a soporific state in which man seeks oblivion and becomes insensate to everything. Rather, it means to become free from the involvement in petty and limited situations and to find peace of mind as a new situation from which one can apprehend things as they really are. Only when mind has become calm can it look out to the world and man without bias. Elsewhere 'Jigs-med gling-pa explains quiescence and the broader perspective of insight in the following manner:

> Quiescence means that the conscious and preconscious thoughts subside in themselves, but if one does not understand

> that the translucent and calm aspect of mind when it is free from the surging billows of restless scrutiny is a self-revealing awareness, translucent in itself, but understands this calm as an utterly insensate state, one is thoroughly mistaken. While the broader perspective of insight is the intensely brilliant cognitiveness of mind being aware of what 'calm' and 'restlessness' mean, and not reifying [what it is aware of], it is a great mistake to engage in an intellectual analysis and propositional judgment of calm and restlessness by failing to understand what insight means.[51]

Finally, if action is fused with the awareness of being it cannot operate in the negation of being which 'Jigs-med gling-pa terms the 'sealing with nothingness'. This means that first we propose an idea and then say that it is nothing.[52] To do so is rank nihilism.

The rNying-ma-pas follow up the central problem of Buddhism, which has been man himself. The goal is to exist in the most intensive way of being human. This goal, in a certain sense, is already present in the ground from which one starts along a path, where the path means essentially how we are going to see ourselves. This demands the highest degree of discernment and discrimination, and it forces man to decide whether he is to be and whether he is to be free or to be at the mercy of dark powers which he himself has released.

---

[51] 'Jigs-med gling-pa, *Gol-shor tshar-gcod seng-ge'i nga-ro*, fol. 19*b*.
[52] *Ibid.*, fol. 22*b*.

Mentalism and Beyond in Buddhist Philosophy

The history of Buddhist philosophical thought can be seen as a gradual progress from what seems to be a kind of naive realism through representative realism towards subjective idealism as far as the Indian setting applies, all of which is summarily discussed in Tibetan works on Buddhist philosophy under the heading of *dngos-smar-ba.*[1] This term may best be translated by 'reductionism' because each system so far mentioned tries to reduce the whole of reality to one or more particular existents (*dgnos-po*). I deliberately avoid the term 'substance' in this connection because this term is exceedingly ambiguous even in Western philosophies and its unqualified (or unqualifiable) use with reference to Eastern ways of thinking would only add to confusion. Moreover, 'substance' would have to be defined in relation to 'matter' which again would raise formidable problems but solve nothing. There seems to be a similar difficulty to pertain to the terms *rdzas* and *dngos-po*. The latter has been translated by me as 'particular existent', and the former is

[1]See for instance Ngag-dbang dpal-ldan's *Grub-mtha' chen mo'i mchan-'grel dKa'-gnad mdud-grol blo-gsal bces-nor*, vol. II (*dngos-smra-ba'i skabs*), where the philosophical views of the Vaibhāṣikas (pp. 1–70 of the Sarnath edition), Sautrāntikas (70–110), and Vijñānavādins (111–230) are discussed as forming one group (*skabs*).

usually understood as meaning 'Matter, material substance'. But if we take *rdzas* in this sense we are forced to classify Buddhist idealism as 'materialism' because 'mind' (*sems*) is said to 'exist *materialiter*' (*rdzas-yod*). Its difference from the avowedly materialistic system of the Vaibhāṣikas is only its monastic tendency. For the Vaibhāṣikas both the 'physical' (*gzugs*) and the 'mental' (*sems*) existed *materialiter* (*rdzas-yod*)[2] and in this respect could claim ultimate validity. They were of the same reality and were not mere incompatibles. But even the differentiation into pluralism (as in the case of the Vaibhāṣikas) and monism (as in the case of the Vijñānavādins) is not a helpful description or classification because it can be argued that the Vaibhāṣikas, too, were monists in the sense that they recognized only one basic stuff (*rdzas*) as absolutely real, while they would be pluralists in recognizing a number of such stuff items giving rise to the fictional notions of the empirically physical and mental. All this shows that the use of Western categories in connection with Eastern patterns of thought is extremely misleading and in most cases reveals a considerable lack of understanding on the part of him who uses these categories.

Instead of slurring over the major differences in philosophical thought in the East and West it seems more profitable to speak of the three major trends in Buddhism (Vaibhāṣika, Sautrāntika, and Vijñānavādin) criticized by the Buddhists themselves for their inadequacies, as representing a kind of 'thingness of thought' which turns even abstracta into 'things' or concrete entities, and either overlooks or is incapable of understanding the functional and operational nature of the thought-process. The critique of the 'reductionist' systems of Buddhist thought

---

[2]As opposed to *btags-yod*. If this distinction between *rdzas-yod* and *btags-yod* holds good for the Vaibhāṣikas as we are told by the Tibetan authors of works dealing with Indian Buddhist thought, the 'nominalistic' trend is not merely a corollary of the allegedly 'idealistic' development, but forms an integral part of Buddhist 'realism'. This again shows that discussions of Buddhist problems in philosophy without previous and careful semantic studies are instances of deliberate obscurantism.

by the Buddhists themselves is therefore basically due to diametrically opposed attitudes which it is not sufficient to characterize as either static or dynamic.

This difference becomes evident by contrasting the views of the bKa'-brgyud-pas and rNying-ma-pas. The former are mentalists, while the latter repudiate the mentalistic reductions. Both start from the central concept of 'Mind' for which the texts use two closely related terms: *sems* and *sems-nyid*. Both terms occur together in one of Saraha's verses which are considered authoritative by both schools. The relevant verse is found in Dohākoṣa 43:

cittekka saala bīaṃ bhava-nivvāṇa vi jaṃsi viphuranti
taṃ cintāmaṇi-rūaṃ paṇamaha icchāphalam dei[3]

The Tibetan Translation is

sems-nyid gcig-pa kun-gyi sa-bon te
gang-la srid dang mya-ngan-'das 'phro-ba
'dod-pa'i 'bras-bu ster-bar byed-pa-yi
yid-bzhin nor 'dra'i sems-la 'phyag-'tshal-lo

Here it will be observed that *citta* is translated by *sems-nyid* and that *taṃ* is rendered by *sems*. The use of the particle *nyid* deserves special attention because it is from here that divergent interpretations derive. Inasmuch as *nyid* emphasizes the preceding word, pointing to the very thing under consideration, the translation of the Tibetan version is:

Mind, indeed, is all alone the seed of everything.
From which the (various) forms of life and Nirvāṇa proceed.
Praise to mind which is similar to the Wish-Fulfilling Gem
Granting one's heart's desires.

The comparison of the Tibetan version with the Prākrit

[3]This verse number is given according to M. Shahidullah, *Les Chants Mystiques de Kāṇha et de Saraha. Les Dohā-koṣa et Les Caryā*. Paris: 1928. This rather slipshod edition fails completely to mark the differences between the Apabhraṃśa version and its Tibetan translation. The Apabhraṃśa version is a bowdlerized text and cannot be claimed to be original.

original shows that the latter does not contain a corresponding emphatic particle *eva.* And since *nyid* has a specific use in Tibetan, the insertion of it is ample proof that the Tibetans translated according to what was intended by the sentence, rather than mechanically.[4]

The bKa'-brgyud-pas do not always seem to have distinguished between the use of *sems* and *sems-nyid* and in this respect, following the Indian tradition, come closest to what is known in philosophical jargon as 'subjective idealism' which is so characteristic of Indian thought. The rNying-ma-pas, also quoting from Indian sources, used them to clarify conceptions already rooted as philosophical ideas in the mental habits of the Tibetans who had already been prepared for the acceptance of the Indian stimuli by the mystic ideas of gShen-rab, the founder of the Bon religion and possibly also by mystic Chinese thought. Some rNying-ma-pas even go so far as to identify gShen-rab with Lao-tzŭ.[5] Whether this identification will withstand criticism is beside the point. It shows that the rNying-ma-pas, of all other Buddhist schools in Tibet, alone were aware of their pre-Buddhist heritage. They make a clear distinction between *sems* and *sems-nyid* which stand for two different things, so to speak.[6]

---

[4]Tibetan translations of Indian texts are noted for their accuracy and this has given rise to the erroneous conception that Tibetan translations were just the original work in a different language. It shall not be denied that mechanical (almost computer-like) translations were made, but they belonged to a later age when the spirit of Buddhism was no longer alive. See the interesting remarks by Dudjom Rinpoche in his *Bod snga-rab-pa gsang-chen rnying-ma'i chos-'byung legs-bshad gsar-pa'i dga'-ston-gyi dbu-'dren gzhung-don*, Kalimpong: 1964, pp. 680 *seq.*

[5]See Blo-bzang chos-kyi nyi-ma dpal-bzang-po's *Grub-mtha' thams-cad-kyi khungs dang 'dad-tshul ston-pa legs 'bshad shel-gyi me-long*, sect. 7, fol. 12*b*. Positive references to Chinese Buddhist thought, rather than its wholesale rejection, have been collected in "Some Aspects of Tibetan Religious Thought," p. 140.

[6]The difference is emphatically asserted in *Bla-ma yang-tig*, section V, fol. 7*a*; and since in rNying-ma-pa parlance *sems nyid* is synonymous with *rig-pa* (as is *sems* with *ma-rig-pa*) the same distinction is discussed with reference to the various synonyms in *Bla-ma yang-tig*, section IV, fols. 41*b seq.* So also *Chos-dbyings rin-po-che'i mdzod-kyi 'grel-pa lung-gi gter-mdzod*, fol. 132*b*; *Theg-pa'i mchog rin-po-che'i mdzod*, fols. 224*b seq.*

The mentalistic position of the bKa'-brgyud-pas is best discussed in Thub-bstan 'bar-ba's *Nges-don phyag-rgya-chen-po'i sgom-rim-gsal-bar byed-pa'i legs-bshad zla-ba'i 'od-zer*, fols. 4*b seq.*:

> All entities of reality are mental
> (*chos thams-cad sems-su bstan-pa*)[7]

"All the entities of reality subsumed under the headings of Saṃsāra, that is, the realm of appearance of possible life forms, and of Nirvāṇa, are (the products of) one's mind (*rang-gi sems*). As is stated in the *Daśabhūmikasūtra*: 'O Buddha sons; this triple world is only mind'; the *Sampuṭa*: "The external and the internal is all fashioned by mind; apart from mind nothing exists'; and by Śabari: 'All the entities of reality are one's mind; except mind there is no other entity and be it an atom!'[8]

"It may be asked, if this is the case what then is meant by 'the appearance of concrete entities' (5a) such as color-forms, sounds and so on, all of which constitute the external apprehendable object (*gzung-ba'i yul*). The answer is that mind (*sems-nyid*)[9] not being aware of itself as constituting a presential value has appeared since beginningless time in the dual aspect of a subject and an object; by its functionalizing activity which assigns an independent status to its own fictions (*der 'dzin-pa'i rtog-pa*), it has built up experientially initiated potentialities of experience and thereby there occurs the appearance of the external world (which belongs solely) to the phenomenon of error (*'khrul-ngor*).

"This is stated in the *Lankāvatārasūtra*:

---

[7]See also sGam-po-pa *Collected Works*, vol. *Nga*, fol. 12*a*: "Since all the entities of the empirical world are one's own mind, everything is mental" (*snang-grags-kyi chos thams-cad ran-gi sems yin-pas thams-cad sems-su shes*). However, a careful reading of sGam-po-pa's work shows that he, unlike his later followers, tended to distinguish between *sems* and *sems-nyid*. See for instance vol. *Ca*, fols. 9*a*–25*a*; *Tha*, fol. 46*b*.

[8]From the *Dohā-koṣa-nāma-mahāmudrā-upadeśa*. Also quoted by sGampo-pa, *loc. cit.*, vol. *Ca*, fol. 4*b*.

[9]*nyid* in *sems-nyid* here takes up the idea of *rang-gi sems*. Its use is quite different in this text from that of the technical language of the rNying-ma-pas.

> Mind hardened by its experience potentialities
> Assumes the appearance of an object:[10]
> To see this very mind (*sems-nyid*) which is not an object
> as an external object is error.

In the *Samputa*:

> The entities of reality are the erring of the mind.
> Apart from mind there are no entities.
> The appearance as entities is the erring mind.

"To give an example: When a storm lashes the sea it becomes like earth or a rock. So when the tendency to err gains in strength there is the appearance of the solidity of external objects. Saraha has expressed it in the following verse:[11]

> When (in winter) still water by the wind is stirred (5b)
> It takes (as ice) the shape and texture of a rock.
> When the deluded are disturbed by interpretative thoughts,
> That which is as yet unpatterned turns very hard and solid.

"How then does this mind (*sems-nyid*) turn into Saṃsāra and Nirvāṇa? Mind (*sems*) becoming deluded by not recognizing the nature of the apprehendable and the apprehending after it has set out on its path of erring, because Saṃsāra, by turning back from this course it becomes Nirvāṇa. As is stated in the *Brtags-gnyis* (*Hevajra*):

> Because of delusion it becomes Saṃsāra,
> In the absence of delusion and Saṃsāra being purified
> Saṃsāra becomes Nirvāṇa.

and in the *Samputa*:

> Engulfed by the darkness of multiple fictions,
> Overpowered by them and madly rushing along,

---

[10]Tibetan verse quotations vary considerably from the Sanskrit version. In this case, only these two lines correspond to the Sanskrit version in X 115 *ab*, the subsequent two lines are not found there.

[11]This is verse 17 of Saraha's *Dohā-koṣa-nāma-caryā-gīti* (*Dohā-mdzod ces bya-ba spyod-pa'i glu*). See the author's *The Royal Song of Saraha*, Berkeley and London: 1973, p. 135.

> Sullied by desires and other passions difficult to control,
> Mind is said to be Saṃsāra by the Spiritual man.
> Radiant in itself, freed from its fictions,
> And cleansed of the dirt of lust and so on,
> When there is neither a project (an apprehendable concretization)
> Nor a projection (a projecting and apprehending process),
> Then it is said to be Nirvāṇa by the lofty-minded one. (6a)

And by Nāgārjuna:

> What is the cause of Saṃsāra
> Is, purified, the cause of Nirvāṇa.

"This shows that the root of faults and virtues is planted by the mind, that they derive from the mind, and that they arise from the mind, as is stated in the *Lankāvatārasūtra*:[12]

> Although the face appears reflected in a mirror
> It appears so without actually being the face.
> Not knowing that mind tends to make an appearance
> The duality of fictions comes about.
> The fictions fed by the experience potentialities
> Spring forth from mind in various ways,
> And manifest themselves to man as an external world.
> They are but the mind of a man of this world.
> What appears as an external world does not exist at all,
> It is mind, rising in various forms.
> What seems to be the physical being, its enjoyment and its situation,
> I call it 'only mind'.

In the *Avataṃsaka*:

> The mind is like an artist
> And the world is created by it.
> All the spheres of the world
> Have been painted by the mind.

---

[12]Here, too, what is given as one coherent quotation in the Tibetan version, is distributed in the Sanskrit *Lankāvatārasūtra* as follows: The first two lines of the quotation correspond to III 74; the remaining lines to X 485–487. Cf. II 32–33.

In the *Ratnamegha*: (6*b*)

> The world is led by mind,
> But the mind does not see the mind.
> Good or evil
> Is built up by the mind.
> Mind is like a fire-brand;
> It surges like waves;
> It is like a forest fire;
> It rushes on like a flood.

In the *Gur*:

> Having turned into possible life-forms[13] since
> beginningless time
> It is fancied as an external world.
> Since everything is the magic working of the mind
> Mind is ever-present.

And

> Apart from mind there is no outer world
> The individual manifestations of color-form and so on
> Are this mind appearing."

It may not be out of place here to make a few general remarks about classifying this line of thought as subjective idealism.[14] The texts seem to state clearly that the world at large is merely

---

[13]*srid-pa* which often appears as the second part in the compound *snang-srid*, rendered by Sarat Chandra Das, *A Tibetan-English Dictionary*, p. 769 as "*saṃsāra*, the visible world," has the specific connotation of 'life-form', referring to the three spheres of desire, form, and formlessness. See Padma dkar-po's *bSre-pho'i lam skor-gyi thog-mar lam dbye-bsdu*, fol. 50*a*. *srid-*(*pa*) is usually contrasted with *zhi-*(*ba*) 'Nirvāṇa'. See *Rang-bzhin rdgogs-pa-chen-po'i lam-gyi cha-lag sdom-pa gsum rnam-par nges-pa'i bstan bcos-kyi tshig-don legs-pa'i 'grel-pa 'Jam-dbyangs dgyes-pa'i zhal-lung*, fol. 3*b*.

[14]It is hardly necessary to point out that 'idealism' in philosophy is a misnomer and should be replaced either by 'idea-ism' as suggested by John Hospers, *A Introduction to Philosophical Analysis*, p. 381, or by 'mentalism' as suggested by C. D. Broad, *The Mind and Its Place in Nature*, *passim*. According to him, idealism is "the doctrine that the nature of the Universe is such that those characteristics which are 'highest' and most valuable *must* either be manifested eternally or *must* be manifested in greater and greater intensity, and in wider and wider extent as time goes on." (*loc. cit.*, p. 654). On this basis all Buddhists have been idealists.

the projection of the finite mind (*sems, rang-gi sems*) and has no external real existence. None of the texts tries to identify an externally real world with the thought or action of a World Mind. But in relating this line of thought to subjective idealism, it also is important to note the role *sems* (*citta*) plays within the total framework of Buddhism. All schools, the Vijñānavādins (or so-called idealists) included, list *sems* (*citta*) among the transitory constituents of reality. It is a 'point-instant' and what we would call the history of a mind would on Buddhist presuppositions be a set of point-instants varying continuously in their quality of temporal position, and the determinate duration of this mind would depend upon the determinate relation between the determinate qualities of temporal position characterizing the first and last point-instants of this set. Accepting for a moment the Buddhist contention that only mind (*sems, sems-tsam*) is real, it follows that it is rather loose talk to equate *sems* with our concept of 'mind' without qualifications. It also becomes evident that in Buddhist idealism which seems to avoid certain ontological-absolutistic implications, *sems* refers to a psychic event as a partless single unit which appears as two, i.e., this event itself and the object. But since the psychic event is the only reality, the unreality of the empirical universe, be this individual minds or physical objects, follows directly from this premise. It is also obvious that the Indian Buddhist idealists whose thought is reflected by the bKa'-brgyud-pas, were above all concerned with epistemology, the relation between the psychic event of the moment with its objective duplicate.[15] Only secondarily were they metaphysically interested, as when they reduced the whole of reality to the one particular existent of *sems* (mind). It seems that the bKa'-brgyud-pas, just as their Indian prototypes, due to their preoccupation with epistemological problems, misunderstood the logical character of the metaphysical premise. They saw *sems* (mind) as a starting-point on which other assertions

---

[15]A valuable analysis of Buddhist epistemology is found in Hemanta Kumar Ganguli, *Philosophy of Logical Construction*, pp. 24 *seq*.

were to be based, in a word, as the basic premise, summed up in the words: "The whole of reality is mental."

However, epistemology is one facet of philosophy, metaphysics another. What distinguishes a metaphysician from other philosophers is not the premise he starts from but the principle of interpretation he brings to bear. He certainly does not claim to reveal truths about a world which lies beyond the realm of the senses. His concern is with how to take what happens here and now or how to get the things of this world into perspective. In other words, a metaphysician is not necessarily a system-builder. This emphasis on metaphysics and the new interpretation offered by it distinguishes the rNying-ma-pas from the bKa'-brgyud-pas.

In his *rDzogs-pa-chen-po sems-nyid ngal-gso* and more so in his commentary on this work, the *rDzogs-pa-chen-po sems-nyid ngal-gso'i shing-rta chen-po*, fols. 370*a seq*. Klong-chen rab-'byams-pa repudiates the mentalistic reduction. His interpretation hinges on the terms *sems-nyid* (*citta eva*), *snang-ba* (*ābhāsa*), and *gzung-'dzin* (*grāhya-grāhaka*). It is significant that he does not open his discussion with the suggestion of the mentalistic premise that the whole of reality is mental, but with declaring that appearance is not a mentalistic phenomenon. For him, 'appearance' is not a correlate to an unknowable thing in itself, nor is it to be identified with semblance, rather it is the slanted views through which an identical thing makes its appearances, as it occurs particularly in perception. That which makes its appearance in these slanted views is *sems-nyid* which is not a mind (*sems*), since mind itself is a slanted view.[16] As we shall see later it is here that the mentalistic premise is transcended. Klong-chen rab-'byams-pa states:

[16]More precisely it is the 'ground' ('being' itself) that appears (*gzhi-snang*), for which *sems-nyid* is a synonymous term. See for instance Klong-chen rab-'byams-pa's *sDe-gsum snying-po'i don-'grel gnas-lugs rin-po-che'i mdzod ces-bya-ba'i 'grel-pa*, fol. 21: *rang-byung-gi ye-shes—gzhi lhun-grub-kyi sangs-rgyas—'gyur-ba med-pa'i chos-dbyings—sems-nyid—rang-bzhin-gyis 'od-gsal-ba—rdzogs-pa chen-po*.

"The refutation of the thesis that appearance is mental: Although observable qualities appear before a mind they are not mental.

All the things that appear as the external world
Appear before a mind but are not this mind.
They are also not found anywhere else.
Although through the power of experience potentialities (*bag-chags*) there appears the duality of the apprehendable (object) (*gzung*) and the apprehending (subject) (*'dzin*)
There has never been any duality of the apprehendable and the apprehending
It is like the reflection of a face in the mirror.

"This is to say, when there is a reflection of the face in a mirror, the polished surface of a mirror serves as the basis for the reflection appearing in it, and the face serves as the emitting agency or the emergence of the observable quality of the face, so that when one's face is reflected in a mirror this reflection is not the face, and yet there is no other projecting agency but the face. Similarly what appears as the variety (of the observable world) on the part of the erring[17] mind, does so appear due to the interrelationship of main and contributory causes. The apparent objects such as mountains and other observable entities, are not mental but apart from their appearance due to the erring tendency of the experience potentialities there is no other thing to be found existing, and this is the appearance of the observable quality.[18] It is the appearance of something non-existent (*med-bzhin snang-ba*),[19] like in the case of a person suffering from an eye disease which makes him see combed out hairs where there are none.

---

[17] *'khrul-pa*. Unlike our 'error' it does not connote culpability. It merely refers to the slanted views we hold.

[18] Klong-chen rab-'byams-pa here argues that the sensible form and size and distance of an objective constituent of perception is determined in part by our predominant interests and beliefs at the moment (*bag-chags*).

[19] *med-pa* as in *med-bzhin snang-ba* and *med-pa gsal-snang* is not the co-implicate of *yod-pa* 'being'. Klong-chen rab-'byams-pa uses it in the sense of the Taoist 本無.

"Someone might argue, if the appearance of mountains and so on is neither external nor internal, what is it then? It is precisely your involvement in what is merely a process of externalization.[20] Since the appearance of the whole of reality subsumed under the headings of Saṃsāra, i.e., the world of appearance and of possible life forms, and of Nirvāṇa, is not found to exist either without (i.e., as an external object) or within (i.e., as an idea or in between ever since it has made its appearance it is described by the eight similies of the apparitional. The *Samādhirājasūtra* says:

> Know all things to be like this:
> When a woman looks at her made-up face
> In a mirror or clear water,
> Although there is a reflection
> It neither is nor is not.

"It is from the appearance of the non-existent (*med-bzhin-du snang-ba*) that the error of the subject-object division with its belief in the reality of its duplicate starts. Here the apprehendable (*gzung-ba*) means the initial object-related phase of the cognitive process (*rtog-pa*), and since absolute subject-being (*sems-nyid*) is such as to possess what is apprehendable (*gzung-bar skyes-pa can*), the apprehending act (*'dzin-pa*) refers to the mental processes that derive subsequently, such as discursive thought and other processes. This is stated in the *sPyan-ras-gzigs brtul-zhugs*: 'It is to be understood that 'apprehendable' (*gzung-ba*) means the mind (*sems*) believing in (the existence of) an object and that 'apprehending act' (*'dzin-pa*) means such mental events as discursive thought'.

"Some stupid people taking pride in their deludedness declare that by apprehendable the appearance of mountains and other objects is understood and that the apprehending act refers to their noetic capacity (*rang-gi shes-pa*). Not much needs to be said about the fallacious reasoning of these dunces. The point is, do these objects appear or do they not before the mind of those who have gone beyond the fictions of subject and object? If they

---

[20] *gnyis-'dzin-las grub-pa kho-nar zhen-pa.*

do, they must appear in the subject-object form, because the object is claimed to be the apprehendable and the cognition of the object as this or that as the (subjective) apprehending act. If they do not, there is a contradiction to the countless statements that what appears before the mind of the spiritually advanced (*'phags-pa*) is like an apparition, that the Arhants among the Śrāvakas see mountains and palaces, and that the Buddhas cognize objects as they are."

The key for understanding what is meant by *sems-nyid* is contained in the statement that this *sems-nyid* possesses what is apprehendable (*gzung-bar skyes-pa-can*). As *sems-nyid* is clearly distinguished from *sems*, which is a mere fiction,[21] it refers to what I shall call 'absolute subject-being', which in spite of the use of the term 'subject' must not be confused with any kind of subjectivism that is inherent in the subjective and even impersonalistic types of idealism.

I have therefore added the word 'being' and hyphenated the term in order to emphasize the existential nature which again must not be confused with the ordinary conception of ontology as the doctrine as *some* being, rather than of being-as-such. The following will be an attempt to clarify the rNying-ma-pas' conception.

'Absolute subject-being' can manifest itself as 'subject' and as 'being' only when it is 'functioning'. Functioning therefore means 'having an object' and consequently 'behaving towards (something)'. In other words, 'having an object' (*gzung-bar skyes-pa-can*) is tantamount to saying 'being a subject' (*sems-nyid*) where 'being' does not stand as a copula joining a subject with its predicate (adjective), but as existence so that 'being' and 'subject' would be interchangeable. Moreover, the

---

[21]See above note 6. The clearest formulation of the difference between *sems-nyid* and *sems* is given in *Bla-ma yang-tig*, section V, fol. 7*a*: *sems-nyid ces smos-pas sems-kyi zad-sa rig-pa 'char-gzhi-nyid-la zer-gyis sems-la mi zer-ro* "*sems-nyid* is spoken of with reference to the rising of an aesthetically satisfying peak awareness where *sems* (mentation) has ceased, not with reference to *sems*."

indefinite article in 'being a subject' must not be understood as indicating a particular subject. The problem is that of 'being subject as such' and 'having object as such'. If on this basis of 'being subject' equalling 'having object', object means to be and if to be means to have object then the object possessed by what is referred to as 'having object' is the primary subject (*sems-nyid*). Hence 'absolute subject-being' does not mean, 'absolutized' being, rather it means being as such as subject which at the same time because of its 'functioning' is not only absolute in so far as it is, but also relative, that is, it is related to something as its object. In this way the absolutism of any idealistic system as well as the relativism of any subjectivism is successfully overcome.

The concept *sems-nyid* 'absolute subject-being', entails certain problems. In contrast to *sems* which is equated with 'unknowing' (*ma-rig-pa*) *sems-nyid* stands for knowledge which again is not this or that kind of knowledge, but knowledge as such (*ye-shes*). This is to say that 'knowledge' is not an addition, but is included in being which, as we have seen, is subject-being functioning through knowledge. In other words, subject-being is an *a priori knowledge*, as indicated by the Tibetan term *ye* ('*a priori*') *shes* ('awareness'). Moreover, absolute presuppositions can evidently not be deduced from further truths without losing this absoluteness. Therefore the texts use the term *rang-byung* 'absolute' (lit., self-originated), in order to avoid the idea that the validity of a set of principles of interpretation can be grounded either deductively or inductively.

One other point to note is that this conception of knowledge is intimately bound up with the central idea of Buddhism being a way. Subject-being is not merely knowledge, it is also the quest for true knowledge. In this quest it is also the subject of possible error (*'khrul-pa*) and knows it, and therefore it can avoid error and bondage and in its knowledge retain its freedom. In other words, error is present as that which is to be denied. Again, freedom is not something to be attained, but is co-extensive with subject-being, just as bondage is limitation and has meaning only towards 'something' as a terminal effect. In so far as 'subject-being' is the same as 'having an object', its freedom is not affected in any way. That is why the texts speak of freedom pervading all phases of man's life.[22]

'Subject-being' (*sems-nyid*) is of course no mind and yet in a sense operates through mind. This is clearly evident from the description of the three aspects under which it may be viewed. Its facticity (*ngo-bo*) is an utter openness (*stong-pa*), its presence (*rang-bzhin*) is luminosity (*gsal-ba*), and its value (*thugs-rje*)[23] is the incessant support (of cognitive activity, *ma-'gag-pa*). This latter point is of special importance as it again shows that value is inseparable from being and since the cognitive process is linked to value in this triple conception, cognition is therefore value-sustained cognition and this is significant with reference to man as a truth-seeking subject. This is evidently implied by such statements as: "Since its facticity is an utter openness, not even the name 'un-knowing' obtains and 'error' has not even postulationally been present; since its presence is spontaneous, awareness shines in a (certain) light; and since value is all-comprehensive, understanding never ceases and is given as the realm of either Saṃsāra or Nirvāṇa."[24] Absolute purity is, of course, an utter openness untainted by any bias or mood, while its presence always lets us see things in a particular light and its all-comprehensiveness constitutes the horizon of meaning.

There are many other problems connected with the rNying-ma-pa interpretation which deserve special analysis as they all will greatly contribute to our as yet scantly knowledge of the development of Buddhist thought. So much, however, seems to become clear from the above analysis. The mind (*sems-nyid*) of

---

[22]*Bla-ma yang-tig*, section V, fol. 61*a* uses the terms *ye-grol*, *yongs-grol*, and *rang-grol* for each aspect of man's total being projected as 'starting-point, way, and goal' respectively.

[23]*thugs-rje*, unlike *snying-rje*, is cognitive. Out of it, as it were, develops cognition (*rig-pa*) and the state of being aware (*ye-shes*). For this reason *thugs-rje* cannot be equated with Sanskrit *karuṇā* or even *mahā-karuṇā* which according to *Abhidharmakośa* VII 33 belongs to the 'worldly' order, while *thugs-rje* in the rNying-ma-pa interpretation belongs to that 'being' (*gzhi*) before there was any 'being' in the sense of a Buddha or a sentient being.

[24]*Theg-pa'i mchog rin-po-che'i mdzod*, fol. 62*b*.

which the rNying-ma-pas are speaking is an absolute fact and is the mind of each of us, though not in the realist's conception of a separation of subject and object into two independent things (thereby turning concrete subject-being into an abstract object), and also not in the idealist's conception of self-knowledge with the disastrous consequence that the self-knowledge of the mind (as an abstract postulate) excludes all knowledge of anything else. It also is not the world-spirit which is but a myth and not a fact, and lastly it is not one stupendous whole which is but another abstraction. Mind (*sems-nyid*) lives in its entirety in every individual and every act of his expressing itself uniquely. This is its very nature as concrete, as indicated by the particle *nyid*.

The Spiritual Teacher in Tibet

The Buddhism of Tibet is commonly referred to as Lamaism. This misleading and inappropriate designation derives from the importance Tibetans attach to the idea of *bla-ma* which literally means 'a potency (*ma*) of highest significance (*bla)*' and which seems to correspond to the India notion of a *guru* or 'spiritual preceptor' who often is the actual object of worship. However, due to the fact that in Tibetan texts *bla-ma* often is the translation of *guru* in Sanskrit works and that Indian works are well known while Tibetan ones are not, the erroneous idea developed that what holds good for the Indian *guru* also applies to the Tibetan *bla-ma* with this difference that the one wears a Hindu garb or none at all and the other wields his influence in a Buddhist setting. It shall not be denied that in Tibetan Buddhism the spiritual teacher is of primary significance, but it is even more important to understand what is meant by 'spiritual teacher' and how he, if indeed he is a person, influences the life of his disciple. Let us see how the idea of 'spiritual teacher' developed.

Mythical language plays an important role in the presentation of religious and metaphysical experience which as power or potency itself 'impels' a person to be and act as its 'representative'. An example is the well known report of the Buddha's enlightenment[1] when the god Brahmā Sahampati urged the Buddha to proclaim his message, much against the will and intention of the newly emerged Buddha. The god Brahmā Sahampati can easily be understood as standing for the 'impelling power' of enlightenment which unlike an absorption in a static absolute as claimed by the Hindu philosophers, is both a vision of reality in a new and more satisfactory light and an activity in consonance with this vision which remains an ever felt presence. Enlightenment, therefore, is a peak experience which is both perceived in itself and yet perceived and reacted to as well as enacted as if it were 'out there', independent of man and persisting beyond his life. Such a peak experience is, to be sure, not egocentered but is felt as a self-validating moment which is so valuable that it makes life worthwhile. This is another way of stating that enlightenment is a continuing dynamic event and not an end. This is clearly borne out by the definition of the word 'enlightenment' (*byang-chub-sems*): "(It is called) pure (*byang*) because Saṃsāra has never had an existence of its own and due to the fact that this very peak experience (*rig-pa*) has been unsullied since its very beginning, (it is called) autonomous (*chub*) because everything positive is spontaneously present in it and its autonomy may manifest itself anywhere in any form (any time); and (it is called) an attitudinal cognition (*sems*) because it encompasses and sheds light on both Saṃsāra and Nirvāṇa due to the fact that it constitutes the horizon of meaning and because it is individually experienceable."[2] In more prosaic words we can say that in the peak experience of enlightenment the vision of reality is tinged with meaning; fact and value have fused. Consequently, vision and action are not mutually exclusive or incompatible. They are facets, not parts, of man's being. Neither can they be added up nor separated: "Vision, total attention, and action are (the facets of) a self-validating peak experience. We speak of

---

[1]See *Majjhima-nikāya*, I, 167 *seq.*, also *Samyutta-nikāya*, I, 136 *seq.*; *Digha-nikāya*, II, 36 *seq*.

[2]*Chos-dbyings rin-po-che'i mdzod-kyi 'grel-pa lung-gi gter-mdzod*, fol. 173*a*.

vision (*lta-ba*) because the peak experience can be perceived with our own eyes. But seeing things in relation to other things is not vision. We speak of total attention (*sgom-pa*) because by steadily caring for the content of the vision the feeling of its presential value will become more and more intense. But attending to the content in relation to everything else in the world is not total attention because it remains unacquainted with the vision. We speak of action (*spyod-pa*) because we remain continually engaged with the presential value. But acting contrariwise is not action because reality is not envisaged and no relation exists to the vision of reality. For this reason vision, total attention and action are not entities that can be added up or separated, precisely because of the fact that the peak experience is observable, can be felt as a presence, and can be reacted to and enacted."[3]

Thus 'impelled' by the 'power' of enlightenment the Buddha became a teacher and unlike a prophet who warns or a preacher who expounds, he grew personally less and less important because he neither imparted nor announced salvation. As a teacher he merely spoke *about* it, pointing to certain facts which everybody can see for himself independently of dogma and scientific hypothesis. The Buddha's doctrine certainly was and is a proclamation of salvation, not however so much of what has occurred or happened but of what must and can be achieved through the doctrine which, by insisting on what can be perceived directly, aims at liberating man from his prejudices and preconceived opinions and thereby lets him regain the openness of mind from which he ordinarily tends to shut himself off. This also is the interpretation of the word *buddha* (*sangs-rgyas*) which became the descriptive term for the man who had had this liberating experience. "Since everything that pertains to error has become exhausted we speak of gone-ness (*sangs*), and of wideness (*rgyas*) in view of the absolute awareness which appreciates everything observable,"[4] and, "when the distorted

---

[3] *Bi-ma snying-tig*, vol. *Ga*, fol. 39*ab*.
[4] *sNying-po don-gyi man-ngag sems-kyi me-long*, fol. 7*a*.

views of ordinary people have been dispersed and an absolute awareness has asserted itself in its encompassingness then there is the broadness of the horizon of meaning because (he who has reached this point) is established on the level of supreme awareness."[5]

Inasmuch as it is the experience of enlightenment that constitutes salvation, the doctrine that effects this insight can continue to operate independently of the teacher who first gave it the coherent form of an interconnected whole. The doctrine was named a 'path' (*lam*). However, this literal translation is extremely inadequate because of our assocating with 'path' the idea of a link connecting two terminal points. The 'path', however, is more than an inert link lying between two points. Looking at it from the outside it may be said to lead to a terminal point, enlightenment, salvation, Nirvāṇa. Looked at from within it is synonymous with 'absolute awareness' (*ye-shes*) and indicates the growth and unfolding of man's being.[6] None of our Western languages possesses a word which can equally be used for the within and the without. Therefore, in each particular case we shall have to specify in which sense the commonly used word 'path' is to be understood. This distinction between the without and the within, with no fixed borders dividing the one from the other, accounts for the distinction between two types of 'spiritual teachers'; the one more specifically termed 'spiritual friend' or 'well-wisher' (*dge-ba'i bshes-gnyen*, Sanskrit *kalyāṇamitra*), the other the *bla-ma* proper. But since the without may be transferred to the within and the within may appear projected into the without, the one can be understood as the other. There is a significant verse which employs both terms, *dge-ba'i bshes-gnyen* and *bla-ma*, which suggests the division between the within and the without, the spiritual and the physical. Translat-

[5]*dPal gsang-ba snying-po'i rgyud don gsal-byed me-long* by gYung-ston rdo-rje dpal-bzang, fol. 17*a*.

[6]*Sa-lam-gyi rnam-bzhag theg-gsum mdzes-rgyan*, *passim*. See also sGam-po-pa, Collected Works, vol. *Ca*, fol. 29*b*: " 'Path' means to give up what is to be given up and to implant its opposite in one's being. 'Goal' means the attainment of the ultimate in giving up and knowledge."

ing the word *bla-ma* by 'spiritual master' we must remind ourselves that we use mythical language and that what the Tibetans understand by *bla-ma* is not necessarily a person. The verse says:

> Always rely on wise spiritual masters
> Because from them a wise man's virtues stem;
> Without fail rely on your well-wishers,
> Like sick persons depending on their physicians for their health.[7]

Bearing in mind this distinction between 'spiritual friend' or 'well-wisher' and *bla-ma*, the idea of the 'spiritual teacher' is basically connected with that of the 'spiritual friend'. In the specific sense of the word, a teacher is an instructor and the subject matter of his instruction in Buddhism is man himself, not as a being opposed to the world he lives in and which he is supposed to dominate in order to destroy it and with its destruction putting an end to himself. Rather does the teaching aim at making man realize his uniqueness of being human, which he is in constant danger of losing, be it that he arrogates superhuman powers or through his actions sinks below the level of a wild beast. This uniqueness of being human with its obligation of acting humanely, so easily lost and forgotten, partakes of the wider context of general impermanence which is brought home to us by the fact that death may strike any time. The awareness of death, instead of filling us with despair, reminds us of our uniqueness and thereby makes us reconsider the way in which we act, whether it helps us to preserve or makes us lose our uniqueness. In this respect the consideration of our actions and their consequences is intimately related to the two preceding topics, uniqueness and impermanence. It also points to the future as of our own making. While the present unsatisfactory situation is the outcome of our previous actions and may well be carried over into the future, it yet challenges us to find a solution which will be more satisfactory.

---

[7]Quoted in the *Thun-mong-gi sngon-'gro sems-sbyong rnam-pa bdun-gyi don-khrid thar-pa'i them-skas*, fol. 33*b*, of the *Klong-chen snying-thig*.

These four topics, the uniqueness of human existence, the impermanence of all that is, the relation between our actions and the situation in which we will find ourselves, and the general unsatisfactoriness of the situation in which we and our fellow beings are caught up, represent the teaching of the 'spiritual friends' to this very day.[8] As these topics are interrelated it is left to the individual teacher to select the one or the other as the starting point of his instruction. For instance, Po-to-ba (1031–1105 A.D.) emphasized impermanence: "The quintessence of spiritual life is the attention to impermanence. When you contemplate the transitoriness by death you lay the foundation for entering the spiritual life, as a corollary you apply yourself to what is wholesome, and lastly you facilitate the understanding of the self-identity of any object seen as a whole."[9] He continues by pointing out the immediate effect it has on the person's life insofar as it makes him lose interest in his individual petty existence and thereby makes him divert his desires which always involved him in Saṃsāra so that he can more easily embark on the 'path' to Nirvāṇa. sNe'u-zur-ba (1042–1167 A.D.), on the other hand, began with an account of Saṃsāra, revolving relentlessly, and then developed the idea of

---

[8]In one way or another all schools of Buddhism discuss the subject matter of guidance according to the sequence of the topics as listed here. Nevertheless the *Blo-sbyong don-bdun-ma*, fol. 2*b*, by Thogs-med bzang-po dpal, mentions only three topics, leaving out the relation between our actions and their outcome. The bKa'-brgyud-pas uniformly deal with all four topics. See for instance such works as the *Phyag-rgya-chen-po lhan-cig-skyes-sbyor-gyi khrid-kyi spyi sdom rtsa-tshig* and the *Nges-don phyag-rgya-chen-po'i khrid-rim gsal-byed de-bzhin-nyid-kyi rang-zhal mngon-sum snang-ba'i me-long*.

The rNying-ma-pas also deal with these four topics but under different headings. With them the individual approach is much more marked than with the other schools of Buddhism. This difference is conspicuous when we compare their *sems-sbyong-bdun* with the dGe-lugs-pas' *blo-sbyong-bdun*. Both deal with the seven features of the purification of mind, but while the latter are ethico-intellectual, the former are metaphysically oriented.

[9]*Legs-par bshad-pa bka'-gdams rin-po-che'i gsung-gi gces-btus nor-bu'i bang-mdzod*, fol. 78*b*. This work contains the summaries and actual quotations from the early Tibetan works on the 'Gradation of the Path' (*lam-rim*) which have since been lost.

the uniqueness of human existence which alone is capable of breaking the vicious circle: "There is no end to Saṃsāra. Since it does not stop by itself we have to wander about in it continuing in its endlessness to this moment. To become frightened and terrified by Saṃsāra when we think that for any being in the six forms of life any pleasure is not real pleasure, is to become involved in the cycle of transmigration. As to breaking this cycle we have to think that since there is no end to Saṃsāra and it will not stop by itself we ourselves have to break it. If we do not do it nobody else can do it for us. Now is the time to break it. If we do not do so now we shall never do so and will have to wander about in it. Certainly it will be difficult to find a human form of life at a later time."[10] The psychological insight is remarkable and characteristic of Buddhism: escapism into a soporific absorption in an absolute is no answer to the problems a man faces and which he has to solve. Both Po-to-ba and sNe'u-zur-ba belonged to the group who came under the spell of Atīśa who infused Buddhism in Tibet with new vigor. In the subsequent centuries the teaching became more organized in first dealing with the immediate situation of man and then elaborating the related topics. There is not a single work in the Tibetan language, dealing with the guidance of man, that does not in one way or another discuss these four subject matters. Most valuable in this respect is the *lam-rim* literature, 'the gradation of the path of spiritual growth extending over three types of men'. Actually, the three types of men are not so many different persons but stages in the growth or stagnation of a single individual.[11] The educational value is obvious; the teaching is graded according to the intellectual acumen of each disciple and to make a person aware of the fact that he is made up of various layers goes a long way to make him realize that he is not an entity fixed once for all but is a continuous variable and therefore capable of growth.

Growth, however, begins when there is fullness of life. That

---

[10]See the work mentioned in the preceding note, fol. 106*b*.

[11]See my *Treasures on the Tibetan Middle Way*, Berkeley: 1971, pp. 12 *seq.*, 80.

is, as the texts declare, when the person belongs to the superior type of man. In other words, the inferior as well as the mediocre types of persons represent stagnant forms of life. Not only is each person here an impoverished individual, he also keeps himself mentally and spiritually impoverished because all his perceptions and actions are anxiety-based. The inferior type is so much engrossed in himself that he cannot see or perceive anything but himself, and the mediocre type, though less engrossed in himself, still is deficiency-motivated and his whole life oscillates between episodic gratifications and frustrations; one moment he feels as if he were in paradise, the next as if he were passing through hell. The superior type, by contrast, is not dominated by the coming-to-rest conception of motivation; he actually becomes more 'interested' and 'active' in a meaningful way which sharply contrasts with the busybodying activity of the deficiency-motivated and anxiety-propelled mediocre type of man. Rather than suppressing, repressing and derogating his emotions, the superior person utilizes and harnesses them in his eagerness to grow. For him the 'spiritual friend' is of primary importance and can give him significant help. Blo-bzang ye-shes, the second Panchen Lama (1663–1737 A.D.), in his *Myur-lam*,[12] is quite explicit that growth and guidance begin with the superior type of man whose main characteristic is his having broken through his deficiency-motivated ego-centeredness and its ensuing intellectual and spiritual stagnation:

"The 'paths' of the inferior and mediocre types of men are not themselves guidance, but are part of the preliminary preparation for the superior person's development and only in this respect are considered to be a guidance. It may be objected that since whatever pertains to the levels of the inferior and mediocre types of men is part and parcel of the level of the superior person, it should be sufficient to deal with the 'path' of the superior man, so why still talk about the 'paths' of the lower ranks? The reply to this objection is that the division into three individualities has

---

[12]The full title of this work is *Byang-chub-lam-gyi rim-pa'i dmar-khrid thams-cad mkhyen-par bgrod-pa'i myur-lam.*

two important bearings on the guidance. First, even without adopting the attitude of an inferior or a mediocre person we have to curb our arrogance of considering ourselves as superior individuals, and secondly, great benefits accrue to any of the three statuses."[13]

Breaking through our self-imposed limitations and curbing our feeling of self-importance is accompanied by or, speaking more precisely, characterized by an interest in others, a feeling for-and-with-others compassion (*snying-rje*). As this term suggests it is our heart (*snying*) that speaks. Since this compassion is born out of the awareness of man's uniqueness and impermanence it is something quite different from the sentimentalism of the do-gooder who merely acts from selfish motives and is blissfully ignorant of the actual needs of the person whom he insults with his charitable gifts.

The 'spiritual friend' or teacher, however, cannot do more than speak to us. He may stir us, particularly when his words are not mere empty phrases and when he by his own life exemplifies what he teaches. The inherent limitation of words is that they can only point to what it is all about, but themselves are not the thing under consideration. sNe'u-zur-ba puts it succinctly:[14] "First we have to think about the words, then about what they are about. Words are like a lamp, what they are about is like pure gold. If in a dark room there is some pure gold we shall certainly not find it without a lamp, although we shall do so with the help of a lamp. Similarly, by relying on what we are told we surely will find what the words are about." Nevertheless, words are mere noises and ineffective unless there is a willingness on our part to act on them. Such willingness is not to be understood as a manifestation of a person's will power which precisely because of its purely subjective character is merely destructive as it operates on the basis of the person's necessarily mistaken perceiving and illusions. Rather it is a responsiveness to a superior power which from now on takes over. Blo-bzang chos-kyi rgyal-mtshan makes the significant statement: "Since various

[13] *Loc. cit.*, fol. 6*a*.

[14] See the work quoted in note 9, fol. 105*a*.

kinds of misery in Saṃsāra which is of formidable power, will continue to be experienced for a long time once I and the sentient beings who in one way or another have been my mother, are born in it unless the specific understanding of the difficulty of obtaining life as a human being is born in me, I pray for spiritual sustenance by my divine master (*bla-ma lha*) in my endeavor to have this specific understanding grow in me and the sentient beings who have been my mother."[15]

The juxtaposition of *bla-ma* and *lha* is of particular importance for the proper understanding of the nature of *bla-ma* which has given Lamaism its name. The term *lha* (Sanskrit *deva*), apart from designating a certain form of life[16] which is as unsatisfactory and transitory as that of a human being because gods (*lha*, *deva*) are merely temporary aspects of life in general, is a label for something in which the sense of the transcendent has found expression. Otherwise elusive and vague it becomes concretely felt and understandable in the form of the *bla-ma* or the *yi-dam*.[17] The latter preserves more of the divine and transcendent, the former has more personalistic traits and therefore fuses more easily with the concrete person who enters and shapes our life as 'spiritual friend' (*dge-ba'i bshes-gnyen*). Ultimately both the *bla-ma* and the *yi-dam* are symbol forms of Buddhahood (*sangs-rgyas*) which each individual is capable of realizing and which speaks to him through these symbol forms. The identity of *yi-dam* and *bla-ma* is well formulated by Blo-bzang ye-shes[18]: "From the *lam-rim* works that belong to the tradition of Bya-yul-pa (1075–1138 A.D.) we learn that anyone who claims

---

[15] *Byang-chub-lam-gyi rim-pa'i dmar-khrid thams-cad mkhyen-par bgrod-pa'i bde-lam*, fol. 6*b*. See also *Myur-lam*, fol. 34*a*.

[16] Usually six forms of life are counted, all of them being unsatisfactory. The three which are less so are the worlds of men, gods, and demons. The thoroughly unsatisfactory forms are animals, hungry spirits, and denizens of hell. For further details see my *Treasures on the Tibetan Middle Way*, p. 13 *seq*.

[17] The various schools of Buddhism in Tibet usually give preference to one among the many *yi-dam*. Those which are more frequently mentioned are Guhyasamāja, Cakrasamvara, Vajrabhairava, Hevajra. Much also depends on the disciple's feeling of affinity.

[18] *Myur-lam*, fol. 27*a*. See also my *The Life and Teaching of Naropa*, Oxford: 1963, p. 107.

that rDo-rje-'chang or any other *yi-dam* exists apart from or even is superior to the *bla-ma* will not achieve any realizations. Further, early one morning when Mar-pa was asleep at Nāropa's place, the great scholar Nāropa manifested the *maṇḍala* of Hevajra in full in the sky and then called Mar-pa: 'My son, don't sleep, get up! Your *yi-dam* Hevajra has arrived in the sky with his entourage. Do you salute me or the *yi-dam*?' When Mar-pa saluted the *yi-dam* Hevajra and his entourage Nāropa said:

> Before there was the *bla-ma*
> There was not even the name of Buddha.
> The Buddhas of a thousand aeons
> Have come into being in dependence of the *bla-ma*.
> The *yi-dam* is the *bla-ma*'s manifestation.

This famous passage to which allusion is often made in oral instructions, clearly circumscribes the importance and significance for the growth of the individual. In addition, it admirably expresses the ambivalent character of the *bla-ma* who is a 'spiritual' teacher in the strict sense of the word because due to his spiritual or mental, rather than physical, nature he is the manifestation and humanly intelligible formulation of Buddhahood which is the as yet unrealized Being of man. At the same time the *bla-ma*, due to his transcendent character, may be envisaged as the *yi-dam* in respect with whom the feeling of transcendence is paramount. And yet the *bla-ma* may be encountered 'projected', as it were, on a human person who enters our life as 'spiritual friend' and 'well-wisher' because he, too, is ultimately a manifestation of Buddhahood. Blo-bzang chos-kyi rgyal-mtshan, in a similar vein as Klong-chen rab-'byams-pa[19] long before him, stated that "our spiritual friends are the very presence of Buddhahood. The Supremely Enlightened One has said in his pre-

---

[19] *rDzogs-pa chen-po sems-nyid ngal-gso'i 'grel-pa shing-rta chen-po*, fol. 136*ab*. The author quotes from the *Nam-mkha' dri-ma-med-pa'i mdo* in which the Buddha addresses Ānanda: "Ānanda, since the Tathāgatas do not themselves appear before the sentient beings, attach yourself particularly to the spiritual friends because they are manifestly present and by teaching the *dharma* sow the seed of liberation."

cious Tantras and Sutras that in this degenerate age the Lord rDo-rje-'chang manifests himself in the form of spiritual friends and acts for the good of sentient beings. Accordingly, our spiritual friends, apart from merely exhibiting different aspects of being, are manifestations of the Lord rDo-rje-'chang in order to attract us who have the bad fortune of being unable to perceive Buddhahood directly."[20]

Thinking in this way of our spiritual friends as the manifested presence of Buddhahood is one way of serving them, the other, which more or less follows from this attitude, being our endeavor to realize for ourselves what they teach us.[21] This shows that learning and growth go together. Learning, in the narrower sense of thinking, consists in carrying over into internal operations the various stimulus-response patterns, such as for instance the one of teacher-disciple, which have arisen in social transactions. Most of these occur on the verbal level—first we have to listen to the words of our spiritual friends, as sNe'u-zur-ba has pointed out. Then thinking of them not as mere words but as meaningful we gradually realize that the meaning we attach to them is our incipient reaction to them plus our feeling-emotional tone. In this way thinking takes on the nature of an inner forum in which social acts—now symbolized—are performed. Inasmuch as the stimulus comes from 'without', from our spiritual friends, they are even more important than the Buddha himself who actually is Buddhahood already realized. bsKal-bzang bstan-'dzin mkhas-grub says: "Since our true spiritual master has come to us in the form which all the Buddhas of the three divisions of time have adopted as their original form in order to guide the sentient beings whose passions are difficult to control, he is in no way different from these Buddhas in view of his possessing all positive qualities and having no defects. Yet from our point of view he is even more

---

[20]*Byang-chub-lam-gyi rim-pa'i dmar-khrid thams-cad mkhyen-par bgrod-pa'i bde-lam*, fol. 4*b*.

[21]See for instance my *sGam-po-pa—The Jewel Ornament of Liberation*, London: 1959, p. 30 *seq*.

significant than the Buddhas. As a rule, the Buddhas do not move from their sphere of ultimate Being[22] and Bliss, yet they show themselves in existential communication[23] to the exceptional, spiritually advanced Bodhisattvas. The Buddhas' existentiality[24] does not become an object of the discursive mind of Śrāvakas, Pratyekabuddhas and ordinary persons, and therefore by way of incarnate beings in the human world they set the beings on the path of maturation and liberation. Although we have not been rejected intentionally because of our distance from these Buddhas, it is simply due to our karma and locklessness that we are not worthy to see the Buddhas directly and to receive the nectar of their words. We are as if in a cave facing north into which the sun does not shine and we roam about in Saṃsāra having no end and there experience untold misery. If at this time when we have found existence as a human being, we were not to encounter true spiritual friends we would have to

---

[22]*chos-sku*. This term corresponds to Sanskrit *dharmakāya* which is either left untranslated or mistranslated by what I call the 'literalist's fallacy'. The Tibetan word *sku* indicates 'existence' in the sense of 'Being'. It almost approximates the existentialist philosopher's conception of 'existence' and 'Being' except that it does not share the latter's subjectivism.

[23]*longs-spyod rdzogs-pa'i sku*. Sanskrit *saṃbhogakāya*. It refers to the level of communication, because it is in this form that the Buddha as 'absolute Being' (*chos-sku*) speaks (*gsung*) to those who are capable of understanding him. The fact that in anthropomorphic representations the Buddha is richly adorned symbolizes the fact that 'communication' enriches. As the existentialist philosophers in the West have shown, communication is incompatible with 'talk', which the longer it lasts the emptier it becomes.

[24]*sku de nyid*. This phrase refers to both *chos-sku* and *longs-(spyod rdzogs-pa'i) sku*. 'Ultimate Being' cannot become an object of thought without losing its character of 'being as such'. Similarly 'communication' cannot become a topic of discourse. 'Ultimate Being' 'communicates' itself through 'meaning fulness'. The latter is the *sprul-pa'i sku*, Sanskrit *nirmāṇakāya*. In other words, because the Buddha as 'being incarnate' (*chos-sku sprul-sku*) communicates (*longs-sku*) with those who are receptive and capable of response he makes them aware of their own 'being' (*chos-sku*). Thus, while *chos-sku* stands for 'ultimate Being', and *longs-sku* for 'existential communication', *sprul-sku* stands for the 'intellectual appreciation of being', constituting 'meaningfulness' on the one hand, and a challenge to existential realization, on the other.

wander about in those unhappy forms of life where not even the sound of the Three Jewels is heard. It is by the grace of our spiritual friends that we understand the profound path opened by them, on which we will easily find liberation from all the misery of Saṃsāra and its evil forms of life, which is the precious citadel of perfect Buddhahood."[25]

The spiritual friend who stimulates us and to whom we respond by listening to and thinking about his words, reappears as the *bla-ma* in the inner forum of thought. Inasmuch as we now deal with meaning rather than with words, even if the *bla-ma*-disciple transaction continues in silent language, the *bla-ma* now continues guiding us, which means that we follow a certain 'path' on which meaning becomes deeper and deeper.[26] The situation that has now developed is well described by sGam-po-pa:

"We think now that, generally speaking, all the misery of Saṃsāra derives from engaging in evil and unwholesome activities, that all happiness derives from engaging in wholesome activities, that our rejecting evil and what is unwholesome and our experiencing what is wholesome at this time when we have

---

[25] *Man-ngag zab-mo yon-tan rin-chen bsdus don*, fol. 6*a*. In the *Legs-par bshad-pa bka'-gdams rin-po-che'i gsung-gi gces-btus nor-bu'i bang mdzod*, fol. 112*a*, Po-to-ba is credited to have made the distinction of "spiritual friends (in the form) of the Buddha, of a spiritually advanced person, and of an ordinary human being. Of these three the last one is the one showing us the greatest kindness, because he leads us out of our unsatisfactory situation."

[26] See the work quoted in note 7. I also refer to verses 40 and 41 of Saraha's Dohas as given in M. Shahidullah, *Les Chants Mystiques de Kāṇha et de Saraha. Les Dohākoṣa et Les Caryā*. (*Textes pour l'étude de Bouddhisme tardif*), Paris: 1928. While in both verses the apabramśa version uses the word *guru*, the Tibetan translation differentiates between *slob-dpon* and *bla-ma*. Since M. Shahidullah does not see this difference his translation is inadmissible. The difference in meaning is thus:

> 40: "Although the nature of the genuine cannot be expressed in words,
> It can be seen with your eyes (opened by) the instruction of the teacher (*slob-dpon*)," and
>
> 41: "When the awareness of the genuine has become pure in its totality,
> The virtues of the *bla-ma* enter your heart."

found the uniqueness of human existence is the presence of the *bla-ma*'s sustaining power, that there has come about the realization of the *yi-dam*, and that we have been caught by the hook of compassion of all the Buddhas and Bodhisattvas."[27]

sGam-po-pa here repeats the idea already found in the *Pañcakrama* that once we begin to think in terms of meaning and thereby have committed ourselves to a way of being and acting we are drawn towards what we really are. The *Pañcakrama* says:

> Let someone be about to fall from the peak of a mountain
> He will fall even if he does not want to.
> He who has obtained helpful instruction by the *bla-ma*'s grace
> Will be liberated even if he does not want it.[28]

Once the *bla-ma* has taken over we are in the process of learning and growth. To the extent that growth consists in doing away with inhibitions and constraints and then permitting the person to '*be* himself' and to see things and other persons equally as themselves, rather than as rubricized de-personalized entities, to that extent the mode of seeing and the way of acting of a person is free and released. Not that freedom has been attained as some classified item, but rather that freedom itself operates in seeing and acting and understanding and so enables the perceiver to see others in their own right. He can thus perceive simultaneously the opposites, the polarities and incompatibles. While in ordinary, selective, rubricizing perception A is A and everything else is not-A, now A and not-A interpenetrate and are like one; every person is simultaneously human and divine, transitory and yet lastingly valuable, male and female, fierce and gentle, stern and benignant, sensuous and ethereal, and this

---

[27]Collected Works, Vol. *Ca*, fol. 44*a*.

[28]*Pañcakrama*, II, 69. Also quoted in *Bla-ma mchod-pa'i khrid-yig gsang-ba'i gnad rnam-par phye-ba snyan-rgyud man-ngag-gi gter-mdzod* by Ye-shes rgyal-myshan, fol. 116*ab*.

This theme that he who has been taken hold of by the *bla-ma* will have to 'grow' even if he wants to remain stagnant and resists growth, is illustrated in a small sketch recently discovered and kept at a temple in Kyoto. It has been reproduced by Sherman E. Lee, *A History of Far Eastern Art*, New York (n.d.), p. 300, no. 386. Mr. Lee, however, has misunderstood the significance of this sketch.

permits much clearer and more insightful perception and understanding of what there is. This is so because the perceptual experience is now organized around the object, not as something to be used and manipulated for this or that more or less selfish purpose, but with which the beholder can fuse into a new and larger whole and to which he reacts with humility, reverence, and even surrender, rather than by imposing himself on it.

The contrast between perceiving more of what there is, concretely and in its intrinsic uniqueness, and categorizing, schematizing, classifying what little we have perceived in ordinary perception, is well brought out by sGam-po-pa and bsKal-bzang bstan-'dzin mkhas-grub. The latter well describes our ordinary perception by which we take in only external qualities, and he speaks of the 'impure character of what appears before us' because it is tainted with our presuppositions, opinons and ready-made judgments: "Now, a Buddha is without any defects and in the possession of all positive qualities. But our spiritual friends have this and that fault deriving from the three poisons and therefore are not Buddhas. If we think in this way it is due to the impure character of our perceptions of what appears before us. Formerly also, due to this circumstance Legs-pa'i Karma saw the deeds of our teacher, the Buddha, as mere chaff; Asanga saw the venerable Maitreya as a bitch; Maitripa saw Śabari, lord of yogis, engaged in such impure acts as slaughtering swine; Nāropa saw Tilopa performing such mad actions as frying fish alive; the novice Tshem-bu-pa saw (the goddess) Vajravarāhī as a leper woman; the *ācārya* Vajraghaṇṭa saw (the goddess) Vajravarāhī as a woman tending swine; and the *ācārya* Buddhajñānapāda saw the *ācārya* Mañjuśrimitra as a householder who had tied the religious garb round his head while tilling his fields."[29]

On the other hand, concrete perceiving of the whole of the object implies that it is seen with reverence and devotion, maybe with selfless love. Certainly, such perceiving is nothing mysterious, although it is of rare and yet totally satisfying occurrence. It is a 'purified' or 'purer' way of seeing from which we

---

[29] *Loc. cit.*, fol. 5*a*. See also *Myur-lam*, fol. 28*a*.

can expect and actually also acquire richness of detail and a many-sided awareness of the object. It is a beginning, not an end, of seeing more and more of the object in its various senses and values. A person who is capable of the profounder perception of the intrinsic qualities of the object does not see something different from what others also see, but he sees *more* of it and *sees* what other people are blind to. Once he continues seeing more of what there is, will he not be truer to himself and actualize his potentiality of becoming an 'enlightened one'? That such profounder perception moves in the same world as do the ordinary and shallow perceptions of most of us and not in a realm of nowhere, and that it also is a mode of seeing where the veil that ordinarily obstructs our vision has been torn, is unmistakably indicated by sGam-po-pa: "To see the face of the *yi-dam* is a vision of our common world in its pure form. Its characteristic is that the veil has only dropped."[30]

The *bla-ma*, as we can now see, is not a mysterious personality popping suddenly out of nowhere as the mystery-monger is apt to believe. The *bla-ma* is our 'spiritual friend' seen in his uniqueness. He is a teacher because he makes us see more and every moment we succeed in getting a wider and more encompassing view we have done what the teacher has tried to make us do and we have felt his presence.

Tibetan Lamas[31] like to refer to the tribulations which aspirants like Mila-ras-pa and Nāropa faced in their search for the *bla-ma*. It seems to us as if their 'spiritual friends' Mar-pa and Tilopa respectively, took an enormous delight in making it difficult for their disciples. The fact is that their tribulations were their struggle with themselves in their attempt to break through their limited vision. This certainly was the nature of Nāropa's visionary experiences. On the other hand, since the

[30]Collected Works, vol. *Nya*, fol. 13*a*.

[31]Tibetan Buddhists are referred to as Lamas, but the use of this word has nothing in common with what is understood by *bla-ma* by the Tibetans. Tibetans do not address the 'Lamas' as *bla-ma*, nor does any 'Lama' style himself as *bla-ma*. If others use the word 'Lama', intending *bla-ma*, in referring to themselves, they do so either out of ignorance or megalomania.

teacher-disciple relationship is a very intimate one, it becomes necessary to test either one. A teacher who gradiloquently speaks about spirituality which then is conspicuously absent in his everyday life dealings, and who is incapable of realizing the disciple's immediate needs, is not a teacher at all. As to the disciples, how many are willing to grow? Will their enthusiasm not die quickly when all is not smooth sailing? And is growth not the most absorbing task which demands of man all that he is? Is it therefore not a sign of educational ability to test a disciple before accepting him and so to avoid the risk of his giving up in no time and returning to his narrow and shallow world?[32]

---

[32]Tibetan texts, therefore, give long lists of the qualities a teacher and a disciple must have if instruction is to be fruitful. See for instance Klong-chen rab-'byams-pa's *rDzogs-pa chen-po sems-nyid ngal-gso'i 'grel-pa shing-rta chen-po*, fol. 132*b seq. Bla-ma yang-tig*, vol. *E*, sect. 4, fol. 55*a seq.*

Tantra and Revelation

The knowledge of man is as the waters, some descending from above, and some springing from beneath; the one informed by the light of nature, the other inspired by divine revelation.—
FRANCIS BACON, *Advancement of Learning*, Book I, Vol. I.

The idea of revelation is found in every religion and has been interpreted in various ways. In the specific Christian conception it is the communication to man of the Divine Will. Here, in course of time, a distinction was made between a 'natural' revelation (*revelatio naturalis*) and a 'supernatural' one (*revelatio supranaturalis* or *divina*). While the former was assumed to be a self-manifestation of the divine in man and nature and to be intelligible through man's natural gift of reason (*lumen naturale*), the latter was claimed to 'transcend' or to be 'outside' nature and human experience. Even if supernatural revelation occurred, it remained inaccessible to reason, whose function was merely to argue and to infer from the evidence of the senses. Reason therefore was contrasted with faith, which was supposed to show man many more of the effects of God. But in being thus contrasted with reason, faith itself suffered a degradation, ranging from the specific form of religious awareness to an excuse for believing anything it liked, and so remained on the level of a child's acceptance of the word of his parents or teachers whom he trusted. The growing rift between reason and faith led to the idea of a double truth, initially meant to further religion but which became a dogma for worldly philosophy (whatever this may have meant or still may mean) and the downfall of both reason and faith. Still, faith is not necessarily an anti-intellectual feat. It goes beyond reason only in the sense that, being the work of the self, it is much bolder in its approach to a goal than is reason, whose scope is much broader than that of faith because its rules are universally applicable.[1]

A further aspect of revelation is brought out in two opposing views about it or, more exactly, about what it does. The widely accepted one is stated by William Temple: "What is offered to man's apprehension in any specific Revelation is not truth concerning God, but the living God himself;"[2] "There is no such thing as revealed truth. There are truths of revelation, that is to say, propositions which express the results of correct thinking concerning revelation; but they are not themselves directly revealed."[3]

The other, which also claims a large following, is laid down in the Westminster Confession that "the Lord" was "pleased" "to commit . . . wholly unto writing" the declaration of His will and in Pope Leo XIII's encyclical, *Providentissimus Deus*, of 1893, that the Holy Scriptures were written at the dictation of the Holy Ghost (*dictante Spiritu Sancto*).

Last, it is generally held that revelation comes in unusual ways, by means not open to the ordinary channels of investigation, and that as a result it yields knowledge which is not ordinarily available. This view is easily shown to be fallacious, as it prejudges and restricts the scope of knowledge and the means of its attainment.

From this short survey it is evident that revelation not only is a process but also has a content stirring man to response. Doubtless, there can be no response independent of the impingement of the divine presence in man's experience, but the ways in which man may respond to the divine call are many. It is

---

[1]On the relation between faith and reason, see also Paul Weiss, *Modes of Being*, Carbondale: Southern Illinois University Press, 1958, pp. 312–13.

[2]William Temple, *Nature, Man, and God*, New York: Macmillan, Co., 1934, p. 322.

[3]*Ibid.*, p. 317.

true that there are people who do not care to listen and who shut themselves off from any communication, but there are others for whom communication with the divine is or will be of preeminent importance. It is, however, doubtful whether the feeling of absolute dependence, which since the time of Schleiermacher has often been claimed to be characteristic of a religious attitude, can be considered communication, in the strict meaning of the word, with the divine. To be an abject slave to the Divine Will, to persevere in blind faith and unquestioning obedience, may be a necessary corollary to a supernatural revelation. But to the extent that supernatural revelation attempts to enforce its authoritarian claim it destroys the individual and even morality, because it does not, and cannot, admit of freedom, least of all of freedom of understanding, which is grounded in man's very act of existing and so makes morality possible. The rejection of supernatural revelation as a form of absolutism is therefore not a sign of irreligion; rather, it is the first step toward a recognition and, through it, a restoration of the dignity of the human individual, who, through his intellect, shares in the realm of the Ideal and is enabled to assent to the divine presence instead of merely submitting himself to it.[4]

Where there is the feeling of dependence, its absoluteness being the sign of some vested interest, not a characteristic, man's response to the divine is strongly marked by the observance of certain rites. This ritual has grown out of the combination of a certain idea with actions appropriate to that idea and retains its character of service. To a certain degree, like magic, it attempts to influence the deity by propitiating it. Yet ritual is more than this. Through it, man also tries to arrive at a new conception of himself as living in a world of law and order of divine origin.

---

[4]It will be obvious that here a clear distinction between 'will' and 'presence' is drawn. The former is a presumptuous, if not blasphemous, concept, as it merely absolutizes man's striving for power and prejudges divine frailties as being of the same kind as human ones but operating on a larger scale. 'Presence' constitutes a value in interaction and thereby remains a living process and admits of individual growth and a broadening of intellectual perspective.

Inasmuch as ritual carries with it its own laws, it finally develops into religious ethics, which become as important for the relation between man and the divine as the ritual itself and which often supersede the latter.

Ethical demeanor contains, in addition, an element of self-reflection which can be developed and transformed into meditation. Meditation is the cornerstone of mysticism, which is a distinct human reaction to the divine presence. Mysticism deliberately avoids all outward show, which it considers sham, because, in transfusing the whole life with religion, it cannot see a separate existence for worship and ritual. It attempts to establish an intimate union of man and God. In this union, however close it may be, the 'terms' of the relation, man and God, may still be presented as external to each other, so that the divine stands over and against man, not as something understood but as that which man is not. But if the divine is the absolute ground of man's being, then it may be doubted whether it can be said to be wholly other than man. There is a point, then, when the relation takes to itself a new quality, which may be called oneness with the divine.

These various ways of man's response to the divine presence characterize the classification of the Buddhist Tantras, as literary works or instruction manuals, into Kriyā-, Caryā-, Yoga-, and Anuttarayoga-Tantras. The classification shows clearly that, in the concrete life of religion, it is our attitude toward God that determines what sort of God we take him to be. It also reveals the critical attitude of Buddhism, which asks, not whether such a God as defined by our attitude toward him exists, but what God means. As a result of this investigation, Buddhism finds that God and man are abstractions from the same whole, which is the infinite fact of being, living in its entirety in each individual and his every act. This is also the meaning of 'Tantra' (*rgyud*), which, apart from designating a certain type of written text, basically and technically is the term denoting the essential and absolutely individual nature of man as a constant possibility, not as something that can be reduced to some entity or other. In this respect, whether he is or becomes a Buddha or is and remains an 'ordinary' being, man *is* his possibilities, in the light of which he has to decide what to become. Being his possibilities, man is 'divine' and so contrasts with his drab concretizations and postulates.[5]

This translation from submission to understanding can be clearly seen from the account given by Mi-pham 'Jam-dbyangs rgya-mtsho:[6]

> This Mantra-Vajrayāna, which is distinguished [from the other spiritual courses] by special properties, comprises four kinds of Tantra, each of which possesses most sublime qualities. They are known as Kriyā-Tantra and so on and have been formulated in view of the four types of mankind, their various degrees of intelligence, the extent and character of their emotionality, and other features.[7]
>
> I. In the Kriyā-Tantra great stress is laid on the observance of outer ablutions, ritual purity, and other ritual actions by body and speech. The god (*lha*) who is the embodiment of a priori awareness (*ye-shes*)[8] is considered to confer favors like a master, while the individual committed to his service receives these benefits like a servant. It is claimed that thereby temporal and lasting realizations are achieved.
>
> Here, too, one distinguishes between (*a*) viewpoint, (*b*) creative imagination,[9] (*c*) conduct, and (*d*) their fruition.

---

[5]'Tantra', as a term for man's total being, is the thesis of Klong-chen rab-'byams-pa, who discusses the multiple meanings of this term in detail in his *Theg-pa'i mchog rin-po-che'i mdzod*, fols. 60*a*–91*a*. (Unless stated otherwise, all quotations from Tibetan texts are from microfilms in the author's possession.)

[6]Mi-pham 'Jam-dbyangs rgya-mtsho, *Grub-mtha' bsdus-pa*, Varanasi: n.d., fols. 27*b* ff.

[7]The classification of the Tantras in this way is found in Klong-chen rab-'byams-pa. *sNags-kyi spyi-don tshangs-dbyangs 'brug-sgra*, Varanasi: 1967, pp. 45–46.

[8]*ye-shes*, Skt. *jñāna*. My use of the term 'a priori' differs from the Kantian conception, as mine does not refer to judgments but to that cognitive event which is prior to judgments.

[9]*sgom*, Skt. *bhāvana*. The rNying-ma-pas interpret this term in two ways. One is the traditional way, corresponding to what is understood by 'meditation' as fixing the mind on a certain topic. This conception is strongly criticized because it implies a 'fixation', the denial of mind's spontaneity and freedom. The second way is precisely this spontaneous activity. As the working of the mind expresses itself in images, I have tried to indicate this aspect by the above translation of *sgom* (*bhāvana*) by 'creative imagination'. On the distinction

(*a*) Although all phenomena are ultimately the same in their actuality, which is the indivisibility of the truths of appearance and nothingness, in our relative world the supreme divine being becomes the embodiment of an a priori awareness in which the radiancy of the evidence of being is directly present in its nature of being free from any defects and in being replete with all values in highest perfection. And so it is considered to be like a master because he confers temporal and lasting benefits on us who receive them like his servants. Since we are not yet perfect as regards our real being and are shrouded in the veils [of unknowing and emotional instability], we feel ourselves dependent upon God. Therefore, since ultimately our identity with and relatively our relation to God is incontestible, the viewpoint of the Kriyā-Tantra is accompanied by the firm belief that, through our perseverance in patterning ourselves after the god's form, speech, and mood, our temporal activities become significant and that ultimately the god's essence is realized by us.

(*b*) Kriyā is known as referring to six divine presences.[10] This, in brief, means that we concern ourselves with such experiences as the visualization of the god's form, the hearing of his message, and the feeling of his mood as well as the manifestation of the god's palace and the emanation and reabsorption of light rays. We then create this mood again and again by repeating the god's specific mantra, as if one's life were at stake, and so cause the god's sustaining power to descend upon us, just as if iron were touched by the philosopher's stone.

(*c*) Inasmuch as the recitation of the mantra is effective in a ritual context, but otherwise remains barren like a seed without water and manure, we must exert ourselves in performing such ritual acts as taking a bath and changing our clothes thrice a day, worshiping and making offerings as detailed in the Tantras.

(*d*) By such efforts as temporal gifts, any of the ordinary attainments are won, such as the body of a Vidyādhara,[11] who is

---

between 'fixation' (meditation) and 'creative imagination', see the *gZhan-'dod bsdus-pa'i bcud-phur* in *Bi-ma snying-tig*, Vol. *Ga*, fols. 34*a*–36*a*.

[10] *lha drug-pa*. The six 'divine presences' are *don-dam-stong-pa'i lha* (the absolute), *sgra'i lha* (its message), *yi-ge'i lha* (its articulation), *gzugs-kyi lha* (its vision), *phyag-rgya'i lha* (the meditator's empathy), and *mtshan-ma'i lha* (the final embodiment).

[11] *rig-'dzin*; literal., 'he who holds to (*'dzin*) the intuitive, aesthetically moving awareness (*rig-pa*) of reality'.

equal in fortune with a god of a sensuous world, and as a lasting result the essence of a god of any of the three action patterns[12] is realized within a period of sixteen human lives.

II. In the Caryā-Tantra, outwardly, ritual purity as effected by ablutions and other observances and, inwardly, creative imaginations are of equal importance. It is claimed that by viewing ourselves and God as being brothers or friends, realizations are won.

Here, too, there is the distinction between (*a*) viewpoint, (*b*) creative imagination, (*c*) conduct, and (*d*) their fruition.

(*a*) Since here the conviction of the identity (of man with God) in the ultimate sense is still stronger than in the Kriyā-Tantra, we and God are of equal status, like brothers or friends. Since temporal and lasting good is realized by reliance on God as he is envisaged as he really is when appearance as a concatenation of interdependent entities has subsided, the viewpoint of the Caryā-Tantra is accompanied by belief in the profoundness of the two truths.[13]

(*b*) Creative imagination means that when we have clearly visualized the God as the embodiment of an a priori awareness in front of ourselves as the individual committed to his service and then repeat his mantra in a steady flow passing to and fro between ourselves and the God and his entourage, finally the God as the embodiment of a priori awareness will come near, and ultimately there is nothing left of logical fictions or propositions claiming truth.

(*c*) This is to observe the various rites of ablution and ritual purity to the best of one's ability.

(*d*) Temporarily, our activities become significant, and, finally, the level of Vajradhara[14] of four action patterns[15] is attained within a period of seven human lives.

---

[12]*rigs*, Skt. *kula*. The three are: *De-bzhin-gshegs-pa'i rigs*, *Padma'i rigs*, and *rDo-rje'i rigs*. According to the *Bla-ma yang-tig*, Vol. V, fol. 3*a*, *rigs* is synonymous with *snying-po* (Skt. *hṛdaya*, *sāra*) and, as a term for the core of man's being, varies in nature with each individual. See also the collected works of Klong-rdol bla-ma Ngag-dbang blo-bzang, *Tibetan Buddhist Studies*, ed. Ven. Dalama, Laxmanpuri, Mussoorie: 1963, I, 50–52.

[13]I.e., appearance and nothingness.

[14]*rdo-rje 'dzin-pa* as distinguished from *rdo-rje-'chang*. The former still implies separateness, the latter absolute self-sameness.

[15]The three patterns as indicated in n. 12, to which is added the *las-kyi rigs* or *rin-chen rigs*.

Further, one speaks of a 'twofold Tantric spiritual course,' because here, inwardly, creative imagination as in the Yoga-Tantra and, outwardly, observances as in the Kriyā-Tantra are equally distributed. Actually, however, the realization of our goal is quicker, because the viewpoint is profounder than in the previous Tantra.

III. The Yoga-Tantra comprises two varieties: (*A*) an outward Yoga-Tantra and (*B*) an inner unsurpassable spiritual course.

(*A*) While here ritual purity and other observances are merely considered to be friends and helpers for the realization of the path, inwardly concern with the working of the mind is stated to be of primary importance. It is claimed that realizations are attained through the contemplation of non-duality when by way of four 'seals' (*phyag-rgya*) and five 'intuitions' (*mngon-par byang-chub*) there has come about a fusion of subjectivity and objectivity, subjectivity being the individual transfigured into a being committed to the service of the god and objectivity being the god as the embodiment of a priori awareness invited to come from his pure realms.

Here, too, there is the division into (*a*) viewpoint, (*b*) creative imagination, (*c*) conduct, and (*d*) their fruition.

(*a*) Since this view of the absolute is superior to that of the two preceding Tantras, we know for certain that we are actually identical like water poured into water. When we concern ourselves with this, the viewpoint is accompanied by the special certainty of the realization of the essence of the god [of our choice] by means of assiduously enacting as the four 'seals' [of our being] the god's nature of (*i*) existing, (*ii*) communicating, (*iii*) thinking, and (*iv*) acting, since all phenomena are manifestations of the working of a mind. This deep absorption empowers us to feel that we *are* the god whom we have visualized.

(*b*) Creative imagination is to 'seal' our three action levels [i.e., body, speech, and thought] and their operations as the expression of the god's act of existing, communicating, knowing, and acting with the four seals of (*i*) *mahāmudrā*, representing the act of existing, (*ii*) *dharmamudrā*, being the act of communicating, (*iii*) *samayamudrā*, being that of thinking, and (*iv*) *karmamudrā*, being our activity as it expresses itself through the emanation and reabsorption of light rays. We perform this act of sealing after we have taken refuge [in the Three Jewels], developed an enlightened attitude and effected out of a sphere of nothingness a transfiguration by means of five 'intuitions'. These are (*i*) the intuition of a lotus and a moon, forming a throne, being the cause factor of the existence of divine realms and habitats; (*ii*) that of letters as the elements of communication being the cause factor of the most sublime message; (*iii*) that of a mood as the cause factor of a temporality which cannot be defined conceptually, but is eternally present; (*iv*) that of perfected form-endowed existence in and with an entourage, being the cause factor of the sublime teacher and his followers; and (*v*) that of the god as embodied a priori awareness, being the cause factor of the very fact of existing or of most exalted awareness.

Even in this ritual activity we resort to deep absorption until the desired realization has been won through mastery and proficiency.

(*c*) Although ritual purity and other observances are practiced from time to time in the proper way, it is through attending to the experience of the inner processes of contemplation and imagination that our activities become more harmonious and steady than they were in practicing the previous forms of Tantra.

(*d*) While for a time the qualities of our experience and understanding improve more and more, finally, within a period of three human lives, the five psychophysical constituents, the five senses, and the five emotive reaction patterns become purified and are turned into the Buddha nature of five Buddha action patterns representing five forms of a priori awareness.[16]

These three Tantras in their totality conceive of the two truths (of appearance and nothingness) as alternations. They insist, however, on the importance of contemplating the ultimate as beyond judgments and propositions when all objective reference has been lost after the relative world of common appearance has been imagined as divine and when afterward the appearance of it as God has been dissolved in itself.

(*B*) Concerning the unsurpassable spiritual course we must first of all know the difference between an outer and inner aspect relating to the triple division into (*i*) starting point, (*ii*) path, and (*iii*) goal.

---

[16] *ādarśajñāna, samatājñāna, pratyavekṣaṇajñāna, kṛtyānuṣṭhānajñāna, dharmatājñāna.*

(*i*) The outer aspect is present when, at the time of the maturing initiations the 'jar-consecration' is of primary importance; the inner one is given when the three higher consecrations figure more prominently.[17]

(*ii*) When creative imagination proceeds in such a way that the Developing and Fulfilment Stages[18] form a unity and not an alternation because the symbol character and the self-same absoluteness of reality are envisaged as not implying any acceptance or rejection, the inner aspect is given. If this is not possible, the outer aspect prevails. As a consequence, when conduct is based on acceptance and rejection concerning the ritual purity in place, food, dress, and so on, the outer aspect obtains; when there is equality, the inner one.

(*iii*) Freedom related to a particular time means that the inner aspect obtains when Buddhahood is realized in this life, the outer one when in a future life.

The general idea underlying the inner aspect of these great Yoga disciplines of the special Tantra is as follows: the totality of reality subsumed under Saṃsāra and Nirvāṇa or appearance and possibility resides in utter absoluteness. Here, 'profoundness' is the purity (of all reality) in having the same value regarding its status of the 'great mean' (*dbu-ma chen-po*)[19] devoid of all judgments and propositions moving within four confines. 'Vastness' is its contemplation in the knowledge of the identity of appearance—that is, the psychophysical constituents, the biotic forces, and sense fields—with the great pure maṇḍala, the five action patterns of Buddhahood, and other features pertaining to it. And so whatever appears need not be rejected, but as a most excellent means that is free in itself, it is turned into a helper for traversing and scaling the paths and levels of spirituality. When in all our actions the unity of 'vastness' as the Developing Stage and 'profoundness' as the Fulfilment Stage, which is a unity that from

---

[17]On these consecrations (confirmation-empowerments), see in particular my *The Life and Teaching of Nāropa*, Oxford: 1963, pp. 143–45.

[18]See *ibid.*, pp. 138–41.

[19]The term *dbu-ma*, Skt. *madhyama*, usually translated 'middle', actually connotes 'central' or 'related to the center'. The qualifying adjectives *chen-po*, Skt. *mahant*, lit. 'great', indicates the absoluteness of the center. This center is the support and point of reference of the whole of nature. In actual life, it is the supreme motivating idea.

> its very beginning has never been joined or separated, is felt as the great absolute a priori awareness in which the two truths (of appearance and nothingness) are indivisible, the highest realization of *mahāmudrā*, integration, or the citadel of rDo-rje-'chang is reached.

These ways in which man reacts to the divine impingement point to an important character of revelation. Its experience may be interpreted as coming from without (being exogenous), or it may be felt as coming from within (being endogenous). This distinction, which is not wholly absent in Christianity, has been clearly stated in Buddhist Tantrism. However, even in its exogenous character, revelation is never absolutistic-supernatural; it always retains its nature of being intelligible to the individual to whom it manifests. Where revelation is regarded as deriving from a source outside ourselves, it addresses itself to those who have not yet ventured beyond the ordinary world of subject and object as two self-contained entities, but where revelation is thought to come from within, it becomes the impetus to self-development, which is an awakening to Buddhahood and commonly described as enlightenment.

Regardless of whether revelation is claimed to come from without or within, it never occurs in a vacuum. It comprises (1) the 'place' where it occurs, (2) the revealing power, (3) the recipient, (4) the subject matter, and (5) the occasion of the revelation. "When place, revealer, assemblage, content, and occasion unite, the religious life begins."[20]

Inasmuch as Buddhism has always stressed the inner life of the spirit, it is only natural that the inner character of revelation should rank foremost and that even the outward one shines in the light of the former. The primary question has not been whether revelation is this or that kind of information but whether it is any kind at all. This again has been bound up with the double question of fact and expression, and with reference to this

---

[20] *Kun-tu-bzang-po'i dgongs-pa zang-thal-las Bi-ma-mi tra'i snyan-brgyud chen-mo rgyal-po-la gdams-pa yang-gsang bla-na-med-pa rdzogs-pa chen-po'i 'grel-pa ye-shes rang-gsal*, fol. 3*b*. (In the following, the title of this text will be given in the abbreviated form *dGongs-pa zang-thal*.)

question the various features of revelation have been discussed in the texts. Certainly, there is something there before it becomes expressed, and as it is expressed, it is created. Insofar as it has been created, it can be said to exist. In this way, fact and expression, existence and creation, are correlatives and have meaning only in the framework of imaginative activity productive of results under the agent's control. It is important to understand 'imaginative activity' and 'agent' correctly and not to misjudge the former as being merely the capacity to redistribute and rearrange materials supplied to it by perception. Nor should we confuse the latter with a solipsistic or pantheistic postulate which in either case overlooks the concrete reality, the absolute fact of the imaginative activity living in its entirety in every individual and every act of his, expressing itself uniquely. This means that the imaginative activity is not *of* some agent but the agent as he expresses himself.

The absolute fact of imaginative activity always refers to a situation of a definite kind, although nobody can say what kind of situation it is until it has become expressed and thereby made clear to him who has had the feeling of there being something. Secondarily, the situation becomes clear to anyone who can understand, and, as the case may be, it is then capable of arousing in him a desire to find a 'way' to feel like the person or divine being who addresses him. Actually, in Tantrism, as the above analysis of man's reaction to the divine impingement has shown, man is one with God, informed throughout by the indwelling of the divine spirit. Only someone who suffers from theophobia because he confuses an abstract concept with the concrete reality can object to the use of the term 'God' in connection with Tantrism, which by dealing with the whole of man's life is both religion and philosophy, the one relating to the life of the soul, the other to that of the mind.[21]

Not only does the absolute fact of imaginative activity refer

---

[21]Of course, the term 'God' is highly ambiguous, and quite a number of people equate God with their idiosyncrasies. There is no reason why this term, having religious significance, should not be retrieved from its abuses by popular superstition.

to a situation, but wherever it moves it never finds anything that is not a fact, individual and unique. So also it reveals nothing that is not a fact. That is to say, in the act of revelation the imaginative activity creates itself in a perpetual discovery of fact and communicates this fact of its being to its environment of fact. Technically this is known as 'self-knowledge' (*rang-rig*), and what is to be understood by this term has been a problem for various philosophies both in the West and in the East. In Tantrism self-knowledge does not mean the mind's static contemplation of its own given nature but the mind's creation of itself by knowing itself to know and, in so doing, also to know the world which it reveals and, in this revelation, creates.

This absolute fact of imaginative activity which creates and reveals itself in a total situation of fact and so communicates itself to that which as part of this whole partakes of the nature of fact is not a process in time as a revelatory act. If it were this, time would appear to be something external to the absolute whole. Rather, the absolute whole is time itself which later on, by the working of the intellect whose function it is to apprehend or construct relations, is split up into the correlatives of temporality and eternity.

As such an absolute whole, the factual character of revelation is described in the Tantric texts as follows:

> The absolute 'place' is the concrete universal, innocent of all logical judgments and assertions, not existing as this or that [abstract particular], and inaccessible to the elements of language, words, and syllables.
>
> The concretely existing revealing agent has neither face nor hands, because no such assertion can be made, as no words, which are the basis of all assertion, are adequate.
>
> The absolute environment for such a revealing agent is the play of the concrete universal, self-created and self-manifesting.
>
> The absolute message to such an environment is self-knowledge. Although it has come into existence it has done so by itself, and although it arises it does so by itself; it has not been created by causes and conditions [external to it], and it has no beginning or end. Although it is there encompassing everything, nothing can fathom it.

In this concrete fact of being, the unity of place, revealing agent, environment, and message is absolute time, having neither beginning nor end.[22]

Fact and expression, which is primarily imaginative activity, are correlative, or, as R. G. Collingwood states it,

> Imagination does not exist in the free state, and itself requires a basis of fact. This basis of fact in turn requires a basis of imagination, for no fact can be known until it has been sought by the imaginative act of questioning, and this question itself requires a further basis of fact, and so *ad infinitum*. This is not an infinite regress only because the two moments, question and answer, are not actually separate. Their distinction is an ideal distinction only, and the presupposition of each by the other is only a way of stating their inseparability.[23]

Now, inseparability is the key word of Tantrism: inseparability of the absolute and relative, of the divine and the human, and, by implication, of fact and expression. The fact of absolute knowledge is expressed through its act of imagination, which ultimately remains self-knowledge; this self-knowledge, as we have seen, never means that there is a self in abstract isolation becoming the ostensible object of this knowledge but that it is the knowledge of a knowing mind by itself. In its act of expression, it effects the concrete act of knowing and through it the refutation of its ostensible content. And so the expression of the fact of knowledge (mind, imaginative activity, aesthetic awareness, or whichever term we may use to refer to fact and expression) is described in this way:[24]

> The absolute 'place' is the citadel 'Precious Mind', the focal point of experiences in which the structural pathways [of possible experiences] gather, in the maṇḍala of our body. Being a 'place' it is the birthplace of all virtues, and being 'absolute' it must be considered as the existence of infinite acts of existing and of being aesthetically aware by this body of unique fortune and purity.

---

[22] *dGongs-pa zang-thal*, fol. 7*a*.

[23] R. G. Collingwood, *Speculum mentis*, Oxford: 1924, p. 80.

[24] *dGongs-pa zang-thal*, fol. 8*a*.

(This intuition) liberates the body's material form from its bondage by atoms.[25] This, then, is the essence of the 'great-perfection doctrine' going beyond all strained endeavors so that by knowing one's body as a 'place' judgments and assertions as to it being something else are abolished.

The absolute revealer in such a 'place' is Samantabhadra, all encompassing, self-existing, the royal self-knowledge. Being 'a revealer' he is the quintessence of perceptivity knowing the whole of Saṃsāra and Nirvāṇa, and being 'absolute' he is knowledge manifesting itself incessantly in various contents. Since this knowledge stands in utter freedom over the variety of contents, our consciousness is liberated from its fetters of (believing in the irreconcilable dualism of) a knowing subject and a known object. This, then, is the essence of the 'great-perfection doctrine' going beyond all strained efforts so that such a revealing power manifests itself by itself.

What is the message transmitted to such an environment? It is the bliss of undivided knowledge resting on (the imaginary world of) pathways (*rtsa*), motility (*rlung*), and creativity (*thig-le*).[26] Being a 'message' it is by virtue of it that there is the awakening to Buddhahood, and being 'absolute' it brings the virtues of Buddhahood to utter perfection by making a vivid experience of anything that man encounters. It liberates our feeling from its fetters of pleasure and pain. This, then, is the essence of the 'great-perfection doctrine' going beyond all strained efforts so that this message (of bliss) exists by itself in itself.

Since in this way 'place' or our body, 'revealing power' or our capacity of aesthetic awareness, 'environment' or our acts of existing and of being aesthetically perceptive, and 'message' or the instruction in the formative means of pathways, motility, and creativity are united in our body this very moment, the realization of Buddhahood becomes a necessity. If this goal of Buddhahood is not attained, it is necessary to practice austerities.

What is meant by 'absoluteness'? The true message, the realm of the specific revealing power, and ourselves as pertaining to a Buddha pattern of action in accordance with our karmic buildup. Moreover, 'absoluteness' is given when interest and

---

[25]In other words, the body is experienced as a Gestalt, not as a postulate.

[26]On the meaning of these terms, see Guenther, *op. cit.*, p. 46, n. 1; pp. 270–72, 273–74.

> devotion concerning the unsurpassable path of mysticism unite. Since (in such a case) there is no obstacle to enlightenment, our volitions, motives, and drives are freed from the shackles of karmic activity, emotive reaction patterns, and their various emotively toned responses. Since in this way our mind in its absolute originality has turned out to be the very fact of being, its place and all that relates to it need not be sought elsewhere. This is known as the self-existing aesthetic perceptivity.

Apart from describing how the 'fact' of knowledge 'expresses' itself and, when it is so seen as expression, constitutes the character of revelation from outside, this account also points to the task of man: to find a way out of the maze of his ideas about himself insofar as they have been judged, falsely, to be real. In psychological and philosophical language which is more akin to the original texts, this means to correct the mind's error about itself so that it can regain its true nature of aesthetic perceptivity. As a distinct form of experience, aesthetic perceptivity refers to and constitutes a whole beyond which there is nothing and in which there is no part that does not refer to or contain the whole. Inasmuch as it is within this whole that experience takes place, this whole may rightly be said to be a 'place' and 'absolute' in the sense that there is nothing besides it. This implies that 'place' is not a certain place *of* a certain thing but this thing itself, which is technically referred to by the expression 'concrete universal' (*chos-nyid*).[27] As such, the concrete universal is

---

[27]This term was first coined by Collingwood. The Tibetan term *chos-nyid* is the translation and interpretation of Skt. *dharmatā*. The suffix *-tā* in Sanskrit forms 'abstracts' and corresponds to the English *-ness*. Due to the influence of Greek thought, we tend to distinguish between horseness and horse, and Western philosophies have set up ingenious systems to unite the concrete and universal. Similar interpretations are found in Hindu systems and Buddhism, if we interpret the latter in terms of the former. Since the Buddhist tradition in India has been dead for nearly a thousand years, while Hindu ideas have continued, it is extremely doubtful whether the rendering of Buddhist technical terms and ideas by Hindu connotations is justifiable. The Tibetans who translated when the Buddhist tradition was still alive may have given a translation which is more to the point and reflects the Buddhist spirit. According to this tradition, then, the 'horseness' is not *of* the 'horse' but the horse which is 'horsy' in relation to other things, which then are technically termed *chos-can* (Skt. *dharmin*).

the unity of the universal and the particular before these two are separated into contrasting principles and are turned into mere abstractions so as to become metaphysical fictions. The concreteness of the whole means that it cannot be viewed as a mere object. It is subject and object together, the subject being a constitutive element in the object, as there would be no object unless there is a subject to know it. The character of the whole as an object is not the abstract objectivity of a world in which the knowing subject has no place but the concrete objectivity which is the correlative of subjectivity. This is clearly stated by Mi-pham 'Jam-dbyangs rgya-mtsho:[28]

> The ground [of all being], insofar as no assertions and judgments about it obtain, is purely transcendent (*ka-dag*); insofar as it is self-lucent, formless, and impartial, without, however, being a mere nothing like empty space, it is immanently spontaneous (*lhun-gyis grub-pa*); and since it is the birthplace of all presential values such as Nirvāṇa and Saṃsāra, it is called all-encompassing compassion (*thugs-rje*).[29] In the language of the 'great-perfection doctrine' it is termed 'that which possesses the three kinds of perceptivity abiding in the prime ground' (*gzhir gnas-kyi ye-shes gsum ldan*). Similarly, in the Sūtras and Tantras it is spoken of as 'evidence of being' (*dbyings*) and 'nothingness' (*stong-pa-nyid*) insofar as no assertions and judgments whatsoever and no defining

[28]Mi-pham 'Jam-dbyangs rgya-mtsho, *gNyug-sems 'od-gsal-gyi don rgyal-ba rig-'dzin brgyud-pa'i lung-bzhin brjod-pa rdo-rje-snying-po*, Varanasi: n.d., fol. 3*a*.

[29]*thugs-rje* ordinarily represents Skt. *karuṇā* when it is used with reference to Buddhahood. Otherwise, Skt. *karuṇā* is in Tibetan *snying-rje*. In rNying-ma-pa texts, the use of *thugs-rje* rarely corresponds to our concept of 'compassion', which closely resembles an emotion. *thugs-rje* is basic to *rig-pa* (aesthetic awareness), which seems to be its derivation. Inasmuch as rNying-ma-pa thought originated when Chinese thought seems to have been well known, it is very likely that *thugs-rje* combines both the Indian idea of 'compassion' and the Chinese Taoist conception of 'responsiveness' (*kan* 感). Chinese influence on early Tibetan ideas is not to be ruled out, and the rNying-ma-pa triad of *ngo-bo, rang-bzhin, thugs-rje* has a close resemblance in usage to the Chinese *t'i* 體, *tzŭ-jan* 自然 and the specific Hwa-yen term *hsiang* 相, and *yung* 用, the first term dealing with ontology, the second with actuality, and the last with cognitiveness.

characteristics obtain; and as 'self-existing a priori perceptivity' (*rang-byung ye-shes*) insofar as it is shining in its own light.

The conception of such an 'object' is the conception of its objectivity determined by knowing the object, and whether it is known truly or erroneously must make a difference to it. This is to say, while the 'object' is the knowing mind itself, the mind's error about itself must distort the object or, what is the same, itself. Such error is, according to the *Bi-ma snying-tig*, similar to mistaking the reflection of one's face in a mirror for an alien face, and so one "strays from true existence (*sku*) into organismic being (*lus*), from the evidence of being (*dbyings*) into [abstract] objectivity (*yul*), and from aesthetic awareness (*rig-pa*) into mentation (*sems*)."[30]

In the concrete world of human thought, the 'fact' of a 'place' of knowledge and experience as the 'concrete universal', resting in itself, revealing itself to itself and by itself, becomes our own body experienced as a Gestalt (*gzugs*), not as an assemblage of atoms which are its 'misplaced' concretizations. Similarly, the fact of knowledge as the mind's knowledge about itself becomes our own consciousness (*rnam-shes*) in its absolutely fundamental and original activity before it becomes involved in its own abstractions of an object alien to and contrasted with a subject. However, consciousness never exists in a vacuum and can never attend to more than a part of a total sensuous-emotional field. Therefore, it works in company with imagination (*'du-shes*) as an idea-forming process whose function it prepares in the sense that, if it is not warped by an error about itself in imagination, we experience ourselves as existing and as knowing rather than as things that may be classified as constituting an 'outer' or 'inner' world. It is customary to contrast thinking, which we associate with consciousness, with feeling, and to a certain extent this distinction is correct. But in the absolute whole where mind is its own object and where the subject is also object, being the one because it is the other,

---

[30]*Bi-ma snying-tig*, Vol. *Nya*, fols. 2*a*–*b*.

thought is feeling and feeling is thought, their differences being held together by an intrinsic unity. What the mind knows, and that with which it transfuses the whole of its being, is feeling (*tshor-ba*). It is described as undivided bliss because the wound of separateness from the whole has been healed and the petty feelings of pleasure and pain have been overcome. Although bliss is thus the subject matter of knowledge, the maxim "don't think, feel" does not apply, because it is the denial of knowledge and through it the denial of itself. Lastly, if knowledge is the life of the mind, its activity (*'du-byed*) is the actualization of Buddhahood, not an involvement in actions and emotional outbursts that tend to harden the mind's error about itself.

The realization of Buddhahood as man's unique task and goal thus turns out to be the total life of self-conscious development. As this process unfolds, be it gradually or instantaneously, the mind comes to know itself through its imagery, which it recognizes as its own creation and which it needs for arriving at its foreordained and pre-existing goal–knowledge. This goal is described as follows: "The absolute place is the evidence of being; the revealing power is omniscient Buddhahood, its essence, perceptivity grown into self-knowledge; the environment is enjoyment in the intellectually inconceivable play of existing and knowing; the message is unfailing great bliss; and time is the presence of comprehending [a world of fact]."[31]

Inasmuch as knowledge 'reveals' the world in which it lives as its environment and which it discovers and creates by its act of self-creation, and inasmuch as this perpetual process of becoming self-conscious occurs here and now 'within' us and so is endogenous to itself, it is justifiable to speak of revelation from within. It will have been noted, however, that such revelation belongs more properly to the level of philosophy as a continual quest for knowledge and not to that of religion proper.

But the transition from philosophy to religion or vice versa is never abrupt. This is so because both participate in the same

---

[31]*dGongs-pa zang thal*, fol. 7*b*.

world of fact, which it is impossible to reduce to narrowly confined, mutually exclusive areas. Therefore, philosophical and religious elements also interpenetrate in Tantrism, which deals with the whole of man, the word 'Tantra' itself being a term for man's total life. It is precisely in the religious sphere and, closely allied to it, in that of art that the sensuous and imaginary elements predominate, and it is here that we feel ourselves to be on more familiar ground. And so the texts also speak of this sphere as of a 'common' one pointing through its imagery to that which, as it were, lies behind it and yet imbues it with life; as Collingwood writes:

> If the mind feels cold without an object other than itself, nothing is simpler for it than to create a palace of art, a world of mythology, a cosmos of abstract conceptual machinery, and so forth. In fact that is precisely what it does when it cannot achieve what it really wants–self-knowledge–without the help of these things. But it is not these things that it wants: it is self-knowledge. For when it has its works of art, what it values in them is not themselves but the glimpses they give of hidden and mysterious beauty. What it worships in the figures of its gods is not these figures themselves in their externality to itself but the revelation through them of something really divine; and so on.[32]

The rich imagery of the spheres of religion and art is linked with the idea of the Buddha's three *kāyas*: *dharmakāya*, *sambhogakāya*, and *nirmāṇakāya*. Rather than give a mere dictionary translation of these terms, which is bound to be meaningless if not utterly nonsensical, it is preferable to retain them as shorthand expressions for complex ideas which can be paraphrased but not 'translated'. Moreover, the Sanskrit term *kāya* is ambiguous, as it may mean what we ordinarily understand by the English word 'body'. The Tibetan language steers clear of the ambiguity by having two terms *sku* and *lus*, whose distinct uses cannot create any uncertainty or misunderstanding. It so happens that, while it is true that most Tibetan texts have been translated from Sanskrit works and that on the

[32] Collingwood, *op. cit.*, p. 281 ff.

basis of these translations there developed an immensely valuable indigenous literature, it is from the Tibetan texts that the Sanskrit terms become intelligible.

Accordingly, the *kāyas* are structures of experience. Although experience is an indivisible absolute whole, three aspects can always be distinguished: a factual, an immediate-intuitive, and a mediating-reflective one. There is, further, a certain interconnection running through these aspects, so that each seemingly successive one is more explicit than the preceding one. As 'structures', these *kāyas* are present to man in an intuitive or immediate form, while as 'contents' they are so deeply embedded in his 'body' that it is impossible to extricate them. It is here that the distinction between *sku* ('structure') and *lus* ('body') becomes most explicit, but, before proceeding with our analysis, the notion of 'body' must be clarified.

When we speak of a 'body' we usually tend to contrast it with a 'mind' which is connected with it in a peculiarly intimate way and animates it. In this view the distinction between body and mind, both of which fall within one and the same whole, the concrete, though infinite, fact of absolute mind, on closer inspection turns out to be an abstraction from absolute mind which has been regarded as a thing in itself so that 'body' and 'mind' became irreconcilable entities. But inasmuch as 'mind', as ordinarily understood on the basis of the mind's abstracting capacity, is merely such an abstraction, there is nothing mental or material about it; in the same way, our 'body', as commonly understood, is neither the one nor the other, whereby the claims about body and mind by either idealism or realism are implicitly refuted. This is an important point that has to be borne in mind constantly, because, in spite of the emphasis on mind in the Buddhist texts, 'body' and 'mind' cannot be interpreted in terms of realism or idealism without qualification. Being abstractions, they are not mere non-entities; they are the mind's ostensible objects which it believes, erroneously, to be real. However, these ostensible objects are not the real object of which the mind has been in search, which is the mind itself, hidden, as it were, behind its ostensible objects. Every ostensible object or abstraction is the mind's error about itself. But no error is complete; it implicitly contains truth. This is because the mind's own nature and state is one of truth, from which it has strayed in its search for itself. Error, therefore, contains truth positively as a warning signal to turn back from a further advance in the direction of error. Because of the truth in error, a mind which is in error can discover that it is so. Through this discovery it conquers error and reaches truth, that is, it comes to itself. Each truth, however, then takes the form which it does to conquer a particular error. This gradation in overcoming error we can realize from comparing the definitions of *sku* and *lus*, of which the dictionaries say that both mean 'body', and also from the relation these two have to each other, comparable to that of 'structure' and 'content' or 'truth' and 'error'.

The word *sku*, which is found as the Tibetan rendering of the Sanskrit word *kāya* in the triad of *dharmakāya* (*chos-*[*kyi*] *sku*), *sambhogakāya* (*longs-*[*spyod-rdzogs-pa'i*] *sku*), and *nirmāṇakāya* (*sprul-*[*pa'i*] *sku*), is explained as follows:

> *chos* means generality and specificity; *kyi* their connection; and *sku* is a pattern of preciousness mysteriously hidden (*rin-po-che gsang-ba'i sbubs-kyi sku*). [In particular,] *chos-sku* [*dharmakāya*] is an actuality which is absolutely nothing as such.
>
> *long-sku* is the enjoyment of the abundance offered through the five kinds of aesthetic awareness (*longs . . . spyod*); *rdzogs* is the perfection of symbols and signs; the *sku* is a pattern of knowledge and vision (*ye-shes sgyu-ma'i sku*).
>
> *sprul-sku* refers to the different shapes of beings who come into existence by four modes of birth, and it manifests itself (*sprul*) in order to educate any being of the six classes of beings; *sku* is a pattern underlying [the beings] against themselves due to inveterate tendencies (*rnam-rtog bag-chags-kyi sku*).[33]

That which is called *lus* and which is commonly translated as 'body', although more exactly it means 'body-mind', 'the body as lived in by the mind', is defined and termed so

[33]*Bi-ma snying-tig*, Vol. Nga, fol. 72*a*.

> because it roams about, is set aside left behind, or does not remain the same. It is by leaving one body behind and migrating to another one that we speak of 'body', and this is because with reference to any body we know that the present body is not our previous one which has been left behind together with its atomic and elementary constituents and because in future also we will take on a new body different from the present one, if we do not know what the body really is. It has four varieties: (i) a precious and mysterious body (*rin-po-che gsang-ba'i lus*) in which *dharmakāya*, *sambhogakāya*, and *nirmāṇakāya* gather; (ii) a body having the character of *a priori* knowledge and of being an apparition (*ye-shes sgyu-ma'i lus*) which exists with reference to the *sambhogakāya*; or the precious one is *dharmakāya* and the one of *a priori* knowledge and apparition is the two form-endowed patterns of being; (iii) a body representing [any being's] dividedness against himself due to inveterate tendencies (*rnam-rtog bag-chags-kyi lus*) which exists in certain formless spheres and when all mental activity has been [temporarily suspended].[34]

The Tibetan terms of the first three 'bodies' are particularly significant, because, except for the substitution of *lus* for *sku*, they use the same words as in the preceding quotation. This shows that *sku* and *lus* are correlative aspects of experience in which immediacy or intuition, and mediation or reflection, and assertion intermingle. This is what has been described above as the structure lying so imbedded in the content that to extricate it is impossible. Ordinarily, however, we are unaware of such imbedded structure until, in collaboration with a guru, the disciple brings it to light. And this happens on what is termed 'the path'.

That which we call our 'body' and of which we may say that it is our 'mind', insofar as our body, *B*, animated by our mind, *M*, behaves in a certain way characteristic of *B* being animated by *M*, is something through which we experience ourselves as existing on various levels, physical, mental, factual. However, in the act of experience, we see ourselves and others as a Gestalt which we subsequently interpret and assert to be either physical

---

[34] *Ibid.*, Vol. Nya, fols. 53*b* ff.

or mental or 'existential'. Thus, experience is both imagination and assertion, and, while the former is neither true nor false of set purpose and is essentially a non-assertive attitude of discovery and exploration, the latter is something dead and done with and constitutes 'error' when it is considered to be the whole of knowledge. But since error is never complete it becomes a challenge because of the truth residing in it. The moment the challenge is understood, the 'path' from error to truth, from assertion to imagination, from content to structure, is traveled. The imagery of the path, however, in the sense that the images are the path, points beyond itself to the underlying absolute reality.

The relation between *sku* ('structure') and *lus* ('body') in connection with the 'path' is as follows:

> 'Structure' (*sku*) is defined as 'in [or with reference to] the body' (*lus-la*). That is to say, we have to do with the body until structure has been realized and this means that the path starts with the body and must be traversed [by separating the impure from the pure], which again means that the goal does not exist as the body. Although this is so, it is sometimes claimed that the goal can be realized immediately without the path being necessary. This, of course, is nonsense, for it is like expecting to possess the goal without preparing for it or without traveling toward it. Besides, the statement in the Guhyamantra texts that the goal must by all means be made the path [of goal realization] is with reference to the three patterns of being (*sku*) becoming the path. If something that is not these three patterns were to be made the path, the statement would be proven to be false, and the fallacy of seeking something unreal by something real would have come up. Therefore, if all the Tantras and instructions of the Guhyamantra declare the three patterns of being and the five kinds of perceptivity to be the goal, here [in the 'great-perfection doctrine'] they are made the path. How to do it has been explained previously.
>
> Further, any given form of a body (*lus-yod*) is not what we understand by structure. There are the bodies of flesh and blood, the product of the five elements [as in the case of men and animals], of knowledge and brilliance [as with the gods], of a numbed mind [as in the intermediate state between death and rebirth], of fancies [as with the spirits], and of massive error [as in the case of

> the denizens of hell]. 'Structure' is spoken of with reference to the body and other features of the six different classes of beings. That is to say, *nirmāṇakāya* is a pattern that is not fixed once for all but corresponds to each of the six kinds of sentient beings and takes on the form of the body which a sentient being believes to be his real body on the level of his being divided against himself and his real nature due to inveterate tendencies (*rnam-rtog bag-chags-kyi lus-yod*). *Sambhogakāya* is the body of a priori knowledge and apparition as it is found in a vision (*ye-shes sgyu-ma'i lus snang-ngo-la grub-par yod*). *Dharmakāya* is a form of a precious and mysterious body (*rin-po-che gsang-ba'i lus-yod*) because it fulfils the beings' spiritual aims by the two form patterns that have come from it.
>
> Since in this way the three patterns of being (*sku*) are the images of the path, ultimately, when the goal has been reached, they do not obtain. If it is argued that then the continuity of spiritual awareness has come to an end, the answer will be that it is not so. Although active spiritual reality (*mdzad-pa*) is not a mind in the ordinary sense of the word (*yul-can*), its spirituality or compassion, unceasing in its power, like the rays of the sun once it has risen, watches over sentient beings with the eyes of omniscience never falling asleep and is present in aiding them. Just as ice and snow melt and flow in abundance when the heat of the summer increases, so the great sustaining power of Buddhahood in sentient beings has grown by itself, and therefore one must know that all the happiness of all sentient beings is the spirituality and compassion of Buddhahood.[35]

From this it follows that *dharmakāya* is the hidden source of man's being, and insofar as he feels this source to be there, it is a value which no words can comprise, but when he concretizes it and asserts it to be, the life-spending source dries up and becomes a dead counter; there is *lus* ('body') instead of *sku* ('structure') or 'organismic being' instead of 'true existence'. So, also, *sambhogakāya* is a structure of sensuous elements of imagery which are felt to give knowledge and in the contemplation of which we feel to have come nearer to knowledge. But here, too,

---

[35] *Ibid.*, Vol. Nga, fols. 79*a* ff.

assertion turns the vision into dogma and the inspiring images into aesthetic idols. Lastly, *nirmāṇakāya*, which as human beings we conceive in human form, is essentially a unifying symbol which challenges us to overcome our dividedness against ourselves and to find ourselves in the life of absolute mind. Each living being participates in and lives through these three patterns of being, but those who do not know that they are doing so give a false account to themselves of their experiences and turn them into 'error'.

Although corresponding to the various levels of man's being, these patterns of being are in a certain way the self-portraiture of the path which always means spiritual development. As such they produce a powerful and very peculiar emotional effect which is felt to come from outside. In this context it is possible to speak of revelation from without, where each pattern appears in a special world of its own, which is woven into the whole. This revelation from without is described in the following words:[36]

> The teaching is the word of the teacher who embodies the three patterns of being: as *dharmakāya* he speaks by way of his sustaining power;[37] as *sambhogakāya* by means of his very fact of being; and as *nirmāṇakāya* in well-articulated words comprising the sixty kinds of modulation.
>
> The 'place' of the *dharmakāya* is the citadel of the evidence of being, the Akaniṣṭha heaven; that of the *sambhogakāya* the pure Ghanavyūha realm; and that of the *nirmāṇakāya* the spheres of Alakāvatī, Tuṣita, Vajrakūṭa, and others.
>
> The revealing power as *dharmakāya* is Samantabhadra; as *sambhogakāya*, Vairocana; and as *nirmāṇakāya* it is threefold: as *dharmakāya* it is Mahāvajradhara or Vajrasattva; as the Vajra pattern it is Vajrapāṇi; and as *nirmāṇakāya* for the education of the six kinds of beings by appropriate means it is the six Buddhas.
>
> The environment means that as *dharmakāya* he transmits his message to the hosts of gods which are the self-manifestation of spiritual awareness and as peaceful and frightful appearances

---

[36] *dGongs-pa zang-thal*, fols. 7*b* ff.

[37] *byin-rlabs*, Skt. *adhiṣṭhāna*. The meaning of this term is very similar to the Thomistic conception of 'conaturality'.

constitute the five action patterns of Buddhahood. As *sambhoga-kāya* he transmits his message by way of symbols and gestures to the assembly of those who have manifested themselves for the sake of sentient beings, the intellectually inconceivable group of the five 'fathers' beginning with Akṣobhya[38] and representing the formative aspect of the spiritual life, the five 'mothers' beginning with Vajradhātvītvīśvarī[39] and representing the discriminative appreciative aspect, the male bodhisattvas Kṣitigarbha[40] and so on as well as the female bodhisattvas Lāsyā[41] and others, all of whom are nothing but the absolute mind of enlightenment. As *nirmāṇa-kāya* he imparts his message by way of articulate speech to the innumerable hosts of transworldly Buddhas, bodhisattvas, and great *śrāvakas* as well as to the countless numbers of form-endowed beings, such as the eight great gods, the protectors, the planets, lunar mansions, the lower gods, serpents, demons, and *gandharvas*, belonging to this world.

The message: the *dharmakāya* promulgates that which is ineffable; the *sambhogakāya*, the six self-existing letters (*oṃ maṇi padme hūm*); and the *nirmāṇakāya*, the innumerable Sūtras and Tantras.

The time: the *dharmakāya* speaks when the profound understanding of reality sets in, and this means that time has no end. The *sambhogakāya* speaks when the concrete universal appears in its distinctness, and this is a pure vision. The *nirmāṇakāya* speaks from the time that an attitude directed to supreme enlightenment has been developed until such time when the world has become empty of sentient beings. Or it speaks from the time when the life

---

[38]The others are Vairocana, Ratnasambhava, Amitābha, and Amoghasiddhi.

[39]The remaining four are: Buddhalocanā, Māmakī, Pāṇḍaravāsinī, and Tārā.

[40]The others are Gaganagarbha, Avalokiteśvara, and Vajrapāṇi. They are the 'intellectual' bodhisattvas, while Mañjuśrī, Samantabhadra, Nivaraṇa-viṣkambhin, and Maitreya are 'functional' bodhisattvas. The distinction between 'intellectual' and 'functional' bodhisattvas is discussed by Rong-zom chos-kyi bzang-po in his *rgyud-rgyal gsang-ba snying-po'i -grel-pa*, fols. 56*b* ff.

[41]She and the other three, Gītimā, Mālemā, and Nṛtyemā, are the female partners of the 'intellectual' bodhisattvas, while Puṣpemā, Dhūpemā, Alokemā, and Gandhemā, are those of the 'functional' ones (see *ibid.*). Their relation to the 'spiritual' Buddhas (*Dhyānibuddhas*) has been detailed in the *Man-ngag snying-gi dgongs-pa'i rgyud rdo-rje-sems-pas gsungs-pa* (*dGongs-pa zang-thal*, Vol. Ke).

span of each being is incalculable in years until the time when it is one hundred years. This promulgation is called the most excellent occasion.

Revelation from without produces a world of imagination; every distinct aspect gives us a cosmology of its own fitted into the scheme of the whole. The danger of such a process is that it tends to become dogmatic and, thereby, absolutized error. However, the fact that this cosmology ultimately is grounded in man's very nature and that this may express itself individually in different forms has never been lost sight of. And this accounts for the fact that religious images vary from pattern to pattern, all of which are interrelated. Thus, we also find the following 'cosmology':[42]

> The *dharmakāya*'s *dharmakāya* is Samantabhadra;[43] the *dharmakāya*'s *sambhogakāya* is Vajradhara; and the *dharmakāya*'s *nirmāṇakāya* is Vajrasattva.
>
> The *sambhogakāya*'s *dharmakāya* is Vairocana; the *sambhogakāya*'s *sambhogakāya* is the five spiritual Buddhas; and the *sambhogakāya*'s *nirmāṇakāya* is Vajrapāṇi.
>
> The *nirmāṇakāya*'s *dharmakāya* is Vajrasattva; the *nirmāṇakāya*'s *sambhogakāya* is the triad of Avalokiteśvara, Vajrapāṇi, and Mañjuśrī; and the *nirmāṇakāya*'s *nirmāṇakāya* is the six Buddhas [in the six worlds of beings].

Exterior revelation in Tantrism is essentially a suggestion of themes, categories, propositions, and symbols which have to be thought out and applied. Exterior revelation, therefore, is not the ultimate in living religiously; it is merely a stimulus. The explication of the propositions and symbols is important for the sake of self-knowledge and self-realization and also for keeping the religious spirit alive. Insofar as exterior revelation is merely a

---

[42]*Bi-ma snying-tig*, Vol. Nga, fols. 72*a* ff.

[43]This name is significant for the claim that religious symbols have to be explicated. On the popular level where exterior revelation prevails, Samantabhadra has anthropomorphic traits, while on the philosophical level, Samantabhadra is a term for the absolute which is a positive value and which, psychologically speaking, indicates the positive character of human nature.

suggestion and, at its best, a promise of truth, but never a conclusion or judgment about truth, its meaning must be explored. Not only does such exploration aim at obtaining what the proposition or symbol promises ('attaining the status of a Vidyādhara or Vajradhara'), it even more so functions as the capacity to relate the whole self (*rgyud*, *tantra*) to its source or ground (*gzhi*) or goal (*'bras-bu*). In this exploration of meaning, exterior revelation as a promising suggestion becomes interior revelation as a supremely illuminating and life-sustaining process (*mngon-par byang-chub*) working through creative imagination (*sgom*).

The Spiritual Guide as Mystic Experience

The concept of 'spiritual teacher' or 'spiritual guide' has been the leading principle in the religious life of the Tibetans who call their form of Buddhism either *sangs-rgyas-kyi chos* or *nang-chos*. The former appellation can be translated as 'The Buddha's Law' if we accept the customary, though wrong, equation of *chos* = *dharma* = law. There is, however, no reason to accept this equation and the translation based on it, because *dharma* does not mean law, but order, sustenance, and the Buddha has not been a law-giver, rather he has drawn attention to what is there and can be observed by everybody without previous acceptance of a theoretical postulate. Another reason for rejecting the customary translation is its inadequacy of conveying the meaning of *sangs-rgyas* or *buddha*. This term is a description of what has happened when a person has been freed from his prejudices and preconceived ideas and has recovered the richness of openness of mind with its vast horizon of meaning. The proper rendering of the Tibetan term *sangs-rgyas-kyi chos* in English would therefore be 'the phenomenon of enlightenment' and 'enlightenment' must be understood as a process-product word as can be seen from the following descriptions where *sangs-rgyas* (Buddha and/or Buddhahood), *rig-pa* (intrinsic perception), *byang-chub-sems* (enlightenment) are used to define each other: "Buddhahood (*sangs-rgyas*) is intrinsic perception (*rig-pa*):"[1] "when intrinsic perception (*rig-pa*) has been freed from minding it is automatically liberated from the deviations of minding and therefore there is no escape from absolute Buddhahood (*sangs-rgyas*), because its very nature which is Buddhahood has become manifest due to its having been freed from obscuring powers;"[2] "the very nature of intrinsic perception (*rig-pa*) abiding in itself is enlightenment (*byang-chub-sems*)."[3] It is important to note and to be constantly aware of the ambiguity of the term *sangs-rgyas* which can mean either 'Buddhahood' (enlightenment) or the person designated 'The Enlightened One' (The Buddha) because Buddhahood, absolute in itself, manifests (expresses) itself in the body-proper of an individual and is manifested (expressed) by the animatedness of the body-proper.

Ambiguousness also attaches to the second term which the Tibetans use to describe their forms of Buddhism. *Nang-chos* can mean the 'insider's faith' in order to distinguish the Buddhists from the non-Buddhists. It also may mean an 'inner process' as opposed to externals. There is thus a unique interpenetration of the phenomenal and absolute and there is no unbridgeable gulf between the two. In other words, this way of thinking recognizes the absolute significance of the phenomenal and rejects the idea that the absolute is something over and above or behind the phenomenal. The absolute is, so to say, the presential value of the phenomenal in a unitary experience. This has tremendous consequences for the human sphere as it tends to cultivate a sense of worth and dignity by changing things and persons into the intrinsically interesting and the intrinsically valuable. The world man lives in is seen as a Buddha-realm of infinite beauty; man himself is a divine being, a god or goddess as the case may be (which of course has nothing to do with deifi-

---

[1]*Chos-dbyings rin-po-che'i mdzod* together with *Chos-dbyings rin-po-che'i mdzod-kyi 'grel-ba lung-gi gter-mdzod*, Klong-chen-pa Dri-med 'od-zer, ed. Tarthang Tulku, Varanasi: 1964, fol. 111*b*.

[2]Fol. 129*a*.

[3]Fol. 21*b*.

cation which is but a confusion of the divine with the human and the arbitrary selection and elevation of a transitory entity into an absolute principle); whatever he possesses or uses is the vehicle of worship; and whatever he does is significant action. This idea of the intrinsic value of man is based on the conviction that, if value is ultimate and not arbitrary, in order to perceive and live by it man must partake in the ultimate. His capacity to discern and to perceive the ultimate is known as 'intrinsic perception' (*rig-pa*) which is the apprehension of the full intrinsic being *and* value of the object or field and brings into action the total being of the percipient. It is contrasted with 'minding' (*sems*) which is essentially a means to metaperceptual ends and which is tied up with man's volitional activities and emotional habits. From this observation follows the idea of man and of sentient beings in general as 'individuals engaged in metaperceptual ends' (*sems-can*). Metaperceptual ends tend to lead man farther and farther away from his intrinsic being and value into the deadening world of things. Rejecting the idea of any static essence (a principle by virtue of which something is what it is), the Buddhists conceived of man *qua* man (*sems-can*) as a continuously on-going act of going astray, of being or, more precisely, becoming 'imperceptive', (*ma-rig-pa*). This going astray is a process which is incidental, not essential and which, therefore, is reversible precisely because of man's 'constitutional ability to become enlightened' (*khams de-bzhin-gshegs-pa'i snying-po, dhātu-tathāgatagarbha*) which acts as it were as a mediator between his absoluteness (*chos-sku*) and his individual nature of a conscious and perceptual being (*sems-can*). Viewed cognitively man's absoluteness manifests itself in and through 'intrinsic perception' and as such is absolute knowledge or enlightenment. It is not a mind which by definition is 'minding', and which is a limitation rather than an openness of mind. Because of the association of knowledge with mind we may speak of man's absoluteness by using the word mind, but we have to bear in mind the distinction between cognitive absoluteness and individual minding as is done in the Tibetan texts by distinguishing between *sems-nyid* and *sems*. "By cognitive absoluteness (*sems-nyid*) we refer to the ground from which intrinsic perception rises, the place where minding (*sems*) has ceased, but not to minding;"[4] "cognitive absoluteness (*sems-nyid*), absolute awareness (*rang-byung-gi ye-shes*) freed from the maze of fictional judgments, is called enlightenment,"[5] and "when (man's) constitutional ability to become enlightened is overshadowed by minding, we speak of a sentient being (*sems-can*)."[6]

Cognitive absoluteness is inextricably interwoven with the idea of the Three Kāyas which are norms and patterns, symbols of interpretation, not 'bodies' as so often stated. Seen ontologically as an utter openness it is the Dharmakāya (*chos-sku*) or Buddhahood as the possibility of actual being and the model of possible actuality; seen empathically it is the Sambhogakāya (*longs-sku*) which brings into prominence the factors of imagination and feeling and which, as it were, reveals the significance of Buddhahood; and seen responsively it is the Nirmāṇakāya (*sprul-sku*), the embodiment of Buddhahood in the concrete individual. But although it is permissible to speak of these patterns or symbols of interpretation they themselves are not representations 'of reality' because there is no relation between the symbolic forms of thought through which we are cognitive, and the so-called things-in-themselves which by definition fall outside experience. "Although cognitive absoluteness may be called Dharmakāya in view of its utter openness, Sambhogakāya in view of its illumining character, and Nirmāṇakāya in view of its responsiveness, its very fact of being is not at all something concrete; (as) intentional structure (i.e., we cannot know without knowing something nor can we do without doing something) it is spontaneously present at all times without getting out of itself or getting into something other than itself, because as the very core (or being) it encompasses Saṃsāra and Nirvāṇa."[7]

This cognitive absoluteness constitutes the ever-present ground and value of man. Here, too, value must be understood as

---

[4] *Bla-ma yang-tig* (n.d., n.pl.), Klong-chen-pa Dri-med 'od-zer, V, fol. 7*a*.
[5] *Chos-dbyings-rin-po-che'i mdzod*, fol. 25*b*.
[6] *Bla-ma yang-tig*, IV, fol. 40*b*.
[7] *Chos-dbyings rin-po-che'i mdzod*, fol. 30*a*.

intrinsic, not as spurious, imposed value-judgment. As the ground of being it may be viewed from various angles, be it as existentially pure awareness, or as being, function and responsiveness. In its first aspect of being-as-such and not as some sort of being it manifests itself as 'existence' in becoming the triple interpretive symbol of Dharmakāya, Sambhogakāya and Nirmāṇakāya and thereby abolishes the traditional ontological claim of a permanent essence (i.e., the being of some being, mistaken for being-as-such): in its second aspect it manifests itself as the 'light' in which we see the world, as when we figuratively say that someone sees everything in a 'rosy light'. This spontaneity abolishes the traditional conception that if being is not some being it must be nihilistic. Most important is its third aspect, responsiveness, which manifests itself as compassion towards every living being and through its vivid sentience abolishes the notion that in life we can deal with abstracts or dead and inert counters.[8] It will be noted that in the Buddhist context compassion is a cognitive power, not a mere sentimentality, and it means more than having an awareness of it that enables us to make a compassionate response to a given situation; rather it is so rooted in our being that we cannot act (i.e., know and feel and act) otherwise than in an immediate and compassionate manner.

This brief outline of the metaphysical background of Tibetan thinking will help to understand the specific nature of the 'spiritual guide' as an inner process of growth with its attendant attitude towards the individual's environment, rather than as the interaction of two individuals. The third chapter of the *Byang-chub-sems-kyi man-ngag rin-chen phreng-ba*[9] bearing the title "mind (i.e., minding as such) rising as the (spiritual) teacher" discusses this point by offering a threefold conception of 'spiritual guide' (*bla-ma*). Here, (a) cognitive absoluteness is the basic (or causal) spiritual guide (*sems-nyid rgyu'i bla-ma*), (b) the effect

---

[8] *gSang-ba bla-na-med-pa 'od-gsal 'rdo-rje-sning-po'i gnas gsum gsal-bar byed-pa'i tshig-don rin-po-che'i mdzod*, Klong-chen-pa Dri-med 'od-zer, fol. 11*a*; *Bla-ma yang-tig*, IV, fol. 131; V, fol. 41.

[9] Vol. 2, fol. 71 of the *rNying-ma'i rgyud-'bum*.

is mind(ing) as spiritual guide (*'bras-bu sems-kyi bla-ma*), and (c) appearance is the spiritual guide as the act which presents to us the things, perceived in their (apparent) authentic reality (*rang-snang chos-nyid bla-ma*).

(a) Cognitive absoluteness "is not someone having perverted aims and being far away from enlightenment through his infatuation with mere fictions of the mind, rather it is a discriminative, insightful and intelligent person who distinguishing between Saṃsāra and Nirvāṇa sees them as frustration and happiness respectively. By taking a causal view of happiness and frustration he realizes them to arise from good and evil. This realization (lit: a mind which inspects) induces conviction, conviction induces effort; this spiritual guide of great effort purifies the three aspects of appreciative discriminative awareness (as brought about by listening to, thinking about, and imaginatively cultivating what pertains to the individual's growth and self-development) and earnestly strives for spiritual integration. By spiritual integration growing stronger and stronger, awareness (*ye-shes*) develops, and the presence of awareness is (the presence of absolute Buddhahood (Dharmakāya). From it the two patterns of (empathatic and embodied) Buddhahood arise automatically without hindrance."

(b) The effect "is man's capacity in all its freshness and genuineness, the way in which the three interpretative symbols of being manifest themselves, its very being being absolute Buddhahood (Dharmakāya), its actuality being emphatic Buddhahood (Sambhogakāya), and its responsiveness being embodied Buddhahood (Nirmāṇakāya). Thus in the very being of man's continuity of 'minding' the teacher is present as the three symbols of interpretation."

(c) Appearance as spiritual guide means that "the five elements (which build the universe and what lives in it) do not use words and letters to point out the spiritual guide, that the spiritual guide also does not do so in pointing out the five sensuous realms and sensual pleasures and other properties of being, but that they point by themselves through their very being so that without resorting to the fictional division into self and other (-than-self), appearance displays reality by its very being."

It is essential to fully understand the significance of appearance which, as the context shows, is not a correlate to an unknowable thing-in-itself and which also cannot be identified with semblance. In Buddhism, appearance is a 'slanted view' (comparable to Husserl's Abschattung), through which an identical thing makes its appearance; it does not replace the thing that appears through it. Therefore reality need not be sought beyond or behind the phenomena; it is here and now. What has been referred to by 'an identical thing' is the 'cognitive absoluteness' (*sems-nyid*) which remains the same, 'identical with itself' (*mnyam-pa*) in all its 'appearances' through which it is known. This idea of 'identicalness-with-itself' in its various manifestations has been summed up by Klong-chen rab-'byams-pa[10] in the words:

> Whatever is an appearance is alike in being an object, a mere flash of (and before) the senses;
> Whatever has manifested itself is alike in being a mind, a traceless inspective cognition;
> Both are alike in their immediate presence, mere fetters by affirmation and negation.
> In reality, what is identical-with-itself in its innermost being, merely appears without being grounded anywhere.
> Objects are alike in their publicness and when investigated can nowhere be traced;
> Minds are alike in their privateness and when examined are (like) the vast expanse of celestial space;
> Both objects and minds are merely pure appearances without existing (in themselves as the one or the other).
> He who understands it thus belongs to the lineage of the All-Positive (Kun-tu bzang-po) and
> Has his place among the best of the Buddha-sons in the heart of intrinsic perception.

[10]*Chos-dbyings rin-po-che'i mdzod*, chapter 11 end.

> Give up all (selfish) longing which fetters you to your strained efforts of rejection and acceptance,
> Because all things are alike in (being claimed to) exist or not to exist,
> In appearing or in being null and void, true or false.
> Expand in absolute self-sameness where no "objects" enter,
> Expand in absolute intrinsic perception where no "mind" enters.

This passage contains a number of highly significant terms and aptly describes what A. H. Maslow has called B-perception and peak-experience. Appearance and its perception is said to proceed without being 'grounded' which means that unlike in ordinary perception where the apparent object is not seen so much *per se* in its uniqueness but selectively as a member of a class, here it is perceived in its intrinsic uniqueness and, as it were, as presenting (*not* representing) the whole of Being. The perceiver is lifted out of the confines of his 'minding' and at the same time is thereby enabled to empathically go into the object which in the absence of a self-centered mind is no longer an ego-related means to a selfish end.

The emphasis on the fact that all things are alike does not mean that one thing is as good as another, but that each thing has its intrinsic uniqueness which remains identical-with-itself regardless of my wishfully affirming or negating it. The intrinsic uniqueness of the apparent object and the freshness of the mind are spiritual guides in the proper sense of the word: the one stimulating, inspiring so that more and more riches are found and enjoyed, the other enacting the values found and thereby setting an example for further actualizations of the values. This is possible because cognitive absoluteness in its humanly more easily understandable and experienceable form of compassionate responsiveness and resonance not only perceives potentialities but also actualizes them. In so doing it is the supreme spiritual guide experienced as 'all-positive'.

Towards an Experience of Being Through Psychological Purification

Purification is a term used in a variety of contexts, but its connotation remains basically the same: to liberate from actual dirt and to release from what is annoying and upsetting. We have only to think of the application of this term in the fields of hygiene or of religion and we note at once that the demarcation between these two spheres is far from clear, the one fuses imperceptibly into the other. Since purification implies the removal of dirt, which is always more than filth, inasmuch as it includes all that interferes with the free flow of life's energy, this term can be applied to other spheres of man's life as well; after all, the various spheres that we single out for scrutiny are but so many facets of a single existent. Of these interlocking spheres, ethics and man's perception of his world are of paramount importance. Not only are we aware of the world we inhabit and see it through 'tainted glasses' or with a 'pure' vision, we also act on the basis of our vision and judge our own and others' action as either 'depraved' or 'noble'.

Traditional ethics, however, particularly in the West, have been marred by a serious misconception of man. Assuming naively that 'good' and 'evil' are fixed qualities or properties, pre-existent and pre-ordained by some transcendental hocus-pocus, they have tended to make man responsible only for the choice he made, but not for the kind of man into which he made himself in so choosing. Next, they concentrated on the supposedly inert relationship between the 'is' and the 'ought'. Since there is not and cannot be any such relationship, by a subtle twist the abstractionist-theoretician turned the 'ought' (or the normative) into the 'is' (or the descriptive) of what was termed Reason, which here revealed itself as what it has often been, not a critical faculty but a euphemism for superstition and a champion of absurdities. Then it is boldly declared: 'This is what a man ought to do because this is what reason says man is'. This reductionism has had devastating consequences for the place of values and meanings in man's life. Overlooking the fact that values are relevant to the very being of man, it has torn them from his being and has treated them as mere quantifiable 'abstractions', becoming more and more meaningless and valueless. On the basis of such a view the gulf between facts and values becomes unbridgeable, and no relationship between them is ever possible. Certainly, whatever is, is, and what 'ought' to be can only be what someone desires, wants, or aspires to bring into being, but it must be noted that the 'what' in what-is and in 'what-I-ought-to-do' or even in 'what-I-ought-to-be', is both something and nothing. In the latter case I am referring to *possible* actions which have not yet been realized into action; in the former case I am referring to what has been a possibility and has become an actuality.

A second point to note is that any 'what' always implies a 'who'. The recognition of the 'who' is not some sort of 'subjectivism', by which term those who are afraid to live their existence try to imply that human existence—by which inner experiences or impressions are meant—are these same experiences as yet not fully understood, but which will eventually be analyzed objectively. And that once bias and 'subjective' interest have been removed, man is nothing but an extended object in a spatial container. The objectivist's fallacy is too ridiculous to need refutation. But because of this fallacy it has not been realized that the 'what' in 'what-I-ought-to-do' refers to both a resolve not yet made and the self-role somehow known before its enactment.

Concretely speaking, any man who feels himself 'impure' and aspires to become 'pure', cannot help but become pure in that particular respect. The self in this self-role is not a pre-existent, unalterable essence, but an emergent self, and like the 'ought' is an object for description. What a man is and what he 'ought' to be are programs in the process of being carried out and there is nobody else but the existing individual to carry out this program. However, we cannot carry out our program of being living individuals without decisive insight into the order of the world in which we exist, and this insight also is always an awareness of our role in establishing this order. In other words, man is not thrown into a world whose order is pre-existent, but in becoming man he is ordering his world in the light of his understanding. Insight emancipates both self and world and returns them to the spontaneous ground from which their experienced concreteness springs, and as such is form-giving as well as self- and world-forming. It is in and through insight that our vision of ourselves and of our world becomes freed from its own dead weight and expands into new dimensions.

It seems to be an inveterate tendency of ours to perceive other persons as well as the world in a way which reveals itself and is felt as a deficiency. We may not be aware of doing so ourselves, but we become keenly aware of it when we are seen in this way. In other words, we compare, judge, approve, disapprove and, above all, use others for self-centered purposes, but we resent being perceived as useful objects interchangeable with other objects or tools, and would prefer to be recognized and accepted for what we are in our complexity. Most of the time we seem to live in a world where classes and concepts have sharp boundaries and are mutually exclusive. Nothing that is conceivable is ever unique or realized as a presence that can open our eyes to what alone is real. This everyday, 'classificatory' perception has an impoverishing effect. The moment we see something embedded in its relationships with everything else in the world and merely as part of it, we have already cut ourselves off from the possibility of seeing it as unique and valuable; our vision has become obstructed, it has become deflected, and we feel uneasy, tainted, 'impure'. In the end, there comes a time when something has to be done about this situation which becomes more and more intolerable as it continues to make itself felt. That something *has* to be done implies that something *can* be done, so that each situation is a possibility for renewal or revision of our world. Then to do something about it, the 'purification', on the one hand, proceeds from a profound disillusionment, not with respect to any particular outcome of the life of thought and acts, but with all possible outcomes. On the other hand and simultaneously with this disillusionment, 'purification' anticipates and leads to a renewal of spontaneity, which is prior to the conceptual and practical, is everywhere present but nowhere found.

One of the first things to be noted is that any situation shows up as something paradoxical. It is both something and nothing. The fact that it is something, a 'what', is shown by its presence; and that it is nothing by its not being a presence *of* something. Its presence is a presentation (*snang-ba*), not a re-presentation, which always presupposes another thing made to appear under some guise. As pure presentation it presents nothing that exists, has existed or will exist (*med-bzhin snang-ba*); it is not even a presentation *of* possibilities, subsisting apart from the presentation and its presence. However, more often than not we approach the situation with abstract conceptual presuppositions concerning what is imaginable and possible, and surreptitiously slip them underneath the presence, assuming the presence to be the appearance *of* the conceptually possible. Not only is the conceivable or conceptually possible not an immediate present and felt presence, it is a distorting, 'tainting' force engendering a host of further distortions standing in the way of our own vision. This is how Klong-chen rab-'byams-pa refers to the situation about which something has to be done (*sbyang-bya*):

> This appearance of the six forms of life as particularly impure,
> Is a presence and yet nothing, a distorted form due to inveterate tendencies,
> Just like the presence of hairs in the vision of someone suffering from cataract of the eyes.
> In the same way as someone has to cleanse the discharge if he wants to get rid of the disease,

> So the person who wants the distorted presentation to become clear must remove the film of extrinsic perception.[1]

As contrasted with intrinsic perception (*rig-pa*), which is concerned with value as fact and fact as value, extrinsic perception (*ma-rig-pa*) is not primarily concerned with the situation in which man finds himself or with the nature of the world as it actually is, but with its systems of categories and constructs through which it filters the experiences, thus deflecting and making them something other than they are (*'khrul-pa*).

The analogy of illness suggests that in order to do something about a situation which is felt to be annoying, the situation has to be diagnosed. However, all too often a so-called diagnosis turns out to be just another kind of classification with no therapeutical value at all. Moreover, a situation is not some abstraction that can be classified and rubricized and passed on like a conceptual system. It is first of all something in which a person is deeply involved. He is an agent in, if not the creator of, the situation about which something is going to be done. It is the existent man who as agent asks the questions about the what and the why. In asking such questions as 'can the situation be resolved' or 'is insight possible', he has already anticipated the answer, because the very questioning presupposes the answer that the situation can be resolved and that insight as counteracting opinion is possible. Questioning, here, is understood as an impulse towards realization, not as a merely rhetorical exercise. Then, in attempting to resolve a situation, the questioner looks for something entirely

---

[1]*rDzogs-pa chen-po sems-nyid ngal-gso*, p. 82 and *rDzogs-pa chen-po sems-nyid ngal-gso'i 'grel-ba shing-rta chen-po*. (Klong-chen rab-'byams-pa's autocommentary), p. 864f.:

khyad-par ma-dag 'gro-drug snang-ba 'di
med-bzhin snang-ba bag-chags 'khrul-pa'i gzugs
rab-rib-can-la skra-shad snang-ba-bzhin
de bsal 'dod-pas bad-kan sbyong-ba ltar
'khrul-snang dag 'dod ma-rig ling-tog bsal

In the following these two works will be abbreviated as SN and SNG respectively. The simile is taken from *Viṃśatikā* 1.

different from what he ordinarily perceives. Strictly speaking, what he looks for cannot even be said to exist; it both is and is not there. He feels uncomfortably incomplete and is impelled by a sense of the incompleteness of his being and knows already that what he looks for is not a spatio-temporal object of his ordinary awareness and that the solution will be achieved only by actual insight which is grounded in and is the very core of his being. At this moment, the questioner, who is usually immersed in his projects with only so much awareness as he needs to effect them, is capable of looking at them from a detached state, free from the peculiar demands of these projects.

In other words, the problem is now that of 'appearance' or supposititious being (*snang-ba*) and of real being (*gnas-lugs*). 'Appearance' is the subject-matter of speculative thought, of shamming, of pretending that something is what it is not and cannot be, of lack of insight or, in terms of perception, extrinsic perception (*ma-rig-pa*). Real being, however, is an ever-spontaneous presence of being and genuine awareness in the sense that genuine awareness (*ye-shes*) is not something added to being, but being itself, and that being is not some fleeting content of genuine awareness, but is this awareness itself.

Thus the attempted resolution of an intolerable situation does not consist in a rearrangement of its conceivable components, but in a total recasting. It is comparable to what happens in regaining aesthetic sensitivity which is basically disengaged and freed from practical and speculative concerns and in its freedom makes speculation as well as bondage the conceivably possible. It is through genuine awareness grounded in man's cognitive being (*rig-pa'i ye-shes*)[2] that the clearing away of all that obstructs direct vision is effected. The first step is the realization that the 'apparent' (*snang-ba*) is 'nothing' (*stong-pa*) and that 'nothingness' or—since 'nothingness' may be understood as mere negativity—the 'open dimension of being' is or becomes

---

[2]This term, characteristic of rNying-ma-pa thought, refers to a cognitive existential experiece, not so much organized in space and time, but remaining strictly within the perception.

the 'apparent', though not in an alternation, but as the realized possibility in all its uniqueness.[3] In this realm, the parts (if they can be called parts) require one another's presence in the whole as a prerequisite to the awareness and sense of presence. Klong-chen rab-'byams-pa begins his discussion of 'doing something about the situation' (*sbyong-byed*) with the words:

> Through the genuine awareness grounded in cognitive being as the counterpart (of categorical thought)
> Recognize the tendency towards Saṃsāra as nothing in itself
> And acknowledge nothingness as the apparent.
> In the non-duality of appearance and nothingness you (then) are aware of the meaning of the two truths.
> By striving for the center, avoiding both extremes,
> Staying neither in worldliness nor in quietude, you are free (in being) in a state (comparable to) space.
> This is what it is ultimately all about:
> Being, absolutely perfect in itself.[4]

Genuine awareness lives in free possibilities of being that have no predeterminate limits; it operates from a creative center and radiates everywhere, to the 'farthest limits of space'. 'Space' has always been a favorite simile. The fact that it was counted among the 'unconditional' factors of reality shows that 'space' was not so much 'objective' or 'geometrical' space, an order of abstract extension where all points are equidistant from each other, but rather man's 'lived' space, the ultimate horizon of his being which goes with him wherever he goes. It is from the

---

[3]*snang-stong*. On this term see Mi-pham's *gNyug-sems skor-gsum* I 23*b*; II 41*a*; III 21*a*; 89*b*; 92*a*; 93*b*. Klong-chen rab-'byams-pa's *Chos-dbyings rin-po-che'i mdzod-kyi 'grel-ba lung-gi gter-mdzod*, fol. 181*a*.

[4]SN, p. 82; SNG, p. 867:

de-yi gnyen-por rig-pa'i ye-shes-kyis
'khor-ba'i bag-chags stong-par la-bzla-zhing
stong-pa'i rang-bzhin snang-bar thag-bcad-de
snang-stong gnyis-med bden-pa gnyis-don shes
mtha'-gnyis gnas bsal dbu-mar bslabs-pa-yis
srid-zhir mi-gnas nam-mkha'i ngang-du grol
'di ni nges-don snying-po'i dam-pa ste
rang-bzhin rdzogs-pa chen-po'i gnas-lugs yin

viewpoint of genuine awareness that man as living man, not as an abstraction in a system, is free or, stating it differently, man is free insofar as he *is*; he is unfree insofar as he conceives himself to be this or that and finds his limits in and by some other this or that.

Appearance as a presence—as long as it is a presence which man knows and feels in such a way that the feeling becomes the presence and the presence becomes the feeling of him who feels and knows—in no way represents or misrepresents something. A presence is just a presence, it is neither *for* man or *against* him. But since we are used to forcing any one of the very aspects which are causing the trouble, while we attempt to resolve the conflict of purpose in ordinary life, we get deeper and deeper into trouble—freely espousing spiritual death and rushing headlong into self-made prisons. Worst of all, we are losing our identity as human beings. Hence the resolution of the problem situation first of all has to stress the human individual rather than his projects which are secondary to him. Hence, also, a person who can extricate himself from his world of concepts, expectations, beliefs, and stereotypes is and becomes a different person from the one who remains 'stuck in the mud'. Klong-chen rab-'byams-pa now says:

> There is neither benefit nor harm in the concrete presence;
> But since you have been fettered in the world by your obsession with taking (the presence) as something,
> There is no point in speculatively going over the various manifestations.
> Rather eradicate this attitude of taking (a presence for what it is not).[5]

The 'concrete presence' here is neither subjective nor objective; it is a reality prior to any dissection which may then be

[5]SN, p. 82; SNG, p. 870:

snang-ba'i dngos-kyis phan-gnod gnyis-su med
der 'dzin zhen-pas srid-par 'ching-bas na
sna-tshogs snang-la brtag-dpyad mi dgos-kyi
'dzin-pa'i sems-kyi rtsa-ba bcad-par mdzod

performed for 'subjective' or 'objective' purposes. The moment we do so, we not only change that which is before us into something other than it is, we ourselves also become something else. Note how we start speaking of *things*! Let us assume we see a painting. The moment we say that it is a painting of a flower or of a bird, we have performed an abstracting act and in this abstracting act we have become a botanist or an ornithologist, a chemist or what-not, and having become 'specialists' we have become unable to see more and more of the many-sidedness of the painting or, for that matter, of a living person. The rule is that we are always preoccupied with our projects, and their 'realization' becomes the criterion of life. Hardly has one goal been reached before another is proposed; too often such a goal-oriented and goal-preoccupied man finds the pressure too intense and the demands too heavy, and he becomes a 'drop-out'. As a matter of fact, the 'drop-out' is the prime example of a person falling from one situation into another, and he does so because he feels insecure and frightened, and because his actions are not supported by insight but by opinions.

In his auto-commentary on the above verse Klong-chen rab-'byams-pa illustrates chasing after goals as well as 'dropping-out' by a quotation from the *Ratnakūṭa*. There these people are, not too flatteringly, likened to dogs pelted with stones:

> A dog that has been frightened by a stone
> Does not run after the man who throws the stone, but after the stone itself.
> Similarly, some mendicants and Brahmins
> Frightened by the sensuous quality (of the world) live in solitude.
> Although they live in solitude,
> If they see sensuous objects
> They are listless and fail to know what goes on within.
> Not knowing what happens in the wake of this evil
> They again are caught up in their 'little world',
> And there again are harmed by sensuous qualities.
> There they may even enjoy the pleasure of gods,
> But when they die and pass from their divine or human state
> They fall into places of evil forms of life.

> Such fools are afflicted by the misery of dying,
> And undergoing a hundred kinds of suffering
> They are, in the words of the Buddha, like dogs chasing a stone.[6]

It is significant that in this passage the man wrapped up in his projects and the 'drop-out' are on the same level; the life of both is not grounded in an awareness of being, but in a pseudo-individuality. The one may have the momentary thrill of satisfaction in having 'achieved' a goal, but since this thrill soon fades, another goal must be set up. The other is just listless, bored and a 'hollow man'. Both are in search of themselves, but the one looks where he cannot find himself, the other has given up looking.

Returning to our example of a painting, no analysis of its canvas, pigment, and brush-strokes could possibly reveal what makes the painting a work of art. Still, there is some connection between the art-work and its aesthetic enactment which, in turn, refers to the very capacity to enact something, a spontaneity that becomes frozen in its expression. Hence, as the originators of the situation in which we find ourselves, we are not standing apart from it, but are its determinant. Every person is his own project, but failing to note the character and nature of 'project', he is easily overpowered by it. Taking his cue from the *Ratnakūṭa*, Klong-chen rab-'byams-pa illustrates it by the analogy of a person who in the act of throwing a stone at a lion is devoured by the lion.[7] This is an apt illustration of how the agent is involved in the situation he has originated and in this awareness he can, as it were, free himself from the compulsiveness of his actions and emotions that lie at the root of his 'folly'.

However, to state that man is the determinant of his situation does not imply any form of subjectivism postulating a self or mind independent from its presence in its presentation. A presence (*snang-ba*) is not something external to my mind (*sems*), nor is it internal to it; neither is my mind standing outside its

---

[6] SNG, p. 872.
[7] SNG, p. 872f.

presence or inside it. Rather, presence is mind as a concrete actualization, and therefore any change in the one is a change in the other. Klong-chen rab-'byams-pa continues:

> The mind has no being of its own in (any) presence.
> It is not found by searching for it; it is not seen by looking for it.
> It has no color, no form, no essence that could be grasped.
> It is neither inside nor outside, has never come into existence or passed out of it at any time.
> It cannot be contrasted with or delimited by anything; it has no basis or substance.
> It cannot be pointed out as 'this is it'; it is beyond any conceivable object. . . .[8]

This use of negative statements is the only means of setting ourselves free from our inveterate tendency to concretize and to elevate our concretizations into eternal principles. It also helps us to regain a directness and immediacy of awareness and feeling, and to avoid their repression for the sake of some fancied spirituality. If there is any spirituality, it must express itself in the concrete presence of lived existence which as a direct and immediate expression is spontaneous and unique. Spontaneity clears activity of its own obstructions and returns it to its own original source. It is very different from ego-centricity or the much vaunted 'self-expression' which means to act on anything that might pop into one's head and, whether the advocates of this self-expression like it or not, is merely neurotic compulsiveness. There is no freshness or originality in it but only deadly repetition. In spontaneity mind stands as a symbol of self-deliverance and, paradoxically, it is more of itself. Klong-chen rab-'byams-pa declares:

---

[8] SN, p. 82; SNG, p. 874:
sems ni snang-la rang-bzhin 'ga' med-de
btsal-bas mi rnyed bltas-pas mthong-ba med
kha-dog dbyibs med ngo-bo ngos gzung-med
phyi dang nang med dus-gsum skye 'gag med
phyogs dang ris med gzhi-rtsa dngos-po-med
'di zhes mi mtshon bsam-yul 'das-pa'i sems

> It is not in the has-been, nor is it on the side of the not-yet;
> It is not in a now, but is a state naturally remaining identical with itself;
> Instead of seeking mind by mind, let be.[9]

The world of spatio-temporal things is one in which one thing is contained in, derived from, and consequent to another. It never is a presence (which is intimately felt), but a demonstration of something or other. It concentrates on the projects initiated by their originator, but leaves the originator out or tries to convert him into a project. By way of contrast, in 'letting be', there is a readiness (which is always spontaneous and not contrived) to perceive and to feel not by interfering with what is present, but by way of acceptance, as when we say that the artist has become his work and his work the artist. In such a moment a person has attained self-identity and simultaneously has transcended himself. But although in such a moment the person may and does feel as if lifted out of space and time, this feeling should not be concretized as something and then contrasted with something else whereby it would become something other than itself and would again be fitted into a conceptual framework. Insofar as man is his situation and even his projects, the temporariness of each situation and of each project does not contradict the non-temporariness of Being. Being is nowhere else than in what there is, it is not something over or behind the 'appearances'. Appearance or 'presence', as interpreted here, probably lasts only a second or so, and all we can say about it is that there is in fact a 'presence'. We cannot say that this presence when taken as an introspective situation contains our empirical self as its objective constituent. Klong-chen rab-'byams-pa therefore says:

> The momentary content dealt with by introspection, affirming or negating,

---

[9]SN, p. 83; SNG, p. 876:
'gag-pa mi dmigs ma-skyes phyogs-na med
da-ltar mi gnas rang-bzhin mnyam-pa'i ngang
sems-kyis sems ma tshol-bar dal-du chug

Is neither outside nor inside, but merely a presence.
The trouble is that what is sought is the seeker himself,
And he can never be caught as his own object.[10]

This inability to find an empirical self or any other self or pure ego as an entity as such or as a content of the mind, serves as a further step towards the realization of a state which somehow precedes all mental operations of the mind as ordinarily understood. Ordinary cognition classifies, particularizes and deals with 'observable qualities' (*rnam-par shes-pa*),[11] and in its operation something always eludes us. We are uneasy and, as it were, know already that there is more to what we perceive in this routine fashion. This knowledge, it seems, has been there all the time (*ye*) but, it also seems, is brought into existence preserving its original freshness (*ye-shes*).[12] However, we have to be very cautious in speaking of 'having been there', for it is not a 'something' that already exists as when we say that a tree or a dog exists, and yet it is not a 'nothing'. 'Something' and 'nothing' are judgments about how we believe a presence to fit into our conceptual system; they are superimposed and fail to perceive things as they really are, shorn of all accessories. Thus the mind (*sems*) forms an opinion about something, and in so doing it adds to and adulterates its operation. It becomes 'subjective' in the usual and

---

[10]SN, p. 83; SNG, p. 877:
dgag-sgrub dran-rig skad-cig yid-kyi yul
snang-tsam-nyid-nas phyi dang nang na'ang med
btsal-bya'i don-gyis tshol-mkhan byas-pas bslad
rang-gis rang-btsal nam-yang rnyed mi 'gyur

[11]In rNying-ma-pa thought *rnam-par shes-pa* is always contrasted with *ye-shes*. The former is a kind of perception (*shes-pa*) in which the object is seen imbedded in its relationships with everything else in the world and classified, judged, and delimited by attending to and rejecting some attributes (*rnam-par*). The latter is a perception in which the object is seen *per se*, uniquely as if it were the sole member of its class. See *gNyug-sems skor-gsum* II 19*b*; *gSang-'grel phyogs-bcu'i mun-sel-gyi spyi-don 'od-gsal snying-po*, fol. 100*a*.

[12]*ye-shes* is a term for a peak-experience as discussed by Abraham H. Maslow, *Toward a Psychology of Being*. As such it is always existential. See also the long discussion of this term by Klong-chen rab-'byams-pa in his *Theg-pa'i mchog rin-po-che'i mdzod*, fol. 232*a*–272*b*.

pejorative sense of the word. But we can also perceive without these subjective adumbrations and be more perceptive, responsive and alert. This experiential fact is referred to by the term *sems-nyid*, which literally translated, would have to be rendered as 'just mind', 'mind-as-such', not as this or that particular mind or empirical self. Actually, as Klong-chen rab-'byams-pa points out elsewhere, in this experience the empirical ego or ordinary mind (*sems*) no longer intrudes and intrinsic awareness is free to operate at its peak. The term thus indicates cognitive absoluteness as experienced fact.[13] Experienced fact cannot be stated in words, we can only point to it by stating what it is not, and even this is to turn experienced fact into described fact. Klong-chen rab-'byams-pa's words are to be understood as referring to experienced fact:

> Without ever coming into existence, genuinely real in itself,
> Cognitive absoluteness, not being present (as something), and not coming to an end,
> Is an open state, since it has no foundation or root (in anything) throughout time.
> Its presence as the unceasing ground for the manifoldness (of the world)
> Has neither substance nor quality in it and hence no eternalism applies,
> Its self-presence never ceases and hence no nihilism is involved.
> Since it is neither a duality nor a non-duality, it is ineffable.
> Since it cannot be established as 'this' it cannot be concretized.
> Know it as naturally pure since its very beginning.[14]

---

[13]In rNying-ma-pa thought *sems* is quite distinct from *sems-nyid*. The former is operative in *ma-rig-pa* 'extrinsic perception, categorizing thought', the latter in *rig-pa* 'intrinsic perception' and *ye-shes* 'peak awareness'. See Bla-ma yang-tig IV 41*b* ff. In other words *sems-nyid* begins when *sems* stops; Bla-ma yang-tig V 7*a*: *'dir sems-nyid ces smos-pas sems-kyi zad-sa rig-pa 'char-gzhi-nyid-la zer-gyis/sems-la mi zer-ro//* "*sems-nyid* is spoken of with reference to the ending of *sems* and the beginning of *rig-pa*, not with reference to *sems*."

[14]SN, p. 83; SNG, p. 878:

ye-nas skye-med rang-bzhin gnyug-ma'i don
mi gnas 'gag-pa med-pa'i sems-nyid ni
dus-gsum gzhi-rtsa med-pas stong-pa'i ngang

The contrast between opinion and knowledge, between 'mind' (*sems*) as the empirical self and cognitive absoluteness (*sems-nyid*) as an identity experience and awareness, implies that it is possible to make the transition from the preoccupation with one's empirical self to actualizing one's capacity to know that we are merely playing certain roles as empirical selves. In actualizing his capacity to know (*sems-nyid*) a person is more himself, but, paradoxically speaking, he is also beyond and above selfhood. The more a person *is* himself (which is not the same as self-aggrandizement), the more free he is of blocks, inhibitions, anxieties, and expectations, and therefore more spontaneous and creative (which is not the same as being whimsical, acting on any random impulse and producing various tools and gadgets). Spontaneous means to be able to respond directly to a total situation without dragging in hopes either as expectation based on past situations (which of course have been different from the present one) or as plans for the future (which again is different from the present). Since to be spontaneous is to be without egocentricity, there is no need to classify a situation in terms of fear or hatred or to evaluate it in terms of good and evil. To be creative, likewise, means to see the world in a fresh vision rather than to try to solve its problems with old solutions.

Certainly, the capacity to know spontaneously and creatively cannot be identified with a particular faculty or segment of life, hence also it cannot be said to 'exist' in the sense we ascribe existence to particular entities, thus introducing a division into that which cannot even be said to be 'one' without falsifying it. Although this capacity is a fact, it would be a mistake to turn it into something existent or subsistent. Again only negative terms, even at the danger of being misunderstood, can indicate what it is all about. Thus Klong-chen rab-'byams-pa sums up the out-

---

sna-tshogs 'char-gzhi ma-'gags snang-ba-la
dngos-po mtshan-mar med-pas rtag-pa med
rang-shar 'gag-pa med-pas chad-pa med
gnyis dang-gnyis-med med-pas brjod-du med
'di zhes 'grub-pa med-pas ngos gzung-med
rang-bzhin gdod-nas dag-par shes-par bya

come of 'purifying one's mind' and arriving at a 'pure state of cognitive capacity' in the words:

> Just as it does not exist (as something) when you analyze it,
> so also it does not exist (as something) when you do not analyze it.
> Pure fact, in itself, not-dual,
> Has nothing to do with good and evil, acceptance or rejection, hopes or fears.
> Hence what is the point of trying to do something with it by singling out (something) and enlarging upon it!
> Don't ever stir up the frantic chase of conceptualism.[15]

The distinction between the conceptualizing and self-narrowing tendency (*sems*) and the capacity of fullest and self-delivering awareness (*sems-nyid*)—which can be actualized by a process of purification, by doing something about an intolerable situation—demonstrates not only man's inherent capability but also provides pressure towards fuller and fuller humanness. It is true that cognitive absoluteness and humanness are abstract terms and like all abstractions fail to convey what it means to be fully aware and to be fully human. At best, the terms can point to ways of being. To be is to be fully aware with no limits to the capacity to know and with no taintedness or bias; it also is to be 'lit up' in the experience of being, taking the highest form of pleasurable excitement; and it also is to be ready to respond in knowledge. But none of these ways of being are essences as postulated (opined) in traditional Western and non-Buddhist Eastern philosophies. Since in existential awareness we are aware of Being—which, unlike postulated being-this or being-that, does not step out of itself into something else (be this another postulated being or non-being) nor change into some-

---

[15] SN, p. 83; SNG, p. 880:

brtags-pas med ltar ma-brtags dus-na'ang med
rang-bzhin gnyis-med gdod-ma'i ngo-bo-la
bzang-ngan blang-dor re-dogs mi dmigs-pas
brtag dang dpyad-pas 'di-la ci byar yod
dus-gsum yid-kyi tshol-khro ma byed zhog

thing other than itself (*'pho-'gyur med-pa*)—such existential awareness is spontaneous (not contrived) and creative (of how we are ordering our world). As Klong-chen rab-'byams-pa says:

> Although cognitive absoluteness may be termed Dharmakāya in view of its open dimension; Sambhogakāya in view of its luminosity, and Nirmāṇakāya in view of its readiness to respond, its very fact of being cannot be grasped as something conceivable. This existential awareness as such is spontaneous, neither stepping out of itself nor changing into something other than itself throughout time, because as the quintessence of Being it encompasses Saṃsāra and Nirvāṇa.[16]

Saṃsāra and Nirvāṇa are judgments *about* Being, but Being itself does not judge.

---

[16]*Chos-dbyings rin-po-che'i mdzod-kyi 'grel-ba lung-gi gter-mdzod*, fol. 30*a*.

Index

TIBETAN

SANSKRIT